# Roman France

## An Archaeological Field Guide

*Jeremy Knight*

TEMPUS

First published 2001

PUBLISHED IN THE UNITED KINGDOM BY:

Tempus Publishing Ltd
The Mill, Brimscombe Port
Stroud, Gloucestershire GL5 2QG
http://www.tempus-publishing.com

PUBLISHED IN THE UNITED STATES OF AMERICA BY:

Arcadia Publishing Inc.
A division of Tempus Publishing Inc.
2 Cumberland Street
Charleston, SC 29401
1-888-313-2665
http://www.arcadiapublishing.com

Tempus books are available in France, Germany and Belgium
from the following addresses:

| | | |
|---|---|---|
| Tempus Publishing Group | Tempus Publishing Group | Tempus Publishing Group |
| 21 Avenue de la République | Gustav-Adolf-Straße 3 | Place de L'Alma 4/5 |
| 37300 Joué-lès-Tours | 99084 Erfurt | 1200 Brussels |
| FRANCE | GERMANY | BELGIUM |

2 8375
936· 4  KNi

British Library Cataloguing in Publication Data.
A catalogue record for this book is available from the British Library.

ISBN 0 7524 1915 3

Typesetting and origination by Tempus Publishing.
PRINTED AND BOUND IN GREAT BRITAIN

# Contents

# Preface

'Our ancestors the Gauls were tall and fair'. This opening sentence of a school history book is the French equivalent of *1066 and All That* in Britain. Both say something of the perceived origins of states that on the one hand sought to create a united Republic out of great cultural, linguistic and political diversity, and on the other derived its royal family and aristocracy from William the Conqueror. The only rivals to the Gauls as national ancestors were the Franks, who had a rather different and more aristocratic social cachet, and the Romans, whose stock rose and fell with the Imperial ambitions of the two Napoleons. Unsurprisingly, Vercingetorix (and Astérix) are the national heroes, not Julius Caesar. To explore such themes however would need a rather different book. My own aims are more modest. They are to provide a reliable guide to Roman France for visitors, students, and anyone, who, like myself, packs their luggage with pocket guides to the birds, insects and ancient sites of whatever country they are visiting. I also hope that people interested in Roman Britain may find it useful to have an account of the nearest and most relevant part of the wider Roman Empire, which can help put its much smaller neighbour into perspective.

As the history of the twentieth century showed, Empire can be a transient thing. The question to ask about the Western Roman Empire may be not why it fell, but how it lasted so long. The first Roman settlement in Gaul was at *Aquae Sextiae* (Aix-en-Provence) in 124 BC, and when the fifth-century bishop Sidonius Apollinaris wrote in the final days of Empire, this was as remote from his own day as Henry V and the battle of Agincourt are from us. Chronologically, my own interpretation of 'Roman France' is even more generous. I have included the more important Iron Age hillforts, more relevant to the story of conquest and assimilation than their British counterparts. Many Roman towns began as hillforts, sometimes overlooking the site of the later Roman town in the plain below. Elsewhere, tribal capitals were replaced by new administrative centres in early Roman times, and names like Augusta Suessionum (Soissons) or Augusta Viromanduorum (St Quentin) emphasised their role as part of the new order. At the other extreme, I have included sites up to the seventh century, when the ancient world really ended. I have also noted some later sites that the visitor is likely to encounter in search of Roman remains. A visitor to the Roman theatre at Lillebonne might be disappointed to learn later that he has missed seeing a castle distinctly relevant to British medieval military architecture. Similarly, anyone visiting the legionary fortress of Aulnay-de-Saintonge might like to be reminded that the village also contains one of the most fascinating Romanesque churches in western France. Generally though, I have merely noted such later sites, not described them.

The arrangement of chapters calls for a word of explanation. Behind the pattern of départements into which France has been divided since 1790 lies a complex historical geography. At the French Revolution, the feudal and ecclesiastical geography of the ancien régime was replaced by a new pattern named after rivers like the Tarn or the Garonne, or geographical features like the Puy de Dôme (a volcanic peak) or the *Vallis Clausa* (Vaucluse). In some areas, these départements replaced a medieval bishopric

*1 France: the Roman Provinces*

which (with boundary adjustments over the centuries) corresponded to the area of a Roman *civitas* and with the territory of a pre-Roman tribe before that. In Brittany and the Loire, in the late Roman province of Lugdunensis III, there is a direct correlation between the areas of pre-Roman tribes and those of modern départements. Here, the writer's task in arranging his material is easy. Such cases are not universal however. The boundaries of the two small southern Roman provinces of Narbonensis Secunda and Alpes-Maritimes bear little relationship either to modern administrative units or to the convenience of the traveller, and the former's seven cities lie in six modern départements. Logically, a work such as this should perhaps divide its material by late Roman provinces, and this might help to bring out the all-important regional variations within Roman France. However, the traveller wishing to look up local Roman sites, or the student working on the archaeological literature of a particular département, would find this confusing. In any case, Roman cities were perhaps sometimes shuffled between provinces at the behest of an administrator, or of local politics, as in modern local government reorganizations. The arrangement of cities and provinces may have been more fluid than is sometimes thought. In practice I have tried to equate late Roman provinces with corresponding groups of modern départements and with traditional provinces like Berry or Gascony, which are still very alive in local consciousness, as the names of innumerable bars and restaurants throughout France testify. I hope that I have avoided the worst anomalies, or at least explained them.

An early church father once said that anyone who claimed to have read the entire works of St Augustine was a proven liar. I make no equivalent claim in respect of the Roman antiquities of France, though over the years I have seen a great many of them, and most of the significant ones. Probably few people would claim to have visited every visible Romano-British site, yet Roman France covers three times the area of Roman Britain.

The sites I have included are both those where there are worthwhile remains to be seen by visitors and those where there is little visible. Some exist within the streetscape of a modern city, like the late Roman walls of Le Mans, the arch at Orange or the Bourse site at Marseilles, or are features of the landscape like the Pont du Gard. Others are on public display like the monuments of English Heritage and its sister bodies (often under the aegis of a local society). At the other pole are sites which are too important to be left out, but where there is nothing to be seen but a flat grassy field. Julian Mitchell once said that an archaeologist was someone who took you somewhere where there was nothing to be seen, and told you in graphic detail what was once to be seen there. An unwary visitor might well be irate at being sent out of this way to visit a featureless field. I have tried to indicate where this is the case, and as a general rule, most sites where there is anything worthwhile to be seen will be marked on the new *Institut Géographique National* maps. On the other hand, though the vast majority of visitors will not need such a reminder, I cannot stress too strongly that many sites are on private land, which should not be ventured onto without the permission of the landowner, and I have tried not to include anything which would encourage trespass or damage to crops.

Sites also change. Key-keepers move house, inscriptions are moved to museums, new areas are excavated and displayed, excavations are filled in. Someone I know once hunted through luxuriant brambles to find a site. Returning some years later, he found it neatly conserved, with notice boards, municipal style paving, and even a street lamp. Urban excavations present another problem, since these are often rescue excavations in advance of development, and 'nothing to be seen' often means 'except a multi-storey car park'. However, I have included urban rescue excavations since these are often the primary evidence for the origins and early history of many French cities.

Why, however, 'Roman France' not 'Roman Gaul'? The present boundaries of France are, after all, political creations of fairly recent date, sometimes arbitrarily dividing units such as Catalonia or Flanders. No less a person than Fernand Braudel quoted with approval a fellow historian's comment that France had been created in the nineteenth century by the railway system and universal primary education. Why not the historically more meaningful boundaries of Gaul? There are several reasons. The 'vasty fields of France' are more than enough to fill any reasonable sized book, without including Belgium, Luxembourg, west Germany, or the complexities of the Rhineland *Limes*. Also, in any broader book, Trier would inevitably play a leading role, yet there is little point in producing a guide in English to Trier when Edith Wightman's book is available.

For most visitors, the familiar yellow Michelin maps at 1cm to 2km (1:200,000), covering France in 36 sheets, will probably be staple fare. Though there is no French equivalent to the British National Grid, it is possible (as in this book) to give an indication of the general location of a site by reference to the map number and fold. Toulouse for example is on M(ichelin map) 82 at fold 8. These are however basically motoring maps, produced by a tyre company, and lack contours and much topographical detail. Also, the system does not work with the very useful Michelin map book, which has its own system, or with the regional maps. The green maps (series vert) of the *Institut Géographique National*, covering France in 72 sheets at 1cm to 1km (1:100,000), are much superior. They are however more expensive and less readily available in Britain. Recent editions show most significant archaeological sites and have a map/fold reference system basically similar to the Michelin. Tours for example is at IGN map 26 at C2. I have used both systems.

Finally, readers may care to be reminded that in French 'Romain' or 'Romaine' (with an i) means Roman, whereas 'Roman' or ' Romane' (without an i) means Romanesque.

# Acknowledgements

My thanks to my friends and colleagues in France and elsewhere have already appeared in my earlier book *The End of Antiquity*, but I am particularly grateful to Professor P.R. Giot for sending me his valued comments on *The End of Antiquity*, along with several offprints of articles which I had missed. Though I had often thought of producing a guidebook to Roman France, the immediate stimulus for the present work came from a suggestion in a review by Andrew Selkirk in *Current Archaeology* and I am very grateful to Peter Kemmis Betty for so readily accepting my proposal for this book.

A number of kind friends have rallied round with help with illustrations, particularly Dini Hardy, Linda Harris, Pierre and Stefan Levi, and Sunshine Mason (the latter two old Montgomery Castle hands), whilst Chris Dunn has very generously allowed me to use a selection of his excellent photographs of sites in southern France. The person who has made this book possible however, in so many different ways, is my partner Annie Burns. This book is for her.

# List of illustrations

# Introduction: Roman France

## Conquest and Empire

Rome first became involved in Gaul in support of her allies, including the Greek city of Marseilles, and to protect the coastal highway from north Italy to Spain, where Rome had strategic interests from the Punic Wars onwards. In 121 BC this ancient 'Road of Hercules', leading ultimately to the Pillars of Hercules at Gibraltar, became the *Via Domitia*, named after Cn. Domitius Ahenobarbus, ancestor of Nero, who annexed the territory of the Allobriges in the Rhône Valley and the Mediterranean coast to create Rome's first transalpine province. The earliest Roman inscription in Gaul is a milestone of Ahenobarbus from his new road, dated to 118 BC, and now in the Archaeological Museum at Narbonne, where in the same year he founded Rome's first citizen colony in Gaul. The new province was invaded by Cimbri and Teutons, but C. Marius defeated the Teutons at Aix-en-Provence (102 BC), traditionally at the Mont-St-Victoire (a modern name) familiar from Cézanne's paintings. It was Marius and his troops ('Marius's mules' as they called themselves), who dug a canal, the Fossa Marianae, through the Rhône delta from below Arles to Fos-sur-Mer, to secure their supply route.

Though Roman territorial control was confined to Provence ('the Province') until the time of Julius Caesar, and the concept of a fixed political frontier may be something of an anachronism, events followed the familiar trajectory of colonial expansion. Each new 'rectification' revealed new threats to the colonial power or its native allies, which called for further intervention. Generals sought professional and political advancement, governors sought to mark their governorship by additions to the empire; the pageantry of empire was immensely popular with the city crowds in Rome and their masters. Merchants in trouble up country could provide a useful *causus belli* and it was said that Roman governors needed to make two fortunes out of their province — one for themselves and one to cover the legal costs of any impeachment by the provincials. Everyone sought a share of the immense riches of Gaul. Even before the conquest, 'Celtic' Gaul provided a seemingly inexhaustible market for the agricultural surplus of the great senatorial estates and vineyards of central Italy, and her wealth in gold and slaves was a powerful attraction.

## Celts and Romans: hillforts and amphorae

This story of conquest and settlement has to be seen against a much longer interaction between the Mediterranean world and a vigorous native culture. Even before the foundation of Marseilles as a colony of Phocea in Asia Minor about 600 BC, Etruscan and Punic trade goods were reaching southern Gaul. The tomb of the 'Princess of Vix' near the oppidum of Mont Lassois (Côte d'Or), now in the museum at Châtillon-sur-Seine, shows how Greek art, seen on the warriors and horsemen of the great crater, and

Celtic thirst, represented by the wine drinking equipment, were combining to influence sixth-century late Hallstatt society. This aristocratic warrior society also created the first major wave of hillfort building in Gaul.

By the time of Caesar, two main traditions of fortification had emerged for major hillforts in Gaul. One, based on earlier types of timbered rampart going back to Hallstatt times, was the *murus gallicus* ('Gallic wall'), described in detail by Caesar himself. Rubble built, it had an internal timber framework joined by iron nails, though these were a later addition to much older traditions of timbered ramparts. They were, said Caesar,

> always built on more or less this plan — baulks of timber are laid along the ground at regular two-foot intervals, along the line of the wall, and at right angles to it. They are fastened to each other by long beams across the mid-points, and covered with rubble, the spaces between the beams being faced with large stones. When these are in position and fastened together, another course is laid on top . . . (the beams) are not in contact with those of the first course, but separated from them by a two-foot course of stones . . . By the addition of further courses, the fabric is raised to the required height. This method of building . . . is not unsightly, with its alternation of timber and stone, each in straight lines (*Gallic War* VII, 2).

The masonry, Caesar added, protected the timbers from fire, whilst the 40ft lateral beams made the rampart proof against battering rams. Many examples are known from excavation, and though Caesar does not specifically mention them, the nails can form a useful archaeological indicator. The large-scale iron mining industry in Berry and Poitou (which again Caesar mentions) would have provided the large amounts of iron needed. The second type of hillfort was of more recent origin, perhaps no earlier than the time of Caesar. It consisted of a single massive dump rampart of earth, fronted by a broad flat bottomed ditch ('like a canal' says Roger Agache). Named the 'Fécamp type' by Sir Mortimer Wheeler after the Camp de Canada in Seine-Maritime, it is widespread in central and northern Gaul and often a *murus gallicus* was succeeded by, or reinforced with, Fécamp style defences.

One purpose of Wheeler's pre-war survey of the hillforts of northern France was to try to link these with the hillforts of southern England, where he had been excavating at Maiden Castle in Dorset. Some, particularly on the chalklands of northern France, are sufficiently alike to bear direct comparison, but overall, differences are more striking than similarities. Multivallate hillforts are extremely rare in France, and the areas enclosed are, by British standards, huge. Maiden Castle encloses just over 19ha, Vieux Reims (Aisne) 170ha, the Camp de César at Villejoubert (Haute-Vienne) 350ha, with an inner enclosure of 120ha. Whilst many are on promontories, with a single rampart cutting off the neck of a headland, so that the area enclosed is largely fortuitous, this raises the question of the purpose of such hillforts and their role in pre-Roman society.

In most areas where data is available, there are many small forts, plus one or two much larger hillforts. The latter are often the only ones within a tribal area, and are sometimes seen as 'tribal capitals' or '*oppida*'. There is much regional variation, but the general pattern is fairly constant. Wheeler's survey found a dozen or more small forts in the 2-4ha range in départements like Calvados or Manche, plus one or two much larger ones. Further south, major *oppida* at places like Bourges, Le Mans and Châteaumeillant developed directly into Roman urban centres. In the mountainous regions of central and southern France, there are many small hillforts, often with drystone defences, usually on a hill overlooking a small river plain, so that the inhabitants could exploit both the upland pastures and the flat arable land below. In Mediterranean Gaul and the Rhône Valley, yet another pattern emerges. Here, cities like Avignon, Cavaillon or Riez begin as defended pre-Roman centres. As in much of the Mediterranean world, occupation moved down to the plain in the early Roman period, often to move back uphill again in more unsettled times.

This does not however explain the purpose of the large *oppida* of central and northern Gaul. Were they permanent 'tribal capitals' or emergency defences thrown up against the Roman legions? Some large *oppida* seem on present evidence to have been only briefly occupied, which might tally with the latter explanation. The hostings recorded by Caesar, when all the warriors of a tribe assembled at an oppidum in a military emergency, might provide a context, though the elaborate and hugely labour and material expensive *muri gallici* hardly look like emergency defences. There is often, of course, a temptation to date a site by reference to an historical figure, as with the innumerable 'Camps de César' scattered through the French countryside, or to a particular military campaign. One class of find however brings together several themes discussed here — Mediterranean contacts with Celtic Gaul; the relationship between Roman commerce and Gallic chieftains in the pre-conquest period; the roles of the Gaulish *oppida* and the problems of their archaeological dating.

The tall cylindrical amphorae known as Dressel type 1, after the German scholar who first studied them, have accumulated a vast literature. They contained the Caecuban and Falernian wines produced on the estates of the late Republican Senatorial aristocracy in central-southern Italy. This was exported in prodigous quantities over much of western Europe. A modern estimate is that between 50,000 and 100,000 hectolitres (1,350,000-2,700,000 gallons) of wine per year were imported into Gaul in the first century BC. According to one Greek writer the going rate in some areas was a slave per amphora. Often the wine was decanted into wooden barrels and the empties discarded, so that at transhipment points like Châlons-sur-Saône many thousand amphorae have been dredged from riverbeds. They are common finds in hillforts, settlement sites and sometimes burials. Two broadly successive types have been identified, and can be dated by their occurrence at better dated sites elsewhere in the Mediterranean or on the Augustan forts of the Rhine frontier. Dressel 1A amphorae date from broadly 150-50 BC and Dressel 1B from roughly 70-10 BC, so that, particularly if there is a good assemblage from a site, it is possible to distinguish sites occupied pre-Caesar from those occupied later.

## Julius Caesar and the Gallic War

Julius Caesar's appointment as governor of Gaul was part of Roman Republican politics, and the rivalry between the conservative senate and the military leaders of the first triumvirate (Caesar, Pompey and Crassus). Caesar was given Cisalpine Gaul (NW Italy) and Illyricum as his province, with four legions. Pompey was given Spain and

Crassus, Syria. Caesar's appointment was for five years (59-54 BC). A few weeks later the senate crucially added Transalpine Gaul (southern France) to his area of command. Caesar's arrival there in March 58 BC coincided with a migration westward of the Helvetii from Switzerland, which threatened to destabilize the area north of his province and alarmed Rome's local allies. It also presented Caesar with a magnificent excuse for enlarging his army. He reinforced the single legion then in Gaul with the three under his command in north Italy, plus two newly raised legions. His six legions now made a formidable army, equally useful against the Gauls and against his rivals in the senate.

Having repulsed the Helvetii, Caesar returned to civilian duties in north Italy, where he could keep in touch with political events in Rome. Rumours of unrest among the Belgae in north Gaul gave him an excellent excuse to raise two more legions. In 57 BC he took his army to the territory of the Remi around modern Reims, who were allies of Rome, and attacked the Suessiones, who surrendered after Caesar had captured their oppidum of *Noviodunum* near Soissons. The Bellovaci retreated to *Bratuspantium* near Beauvais, but then surrendered, as did the Ambiani. The Nervii, Atrebates and Viromandui risked a pitched battle, but were defeated after heavy fighting. Following this, the tribes of Brittany and the Loire submitted, and Caesar returned to Italy, where 15 days of official celebrations marked his victory. Due to the excellent natural communication routes within France, an invading army, once it has secured a military decision, can quickly overrun the country. This was as true for Caesar in 57 BC as it was for the Germans in 1940 or the Anglo-Americans in 1944. Caesar's conquest of Gaul was largely complete, and his remaining years in Gaul were mostly taken up with 'revolts' (as he chose to represent them) by tribes who had submitted expecting the loose overlordship they were used to, but found to their cost what Roman rule actually entailed.

The first to rise were the Veneti of southern Brittany, who had a fleet of solidly-built Atlantic merchant ships for trade with Britain. They presented Caesar with a problem. The tribes of Belgic Gaul had done much of Caesar's work for him by gathering their forces and treasure into a central oppidum, which he could then assault with his legions. The Veneti on the other hand had numerous cliff castles on the ends of promontories and headlands, as Caesar describes, of a kind which the visitor to Morbihan (or to the coasts of Atlantic Britain and Ireland) can see for himself today. Only after the Romans had defeated the Veneti in a sea battle were they able to subdue them. Caesar's subsequent executions of the tribal leaders, and mass deportations into slavery, were worthy of the twentieth century.

In the same year (56 BC), two of Caesar's generals attacked Normandy and Aquitaine. The tribes of Manche, Eure and Calvados under Viridovix attacked the camp of Q. Titurius Sabinus, but were defeated. At the same time, Publius Crassus reduced Aquitaine. The only tribes to resist with any success were the Morini and Menapii of Flanders, who retreated into their forests and coastal marshes. The next two years were taken up with German affairs and Caesar's two abortive invasions of Britain. In 54 he suffered a severe setback when the Eburones of Alsace-Lorraine destroyed a legion under Sabinus and Cotta, killing both commanders, and the fighting spread to neighbouring tribes, including the Treveri, Nervii and Menapii.

By 52 BC this rising had been suppressed, but almost immediately a new outbreak began with a massacre of Roman traders in Orléans. Leadership was assumed by

Vercingetorix, a young Arvernian noble, who proved a skilful commander, with a formidable coalition of tribes, from Sens and Paris, through Maine, Anjou and Touraine as far as the Vendée and Dordogne. Caesar captured a series of major *oppida*, culminating in a long siege of Bourges. When he attacked Vercingetorix's stronghold of Gergovia however, he was repulsed with heavy losses, and the Gauls stormed the Roman supply base at Nevers, capturing much of Caesar's corn supply, and freeing the hostages held there. Caesar even considered retreating to Provence, but instead joined forces with Labienus, who had defeated the tribes around Paris. Vercingetorix now assembled his forces at Bibracte (Mont Beuvray), eventually retreating to Alesia (Alise-sur-Reine), which Caesar besieged with ten-mile siege lines, with camps, fortlets, timber towers and rows of sharpened stakes in concealed pits. A parallel siege line faced outwards to prevent surprise attacks. When Vercingetorix saw that further resistance was hopeless, he surrendered. Though the war was to drag on for another two years, with sieges like that of Uxellodunum (Lot), Gaulish resistance was largely over.

One telling comment on the nature of the Caesarian conquest is the disappearance from circulation of the previously plentiful Gallic gold coinage. Roman historians remarked on the vast amounts of gold bullion that Caesar brought back from Gaul. Suetonius wrote: 'he pillaged shrines and temples of the gods filled with offerings and more often sacked towns for the plunder than for any fault on their part. As a result, he had more gold than he knew what to do with.' (*Div. Jul.* 54. 2).

## New beginnings: Gaul after Caesar

Following Caesar's departure in 50 BC, a large military presence was still required, and Gaul was governed by soldiers like Aulus Hirtius (who wrote the last book of Caesar's Commentaries), Munatius Plancus, who founded Roman colonies at Lyon and at Augst in Switzerland, and, after Octavian had secured Gaul from Antony in 40 BC, Marcus Agrippa. Advances were already being made in such things as civil government and the road system. Augustus's visit in 27 BC saw the division of Gaul along the lines of Caesar's famous tag 'all Gaul is divided into three parts', into the provinces of Aquitania, Lugdunensis and Belgica (the 'Three Gauls'), in addition to the already existing Narbonensis. The changes that followed would have taken some decades, but new administrative centres for Gallic tribes were established, with names such as *Caesaromagus* 'Caesar's Market' (Beauvais); *Augustomagus* (Senlis); or *Augusta Vermanduorum* (St Quentin). A member of the Imperial family such as the future Emperor Tiberius, his brother Drusus, or Germanicus served as a sort of Governor General in the Three Gauls, with Legates appointed by the Emperor as governors in Lyon (Lugdunensis), Reims (Belgica), and probably Saintes (Aquitanica). Narbonensis was a civilian Senatorial province and from 22 BC Upper and Lower Germany were governed by their military commanders, but did not become formal provinces until the time of Domitian.

Augustus was in Gaul from 15-13 BC and in the year after his departure the great altar of the *Concilium Galliarum*, the annual Council of the Gauls at Condate, the confluence of Rhône and Saône outside Lyon, was consecrated. The first high priest was an Aeduan, C. Julius Vercondaridubnus, from a tribe which had always been allies of Rome. His names suggest that he or his father had been granted Roman citizenship by Julius Caesar. A second altar and temple followed soon after at Cologne, for Augustus's projected new province of *Germania*. From 10 BC Lyon became one of the principal mints for the coinage of the Empire.

The depleted Gallic aristocracy received new recruits. Some, from families with a military tradition, were given command of auxiliary regiments, often Gallic cavalry *Alae* which became part of the Roman army list, with titles incorporating the names of their founders, like the *Ala Classiciana* of Julius Classicianus, or the *Ala Indiana Gallorum* of his father-in-law, Julius Indus, the equivalent of Hodson's Horse or Skinner's Horse in British India. Those who stayed at home, or were not able to aspire to a career in Imperial service, could hope for the privileges and status of Roman citizenship, a status which could be enhanced by office holding or meeting the cost of public buildings in their native city. They might even hope to represent their tribe in the *Concilium Galliarum*.

Further south, the Roman Colonies of Gallia Narbonensis received settlements of legionary veterans, who were given land allotments in the surrounding countryside. Veterans of Legio II Gallica were settled at Orange, those of the 6th Legion at Arles, and of the 7th Legion at Béziers. The 8th were at Fréjus, the 10th at Narbonne. Some colonies, and other privileged cities, were given permission to erect imposing city walls like those of the late Republican cities of north Italy. Paradoxically, it was the more Romanized south that saw the greatest disruption of the settlement pattern by land confiscations. The settlement of legionary veterans involved the confiscation or compulsory purchase of the surrounding countryside over a large area, and its laying out in a grid of land allotments (centuriation). The system was not really practical in inland Gaul, for the veterans would be used to Mediterranean ways of farming, and the area was still too unsettled to risk the revolts that large scale confiscations might trigger off (as they did later in Britain).

Anyone interested in Roman military archaeology will turn to the Rhine and Danube frontiers, or to Britain rather than to France, but there are a number of important and relatively little known military sites. The only permanent legionary fortress within France's present political boundaries, that of *VIII Augusta* at Strasbourg, belongs with the Rhine frontier in Germany, but two early legionary camps, first identified from tombstones and stamped tiles, have now been extensively excavated. The timber built fortress at Aulnay de Saintonge (Charente-Maritime) held 2,000 men from the Rhineland legions *XIV Gemina* and *II Augusta* in AD 20-30 after a revolt in the Loire valley. Twenty years later both legions took part in Claudius's invasion of Britain. Mirabeau (Côte d'Or) was the stone-built fortress of *VIII Augusta*, occupied AD 70-90 (contemporary with the early phases of Caeleon, York and Chester), before Domitian moved the legion to Strasbourg.

## The making of the cities — Augustus to Trajan

Under Augustus and his successor Tiberius (AD 14-37), cities like Lyon and Argenton-sur-Creuse (Indre) in central Gaul acquired stone theatres, and monumental sculptured arches appeared. That on the bridge at Saintes (Charente-Maritime), capital of Gallia Aquitanica, was erected by C. Julius Rufus, Priest of Rome and Augustus, in honour of living and recently dead members of the Imperial family. That at Orange (Vaucluse),

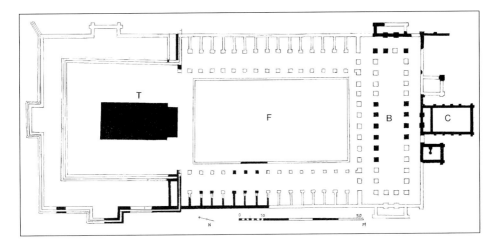

2 *Feurs (Loire) Excavated plan of the tripartite forum complex of AD 10-30, with council chamber (C), civic basilica (B), forum with shops (F) and temple (T). After Valette and Guichard*

veteran colony of *Legio II Gallica*, followed in 26-7. Rufus also paid for the amphitheatre of the Three Gauls at Condate outside Lyon. Feurs (Loire) has the earliest datable example (AD 10-30) of one of the most characteristic urban building types of north Italy and Gaul. This was the tripartite forum-basilica complex, with a transverse basilica (town hall and magistrate's court) at one end, a colonnaded forum in the centre, and a temple in a monumental precinct at the other (**2**). The earlier Augustan forum and basilica at Ruscino (Pyrénées-Orientales) of 25-20 BC is similar, but lacks the temple.

Tiberius's reign saw steady growth in the Gallic economy. At Paris, the *nautae* or river boatmen of the Seine dedicated a Jupiter column (the earliest known) to him. If, as Paul Middleton has argued, much of their business was concerned with bulk shipments of foodstuffs to the army of the Rhine, the reason for their gratitude is obvious, though this does not explain why the butchers of Périgueux should have set up an altar. In central Gaul the suburb of St Romain en Gal at Vienne was laid out in his reign, with drainage, water supply and large Italian type peristyle houses. Limoges and Bordeaux had aqueducts under Tiberius, and Lyon and Périgueux under Claudius. Smaller towns like Néris-les-Bains (Allier) and Argenton-sur-Creuse were already flourishing, the latter with early stone houses, and the potteries at Lezoux began production. There was a rising among the Andecavi and Turones in AD 21, which spread to the Treveri and Aedui, put down by a detachment of the Rhine legions (the fort at Aulnay de Saintonge probably relates to this), but such affairs did not interrupt the steady rise in prosperity.

Both Caligula (37-41) and Claudius (41-54) spent time in Lyon, Claudius being born there. Inscriptions in widely separated parts of Gaul show that masons and building stone were now more widely available, possibly with official encouragement, to wealthy local magnates who wished to ornament their cities. Theatres were built at Evreux (Eure) and Feurs (Loire), both by Priests of Rome and Augustus, the latter replacing a timber theatre. Saintes acquired an amphitheatre. In the north, towns like Bavai now had street grids and Amiens already covered 60ha.

Some Gauls from Narbonensis were already integrating into the Empire at the highest levels. Tacitus (*Annals* 11, 1-3) describes the downfall of the Gallic senator Valerius Asiaticus under Claudius. A native of Vienne, and twice consul, he was a man of great wealth, with wide and powerful connections in Gaul. He also owned much property in Rome itself, including the Gardens of Lucullus, and served with distinction on Claudius's British expedition. These merits were enough to condemn him. In AD 47 he was forced to commit suicide on fabricated charges of treason and adultery. One Gallic family given citizenship by Pompey took the name Afranius from one of his generals and settled at Voison. Sextus Afranius Burrus, born shortly before the birth of Christ, served Tiberius and Claudius as steward of the Imperial properties and helped secure a smooth succession to the throne for Claudius's son Nero in 54. He became praetorian prefect, and he and the Spanish-born Seneca were Nero's chief advisers in the earlier and happier part of his reign. An inscription records how Burrus became patron of his native town (ILS 1321).

The rule of the Flavian Emperors Vespasian, Titus and Domitian (69-96) saw the consolidation of Roman Gaul, both in town and country. Edith Wightman estimated that half the villas in Gallia Belgica were built in the later first century, and when the countrymen of these areas went to market, they would find newly-built forums, with their associated temples, in cities like Paris, Amiens or Bavai. Further south, in Voison-la-Romain, the streets of shops, and large courtyard houses built around gardens and pools, began at this time. The Flavian period also saw a fashion for large monumental amphitheatres, no doubt following the inauguration of the Colosseum at Rome in AD 80. Though not closely dated, those at Nîmes and Arles (perhaps by the same architect) and the 'Grand Amphitheatre' at Metz seem to date from this time.

## Second-century apogee : Hadrian to the Severi

In 121, Hadrian (117-138) passed through Gaul en route to Britain, and was there again in the following year. As elsewhere in the north-west provinces, one of his major concerns was to encourage urban life, and the religious cults and temples that went with it. Lyon, effective capital of the Three Gauls, particularly benefited. At *Condate*, meeting place of the Council of the Gauls, he enlarged the amphitheatre, and probably built or rebuilt the temple, revising its dedication, and making it, rather than the associated altar, focus of the cult. It was no longer the Temple of Rome and Augustus, but of Rome and all past Emperors of good repute. He replaced the pillars carrying Victory figures each side of the altar with columns of Egyptian syentite from the Mons Claudianus quarries, and these survive, now supporting the cupola of the church of St Martin d'Ainay.

On Fouvière, the monumental complex at the centre of *Lugdunum*, he doubled the size of the Augustan theatre, and gave it elaborate architectural decoration in white marble. His most impressive gift to Lyon however was the Gier aqueduct. The city already had three aqueducts, one the gift of Claudius, but the engineering problems of bringing water to the Hill of Fouvière had so far proved too difficult. Hadrian brought water from the hills 50km west of the city through a series of conduits and aqueduct bridges in reticulated masonry (the actual constructed length was around 80km) to a complex of reservoirs on top of the hill. As a work of building and engineering it bears comparison with Hadrian's Wall. A reminder of the careful planning that lay behind it is given by an inscription of Hadrian found near the aqueduct (and now preserved in a village school) delimiting the area within which water supplies were protected.

An unexpected trace of Hadrian in Gaul was found in an inscription at Apt (Vaucluse) in 1604. Verses, seemingly by Hadrian himself, recorded the burial place of his horse Borysthenes. This tallies with Cassius Dio's statement that when Borysthenes died in Gaul, Hadrian set up a tomb with an inscribed tomb slab. It is perhaps not surprising that some historians have regarded this remarkable find with reservations. Hadrian was certainly in the area however, and nearby Avignon received some benefit from him, for it added his name to their own — *Colonia Julia Hadriana Avenio*. At Nîmes, news reached him of the death of Plotina, widow of Trajan, and he is said to have ordered a basilica to be built in her honour. At Narbonne, he may have completed the great temple of Carrara marble dedicated to the Capitoline gods Jupiter, Juno and Minerva. A monumental Hadrianic inscription in Carrara marble was found reused in a medieval village church, but could be from some other building. Inscriptions of this quality were often cut on fine marble, even where the building concerned was of less costly material. There are other traces of building works under Hadrian at Tours and Périgueux.

One very different enterprise which may have owed something to Hadrian was the Breton *garum* (fish sauce) industry. Though fish processing tanks are widespread on the west Mediterranean and Atlantic coasts, the industry did not arrive in Armorica until Hadrianic times, perhaps attracted by the nearness of the British and German armies. An association of Roman citizens in Finistère may be connected with the industry, which probably relied on official army contracts rather than on private mercantile enterprise, and Hadrian may well have encouraged an industry that ensured a regular supply of this much appreciated foodstuff for his armies.

In contrast to Hadrian's tireless travels to every corner of his Empire, his successor Antoninus Pius (138-61) never left Italy, whilst Pius's adopted heir Marcus Aurelius (161-80) spent much of his reign campaigning on the Danube frontier. The Antonini were a Nîmes family, descended from Italian settlers. Their rule was the high summer of Empire. Not only were monumental buildings with costly sculpture in Antonine baroque style going up throughout Gaul, but the local aristocracy were showing their wealth, self-confidence and loyalty by paying for them. At Eu on the Channel coast about AD 170, Lucius Cerialius Rectus gave a new proscenium for the rural theatre of the *Pagus Cataslugi*, with a prominent inscription recording the fact. When Amiens was ravaged by fire about the same time, the forum and baths were promptly rebuilt in monumental style. Among the Bellovaci of Oise, a temple complex with elaborate sculpture and Corinthian columns was built at Mont Capron outside Beauvais, and the rural cult centre at Champlieu acquired a fine new temple, as did that at Ribemont-sur-Ancre among the Ambiani. At Yzeures near Tours another local magnate set up an altar and column with sculptures of the days of the week, and of battles between gods and giants, dedicated to Mercury and the divinities of Marcus Aurelius and Commodus.

These examples are taken from one region of Gaul, and could be extended. The grand buildings and costly sculpture paid for by a rich and self-confident middle class may remind the British reader of the High Victorians. As in the late Victorian period however, it is possible to see, at least with hindsight, the first shadows of coming change. There had been barbarian invasions of the Empire before, but Marcus Aurelius's protracted campaigns on the Danube led to an ominous debasement of the silver coinage.

It is more difficult to assess the significance of religious change, but beside the paradox of the pacific philosopher-emperor Marcus Aurelius who spent his days on military campaigns, can be set the growing popularity of Eastern mystery cults. A collection of altars to the Great Mother found under the chancel of Lectoure cathedral in the seventeenth century record the bull-sacrifice ceremonies of the *Taurobolium*. Similar altars are known from many sites in southern Gaul and the Rhône valley. At Tain l'Hermitage (Drôme) a taurobolium altar stands in the centre of the village, in the Place de Taurobole. These, or the sculptures from the Temple of Mithras at Nuits St Georges (Côte d'Or), suggest that some were now finding the state religion of the Olympian gods no longer satisfying in a changing and perhaps anxious environment. The Mithraic shrine at Bourg-St-Andreol (Ardèche) was founded by a group of Greek traders, and a recent study of the Nuits St Georges material has emphasised its oriental influences, suggesting that the Mithraeum may have been founded by traders from Italy or the east. It is no coincidence that the first recorded community of Christians in the west outside Italy, that at Lyon in 177, consisted largely of Greek immigrants from Asia Minor. The rare traces of third-century Christianity in Gaul, or the cities whose bishops attended the Council of Arles in 314, correspond well in distribution with that of the taurobolium altars.

## The third century

Change was not sudden however. Under Severus and his successors (193-235) building activity continued, though at a slower pace. There were new bath buildings in Paris (the Cluny Baths) and at Vieux in Normandy (finished in 238), and a monumental complex, perhaps another large public baths, at Beauvais. At Bitburg on the Rhine, Lucius Ammatius Gambaro gave a proscenium and tribunal to the rural cult theatre, dedicated to Jupiter Optimus Maximus and the divinity of Septimius Severus and Caracalla. Such munificence was becoming less common however. Severus's notorious confiscations of the property of supporters of his rival Clodius Albinus would have damaged the prosperity of the Gallic aristocracy. The abandonment of much of the Fouvière complex at Lyon could have been due to the confiscation of its revenues and endowments by Severus, and the annual assembly of the Gallic tribes at the altar of Rome and Augustus outside Lyon declined sharply after 200. This downturn was not confined to Gaul. In North Africa for example, the erection of monumental buildings paid for by local magnates ended with the last of the Severans.

When Severus Alexander, last of the dynasty, was murdered by his own troops, he was the fourth successive Emperor to die by violence in 18 years, and there were to be many others in the years ahead. In the absence of any fixed succession law, whilst Emperors like Hadrian or Pius could appoint their successor by adoption, in a crisis, any regional army commander had before him the shining examples of Vespasian and Severus as precedents for a coup. There is little need to follow the third-century crisis in detail here, save to note that its symptoms were internal rather than the result of barbarian invasion. They included urban stagnation and decline, an empty countryside, and the replacement of a solid currency with a mass of worthless alloy. The huge hoards of this found buried on sites throughout Britain and Gaul reflect its valuelessness as a means of exchange rather than any fear of barbarian invasions.

Cumulative evidence from a growing number of cities, particularly in the south, shows the abandonment of whole areas of large houses in once prosperous cities in the course of the third century. At Marseilles, a series of rescue excavations has shown that the area above the Vieux Port lay empty in the late Empire and there is now similar evidence from third-century Arles. In Vienne, the prosperous cross-river suburbs of Ste Colombe and Saint-Romain-en-Gal were abandoned, and at Aix-en-Provence houses which had acquired luxurious mosaic pavements during the second century were deserted early in the third. Further north, cities like Amiens and Boulogne shrank radically, despite their key positions behind the Rhine frontier. Away from the cities, field survey in areas as far apart as west Germany and central Italy show how the number of late Roman rural sites was a fraction of those occupied before 200. The reasons for this recession are not clear. The old explanation of 'barbarian invasions' no longer holds, if only because we can now see that the process was well advanced long before any such invasion. Local magnates, in the changed circumstances of the third century, probably found participation in local government an expensive burden rather than a source of family prestige, and withdrew to their villas. The towns had a limited economic base, with manufacturing industries concentrated in small country towns rather than in the cities. Since most local magnates probably now lived on their estates, the best modern analogy might be a Regency spa or a seaside town permanently deserted by its summer visitors.

The efforts of a series of able third-century soldier-emperors to reform the army, reverse the decline of the coinage, fortify a few cities as strategic strongpoints (Aurelian's walls around Rome are still one of the marvels of the city) and to impose unity against dissident groups such as Christians, failed. This was in the face of continual army coups and barbarian invasions by Goths on the Danube, Alemanni on the upper Rhine, and a new people, the Franks, in the Low Countries. For a while, Gaul was ruled by its own Emperors. Postumus and his successors lasted for 14 years, at a time when much of the east was controlled by the rulers of Palmyra. The Empire might have seemed in danger of permanent fragmentation, but the real lesson of the 'Gallic Empire' was the need for an Emperor on the spot on dangerous frontiers if crises were to be contained.

Despite these crises, a certain amount was achieved. Gallienus (253-68) deprived the gentleman amateurs of the senate of their monopoly of high military command, and placed it in the hands of professional soldiers. The army itself was reorganised, with a rapid reaction force of cavalry based in N Italy. The provision of its foodstuff and supplies, the *annona militaris*, became a first priority. A start was made on the reform of the coinage. From Gallienus and his father Valerian onwards, it was realized that the frontiers of the Empire were too extended to be guarded by one ruler (the absence of the emperor from a threatened frontier was a frequent cause of army self-help revolts), and the practice arose of separate eastern and western emperors. When stability was finally restored by Diocletian from 284 onwards, all these were to become characteristic features of the late Empire.

## The age of anxiety: Diocletian to Valentinian

Diocletian's collegiate system of eastern and western senior emperors (Augusti), each with a junior emperor (Caesar) as heir apparent, restored political stability until his voluntary retirement in 305 led to quarrels among his successors, the final victor being Constantine the Great (308-37). Constantine reversed Diocletian's persecution of Christianity, which became the new state church.

Diocletian's reorganization of the provincial structure, like much of his policy, aimed to create a hierarchy of civilian and military office holding, making coups by an individual more difficult, and ensuring closer control of local communities for the collection of tax and the *annona*. Throughout the Empire, provinces were divided into smaller units. Lugdunensis, Narbonensis, Belgica and Aquitania were all divided in half, with capitals at Rouen (Lugdunensis Secunda), Aix-en-Provence (Narbonensis Secunda), Trier (Belgica Prima, with Reims, the old capital, as the head of Belgica Secunda) and Bordeaux (Aquitanica Secunda). In the late fourth century, under Gratian or possibly Magnus Maximus, Lugdunensis was further divided, with new provinces based on Tours (Lugdunensis III) and Sens (Lugdunensis IV). Vienne was the capital of Viennensis in the Rhône valley and Besançon of Maxima Sequanorum in the Jura region.

The cities that made up these provinces were now much changed. Many public buildings had been demolished, perhaps because local magistrates could no longer afford to pay for their upkeep. Often the stonework was stockpiled for use in the new town walls. The towns had shrunk in size, because of depopulation, or because town life was no longer seen as attractive. In some areas, palatial fourth-century rural villas show that the local aristocracy was far from bankrupt, but saw no advantage any longer in urban office holding. Where inscriptions do record new building work (often repairs or additions to existing buildings), the donor is no longer a local magnate, but the *praeses* or governor. Major new works were mostly a matter of Imperial largesse. The Constantinian baths at Arles may have been part of an Imperial palace complex and a lost inscription records Constantine's gift of another bathhouse to the capital of Belgica Secunda at Reims. Basilicas at Trier and Metz, and known from literary sources at Tours, were probably audience or judicial halls for the provincial governor. The town walls, which are often the main surviving structures from these late Roman towns, show a similar degree of official direction.

The walls were built in a uniform structural technique that suggests central organization and planning, and the employment of experienced engineers and builders moving from one job to another like modern motorway engineers. Stephen Johnson has shown that the town walls of a province often have a family resemblance suggesting that building was organised at a provincial level under the governor. There is also some indication that within some provinces the area enclosed may not have depended entirely on the size of the town, but may have approximated to a standard size.

Building a town wall of this kind would have needed detailed organization and planning. Meetings between the governor, the military engineers and the city authorities would have decided on the line of the wall and the demolition of any buildings that stood in its way. Unwanted public buildings, like a Victorian town hall or railway station in a modern city, or a long disused cemetery, would provide both land for the line of the wall and useful building material. These would be demolished and the stone stockpiled for reuse. Construction began with the digging of a large foundation trench along the line of the wall. This was then filled with the most massive available pieces of stonework — column drums, fragments of sculptured cornice, tombstones, even statues and inscriptions, laid without mortar. Sometimes part of a standing building would be left and incorporated in the line of the wall. At Bourges, an apsed fountain house was encased in the masonry, and earlier monumental arches often only survive because they were incorporated in the late Roman walls of their city. The building of the wall then began. The massive foundation courses would be carried up for some distance in large squared masonry to provide a solid and siege proof base. Above this, the two outside faces were built up for some feet in *petit appareil* — the small squared masonry blocks laid in neat courses, and of a convenient size for handling, which had been standard, particularly in Roman military work, for centuries. Often, this used a pinkish waterproof mortar incorporating crushed tile. The space between the faces was then filled with dry laid rubble, and wet mortar, usually white, poured around it like concrete. The lift of masonry would then be levelled up with a usually triple course of tiles capping the facing stones. Once the wall reached a certain height, wooden scaffolding was needed, and square putlog holes for its beams would be incorporated in the tile courses. The tiles would hasten building by allowing the water content of the mortar to evaporate more quickly, and form a base for the next section of dry built rubble.

The walls were protected by towers from which the ground in front could be swept by covering fire. These varied in type. Sometimes square, but more usually round-fronted, they could either span the curtain wall, so that it joined the tower mid-face, or were wholly external. They were usually solid in their lower part, as far as the wall walk. Where the upper parts survive, as at Le Mans, Senlis or Bourges, there were two upper floors above the curtain wall, each with three large arched openings facing outwards for defence. Arrow loops, though known to the ancient Greeks, do not occur.

A late Roman document, the *Notitia Galliarum*, lists 115 Gallic cities, plus a few lesser towns, under their respective provinces. It is later than 383, for Grenoble is named *Gratianopolis*, after Gratian. Jill Harries has suggested that it may have been drawn up under Magnus Maximus (383-8). Many people (myself included) have mapped the *Notitia* as the political geography of late Roman Gaul, but this geography may have been more fluid than is sometimes realised. Several major cities had once been mere *vici*, including Boulogne and Grenoble. The latter, at a strategic river crossing on the overland route from Italy into Gaul, was given defences by Diocletian before being renamed *Gratianopolis* and promoted to civitas status. Conversely, places like Cassel in Flanders or Vieux in Normandy failed to develop as cities. By the *Notitia*, both had been absorbed by their neighbours. Jublains (Mayenne) appears in the *Notitia Galliarum* as the *Civitas Diablintum*, yet apart from the late Roman fort, the remains are those of a vicus, or a rural cult centre. Its territory looks as if carved out of that of the Cenomanni of Le Mans, and it may have been a vicus of Le Mans for much of its life, raised to civitas status in the late Empire for administrative or political reasons.

The *Notitia Galliarum*, probably in origin a civil document, was used (as its preface tells us) in ecclesiastical controversies over precedence and status, since the Church based its pattern of bishoprics on that of late Roman civil administration. Some entries may be later ecclesiastical emendations, relating not to late Roman civil government but to fifth- or sixth-century bishoprics. In Medieval times, antiquarian debates over the Roman status of a particular city were a staple of such arguments, and early accounts of Roman ruins by medieval writers were often ammunition in such quarrels, designed to show the antiquity and status of a particular see.

# The fifth century

In Britain, the period after the usurpation of Constantine III (407-11) saw the rapid eclipse of the Roman economy. The Roman state no longer paid troops and officials, coin ceased to enter the country or to circulate, and the pottery industry rapidly declined to extinction, though we have a few shadowy glimpses of a continuing homegrown civil administration, and of a Church not unlike that in contemporary Gaul. In Gaul, despite the invasions of the Goths, Vandals and Burgundians and the gradual expansion of the Franks into north Gaul, conditions were very different. New types of coinage circulated, as did the products of a recognisably Roman pottery industry. In the north, red-slipped pottery from the Argonne continued the tradition of *terra sigillata* ('samian ware'). In southern Gaul there were stamp-decorated orange or grey slipped wares (*sigillée paléochrétienne grise et orangée*), supplemented by coarse-ware jars, bowls and jugs in Gallo-Roman tradition, produced in various local centres and fabrics. Large amounts of oil and wine from North Africa continued to arrive at Mediterranean ports in characteristic amphorae, accompanied by red-slipped table vessels (African red-slip ware) and by lesser amounts of similar imports from the East Mediterranean, some of which even reached western Britain and Ireland.

A generation after the barbarian invasions of 406-7, the Roman Generalissimo Flavius Aetius kept up a precarious balancing act with Goths, Franks, Gallo-Romans, Burgundians and Huns until his murder by Valentinian III in 454. When Valentinian was killed by two of Aetius's soldiers in the following year, many saw this as the end of the western Empire. In any case Gaul was now low in the order of priorities of the increasingly shadowy western Emperors who survived in Italy until 476, or the eastern Emperors who exercised more realistic power from Constantinople. Traditionalists like Sidonius Apollinaris still kept up something of the old ways; classical erudition of a somewhat stilted kind, aristocratic letter writing, country villas (where one suspects the roofs leaked) and loyalty to an ideal of Empire which was increasingly far from reality. However, Sidonius's real status lay not in his role as a Roman senator, but as bishop of Clermont Ferrand.

The cities had by now undergone a transformation. Inside their walls was the cathedral complex, with the cathedral itself, the bishop's palace and a baptistery. These were often associated with a piazza in which crowds from all over the civitas territory would gather on the major feasts of the Church, when baptism was administered. The cathedrals themselves have been rebuilt over the centuries, and none survive above ground, save for part of the great double-cathedral complex in the late Roman Imperial city of Trier. Others have been found by excavation, as at Lyon or at Geneva, where a large fourth-century double cathedral and baptistery are displayed in an archaeological basement under the present cathedral. A number of fifth-/sixth-century baptisteries survive in southern Gaul. Most are centrally-planned octagonal rotundas, with internal corner niches and a ring of reused Roman columns around the central baptismal basin, which was sunk in the floor, with steps leading down. This architecture, common in monumental bath buildings from the first century onwards, and in Imperial mausolea, was easily adapted for baptisteries.

Outside the walls were the cemeteries, and in some cities, the graves of Christian martyrs. Roman law, going back to early times, insisted on burial outside the city, for the presence of the dead was regarded as polluting, in a ritual rather than a hygienic sense. The relatively few Gallic Christian martyrs had been buried outside the city in the normal way. The Christians within the city celebrated their 'heavenly birthday' with feasting and religious ceremonies (rather to the annoyance of St Augustine), just as an ordinary family remembered their dead. In the course of time, the *cella memoria* or tomb chapel was replaced by a church, which in some cases developed into an important medieval monastery. The fifth and sixth centuries also saw a flowering of late antique art in south-west Gaul in the form of sculptured sarcophagi of marble from St Béat and other quarries in the Pyrenees. They incorporated human figures, strigil patterns and plant scrolls, some closely related in style to the late mosaics from some of the great Aquitanian villas. Over 200 are known (for catalogues see Ward Perkins 1938, and James 1977, 301-42). They are a surprising testimony to the wealth and patronage of the Aquitanian late Gallo-Roman élite, as well as to the vitality of the new Christian centres.

Recent excavations in cities like Marseilles and Arles have revealed a similar late antique urban flowering, with crowded earth-floored buildings of the fifth to seventh centuries whose relatively insubstantial remains might well have been missed by earlier excavators. The finds from Marseilles give archaeological substance to Pirenne's picture of a flourishing trading port there in this period, whilst excavations in Saint-Bertrand-de-Comminges, at the foot of the Pyrenees, are producing another interesting picture of fifth-century activity. A large house in a central position next to official buildings and a market square was presumably the residence of a local magnate. It continued in occupation in the fifth century, and even acquired a new mosaic pavement. The market square may have continued as a centre of economic activity, as is suggested by a marked concentration of *sigillée paléochrétienne grise*, while east of the house an early fifth-century Christian church was built on part of its garden. To British readers, the combination of fifth-century magnate dwelling, market centre and church may recall Wroxeter.

## Buildings of the city: theatres, amphitheatres, fora and baths

For a Greek or Roman, civilization was synonymous with city life, and to function, a city needed certain amenities. These included a Roman forum or Greek agora; a basilica with law-courts, council chamber and civic offices; temples to the gods (for public rituals rather than private worship) and baths for relaxation. A theatre and amphitheatre were usual, and larger cities, particularly Imperial or provincial capitals, might boast a circus for chariot racing. These buildings were not simply utilitarian. To reverse a phrase of Gibbon's, they were intended for ostentation as well as for use. A magnate and landowner would sit in the council chamber with his peers, take a conspicuous role in public ceremonies at the temples, and use his reserved front row seat at the theatre or amphitheatre not only to see, but to be seen. Statues in the forum and inscriptions on public buildings might emphasise both the status of his family and their loyalty to Rome, the more so since many such buildings were paid for by such people, as the inscriptions reminded everyone. One major reason for the shrinkage of Gallo-Roman cities in the late Empire may have been that such people now saw urban office holding not as prestigious, but as an expensive and unrewarding burden.

Early drawings and other records show that in the sixteenth and seventeenth centuries, many French cities still retained impressive remains of amphitheatres, sometimes used in medieval times for meetings of the citizens, or for religious pageants. At least 25 existed. The earliest are the military amphitheatre at Fréjus and the Claudian examples at Saintes and Feurs. After the completion of the Flavian Amphitheatre (Colosseum) in Rome in AD 80, grand amphitheatres became fashionable, and those at Arles and Nîmes date from this time. If only thanks to Hollywood, there is little need to explain what a Roman amphitheatre was used for, and the explanation of particular features is best left to the description of individual sites where they can be seen.

In the larger cities, theatre and amphitheatre often stood close together, sometimes with a circus for chariot racing and a large set of public baths, forming a leisure and recreation complex on the edge of town. Theatres of Greek pattern were already being built under Augustus, as in Lyon and Arles, whilst by the time of Claudius even some small northern towns like Evreux had their theatre. Not all cities could afford such a grand complex however, and still less could the many rural cult centres. By the second century, an economical solution had emerged. The classical Graeco-Roman theatre had tiers of seats around a flat semicircular space known as the orchestra, with the stage and the stage facade (*Scenae frons*) behind. In Classical Greek drama, the orchestra had been used for the chorus. It was now used to seat distinguished members of the audience. The combined theatre-amphitheatre characteristic of 'Celtic' Gaul (sometimes called a 'cockpit-theatre') enlarged the orchestra into an oval arena, like that of an amphitheatre, and moved the stage building back to make room for it. The result could be used for theatrical events, but was also a fully functional amphitheatre. Examples can be seen for example at Lillebonne, Paris (which also had a classical theatre), Sanxay and St Albans (for a catalogue, with distribution map and comparative plans see Kenyon (1934), 242-53).

The Gallo-Roman city quickly devised a characteristic form of forum complex, based on north Italian models, and ultimately perhaps on the Forum of Augustus in Rome. This differed from that familiar in Britain, which resembles more than anything else the headquarters building of a legionary fortress (a matter of common origins rather than of derivation one from the other). The Gallo-Roman forum was tripartite, with a central colonnaded piazza or forum flanked at one end by a basilica set lengthwise, and at the other by a classical temple in a formal precinct or temenos. The basilica was a large aisled hall, rather like the nave of a church, serving as town hall and lawcourts. Sometimes, as at Arles or Bavai, where the complex (usually at the lower temple end), was on sloping ground, this might be levelled up by ranges of vaulted underground chambers (*cryptoporticus*). Tripartite fora of this kind are known from many cities, but two early examples are useful as evidence for their origins. That at Château Roussillon dates from about 25-20 BC. Its lower end, instead of leading to the temple precinct, is closed off with a row of shops. The later example (AD 10-20) excavated at Feurs shows the fully developed tripartite type.

One of the earliest bath buildings in Gaul, of about 40 BC, is that at Glanum. Of the so-called 'Pompeian' type, it has a simple 'straight through' plan, with three barrel-vaulted rooms side by side — cold (*frigidarium*), warm (*tepidarium*) and hot (*caldarium*), with an apse at one end and a hot bath at the other. To the south was a colonnaded *palaestra* or courtyard for ball games and exercise and a large rectangular swimming pool. This (Krencker's 'Row type'), with various modifications, remained popular in

Gaul. Sometimes an extra warm room was added, making four in all, as at Drevant, or Cimiez. Elsewhere a more elaborate *caldarium*, with a large apse at one end, was added parallel to the main range, as at Talmont or the North Baths at Saint-Bertrand-de-Comminges. This 'ring type' enabled bathers to enjoy a circuit of rooms of varying temperature, from cold to hot and back again, without retracing their steps through the same set of rooms. The fully developed 'Imperial' plan, as seen in the great bath complexes of Rome, and marked by a strong bilateral symmetry around a central axis, can be seen in the Severan Cluny Baths in Paris, and in the now incomplete Constantinian North Baths at Arles.

## Building techniques

Whilst it might seem pedantic to use French or Latin terms for types of Roman masonry, this is done for brevity, since it is often hard to find English terms which are not both clumsy and twice as long. So far as I am aware there is no modern definitive study of Gallo-Roman building techniques, but there are several distinctive types of masonry which the visitor will encounter, and which need a word of explanation.

Most common is *petit appareil* ('small square blocks'), with a stone rubble core and facings of neatly squared and coursed blocks of stone of uniform size. *Opus mixtum* ('mixed work') combines this with levelling bands of brickwork, in the form of two or three courses of flat tiles at regular intervals. This is particularly characteristic of the late Empire, as in late Roman city walls. Older scholars, like Grenier, thought that it did not occur before about the time of Hadrian, and used it to date buildings found in older excavations, where evidence was otherwise scarce. This may be true as a rule of thumb, but it was used earlier, at least sporadically. Both types of masonry often show *putlog holes* (for once there is an English term). These are horizontal rows of small square holes in the stone facing, used to carry the timber beams supporting the scaffolding used in construction, and left open for ease of maintenance and repairs. In the writer's experience, the most commonly asked question by visitors to Roman or medieval buildings is 'what are those holes for?'.

Two other techniques are less common. Both are far more usual in Italy, and when they are met with in Gaul, it is worth looking for a reason. Load-bearing brickwork (i.e. walls entirely of brick) is normal in Roman Italy. Toulouse has a long tradition of building in brick, from Roman times to the present, because of a lack of local building stone. The city walls, now with an archaeomagnetic date of about AD 30, are of brick, as is the late first-/early second-century complex at St Michel du Touch outside the city, with its large bath complex and amphitheatre. The late Roman basilicas at Trier and Metz are also of brick (and use identical brick stamps). These are probably official Imperial, not civilian, buildings, and might have used imported craftsmen. Something of the sort might also account for the use of *opus reticulatum* ('work like a fishing net') in Hadrian's Gier aqueduct at Lyon. This consists of a facing of diamond-shaped stones, giving a diagonal pattern to the wall face. Common in Italy from an early date, it occurs sporadically in Gaul. Hadrian is believed to have travelled with an entourage of architects and builders, and the Gier aqueduct could reflect this.

# The countryside

With such imposing urban monuments, it is easy to forget that the vast majority of the Gallo-Roman population were not town dwellers, but lived in rural areas, and worked the land. The most important element of the rural economy, the villa, is grossly under represented in what follows, since few have been conserved and displayed, and those which have are mostly opulent 'luxury' villas, far from typical of the full range of Gallo-Roman farmhouses. 'Villa' in Latin means 'farm', and like modern farms, these could range from cottages to châteaux. There are several excellent books on Roman villas, and in the space available, it is more useful to concentrate on other less familiar aspects of the rural scene, and ones which have left much to see above ground.

In the Mediterranean world, towns are usually fairly closely spaced on the available agricultural land. Even today, townsfolk travel out each day to work land in the surrounding countryside, returning home to town at night. There is little need for secondary centres of population, and the Greek city-state could include within its walls almost its entire population. When this idea was transplanted to northern climes by Augustus, it was necessary to make adjustments. With a different agricultural regime, and fewer and more widely spaced towns, an infrastructure of rural market and administrative centres became necessary, as in Italy. The Pictones for example, with their capital at Poitiers, covered the area of three modern départements. An infrastructure of smaller secondary settlements already existed in Gaul from Iron Age times, and it was only necessary to adopt and expand this. This involved a system of *pagi* or rural districts and *vici* or small market towns. A local magnate could hold office in a vicus or a pagus just as he could in a 'civitas capital'. Both terms are found on inscriptions, and *vicus* in place names. However, it was a third element, the rural cult centre, which has left most archaeological traces in the French countryside.

Rural cult centres are usually sited beside a road or road junction close to the boundaries of two or more *civitates*. Some were already important religious centres before the Roman conquest, as the extraordinary charnel heap of carefully sorted human sacrifice victims, minus their skulls, at Ribemont sur Ancre shows. Others have produced many Iron Age coins, presumably offerings. Others were close to major Iron Age *oppida*. The system was probably reorganized under official encouragement in early Roman times, and new sites added. Names like *Germanicomagus* 'Germanicus's market' (Bouchards, Charente) or *Claudiomagus* ' Claudius's market' (Clion, Indre et Loire) suggest officially chartered markets like those of medieval towns. The system was separate from the network of *vici*, which provided the network of weekly provision markets, but the *concilabulae* (which may have been the name of these cult centres), and their periodic fairs on religious festivals, when traders and peddlers would attend, no doubt saw a great deal of rural business transacted. Provost has shown how those of the Loire were spaced at regular intervals of around 70km, so that no one was more than a day's journey, there and back, from such a centre.

One of the most surprising aspects of these sites is their architectural sophistication and size. When fully excavated, they include at least one Classical or Romano-Celtic temple in a monumental precinct or *temenos*; a piazza in which large crowds could gather; a theatre which can sometimes be as large as those at Nîmes or Orange, or one of the theatre-amphitheatres characteristic of 'Celtic' Gaul; public baths; a varying number of residential buildings and often subsidiary smaller temples. At its peak,

Ribemont-sur-Ancre covered 25ha. The clue to their social purpose is provided by a series of loyal dedications to the Genius or guiding spirit of the Emperor, and to the god of the shrine, by local magnates, which also record the gift of a stage front or the like by the magnate. Thus at Nizy-le-Comte (Aisne), Lucius Magius Secundus dedicated a proscenium to the numen of Augustus and to Apollo for the Pagus Vennectius, whilst at Bitburg on the Rhine, Lucius Ammatius Gamburio gave a proscenium and tribunal to Jupiter and the numen of Severus and Caracalla, together with two annual spring games. The *concilabulae* were thus part of a social mechanism linking land-owning magnates to Rome and the Emperor, emphasising their status within the community by public ceremonies, office holding and ostentatious gifts of public building work.

# 1 Normandy
## (Lugdunensis Secunda)

Normandy is the obvious starting point for any exploration of France, not only because many British visitors will arrive here, but also for the closely related reason that links it with two of the most familiar dates in British history. Indeed, a Latin inscription on an elegant modern memorial in Caen aptly links the two when it reminds us how the Normans crossed the Channel to conquer Britain in 1066, only for the British to return to liberate Normandy in 1944.

In the Iron Age, the area was the territory of eight major peoples, whose distribution corresponds with that of major towns and cities of Normandy-Bayeux, Caen and Lisieux in Calvados; Evreux in Eure; St Lô in Manche; Seez in Orne and Lillebonne and Rouen in Seine Maritime. Normandy, particularly the chalk country of the Pays de Caux, contains a number of outstanding hillforts, which often recall those of southern England. Wheeler's pre-war survey of these brought out how in some cases a single large hillfort can be identified within a tribal territory, and may have been the *chef lieu* of that tribe and perhaps predecessor of the Roman civitas capital before the area was conquered by Caesar's general Titurius Sabinus in 56 BC.

Because nearly all these civitas capitals developed into flourishing medieval and modern cities, few standing Roman monuments survive, though the theatre-amphitheatre at Lillebonne and the late Roman walls of Evreux are outstanding exceptions. Slighter traces of late Roman town walls survive elsewhere, and Stephen Johnson has shown how, as at Bayeux, Evreux and Lisieux, they enclose rectangular areas with the characteristic 'playing card' shape of early Roman forts. This may reflect both the influence of the 'Classis Britannica' fort at Boulogne, and the way in which the building of town walls may have been organized on a provincial basis under the supervision of the governor.

*Guide Répetoire* 18 (1968) Calvados, Manche and Orne and 19 (1968) Seine-Maritime and Eure.

## CALVADOS

The modern département included three Roman civitates, those of the Baiocasses of Bayeux in the W, the Vidocasses of Vieux near Caen in the centre, and the Lexovii of Lisieux in the E, though by the late Empire the Vidocasses had disappeared as a separate unit. Wheeler's hillfort survey revealed many small pre-Roman defended sites, usually promontory forts, in the 2-4ha range, but only two major hillforts, Castillon (35ha) SW of Bayeux and St Désir (160ha) outside Lisieux. Neither has been tested by extensive excavation, but the possibility that they represent the pre-Roman tribal centres of the Baiocasses and Lexovii is strong.

F. Delacampagne, *Carte Archéologique de la Gaule* 14 (1990).

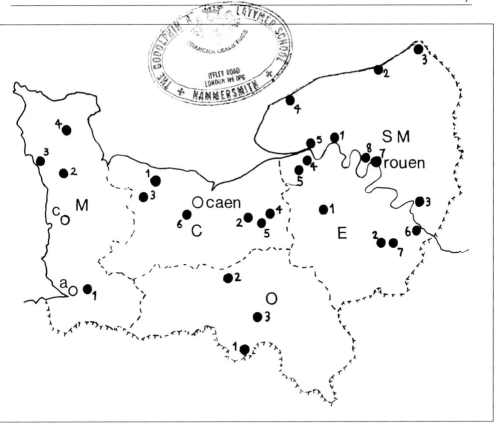

3   Normandy (Lugdunensis Secunda)

**C** Calvados *1 Bayeux 2 Cambremer 3 Castillon 4 Lisieux 5 St Désir 6 Vieux*

**E** Eure *1 Berthouville 2 Evreux 3 Les Andelys 4 Quillebeuf sur Seine 5 St Sampson de la Roque 6 Vernon 7 Vieil-Evreux*

**M** Manche *1 Petit Celland 2 Mont-Castre 3 Port Bail 4 Valonges a Avranches c Coutances*

**O** Orne *1 Alençon 2 Merri 3 Sees*

**SM** Seine Martime *1 Caudebec 2 Cité des Limes 3 Eu 4 Fécamp 5 Lillebonne 6 Quiévrecourt 7 Rouen 8 St Martin de Boscherville*

## Bayeux (Augustodunum)
M54 10 IGN06 C9

Cantonal capital of the Baiocasses. Fragments of late Roman town walls of petit appareil with brick levelling courses, built into later walls, enclose a rectangular area of 9ha, with the 'playing card shape' typical of early Roman forts, also used in this area for urban defences. Blanchet 36, Johnson 1983, 87, fig 27.

## Cambremer Hillfort
M54 17 IGN18 A5

The promontory fort of Château des Anglais stands on the summit of Mont Argis west of Cambremer, overlooking the Auge valley. It is of the 'Fécamp' series, with a single bank rising 10m above the broad ditch, and enclosing some 24ha. Though smaller than Castillon or Malicorne, it is included here since it belongs with these major

sites rather than with the smaller defended enclosures. Its relationship to Malicorne, 13km away, is unknown.
Bender 1986, 166.

## Castillon Hillfort
M54 14 IGN06 C8

Castillon is on a low-lying promontory between two streams. Surrounding the modern village is the bank and ditch of a 35ha hillfort, with a broad shallow ditch of 'Fécamp' type, but a *murus gallicus* rampart. Limited excavation showed that this had a stone facing and a nailed timber framework like that at Petit Celland in Manche.
Wheeler and Richardson 1957 116-17. Gourvest 'L'Oppidum de Castillon (Calvados)', *Annales de Normandie* II, I (1961), 99-103.

## Lisieux (Noviomagus)
M55 13 IGN18 A6

The capital of the Lexovii had the usual amenities, including an amphitheatre west of the city at St Désir, and large public baths, excavated in the 1980s. These were built in the late first century and underwent several modifications before being demolished in the late third. Of the town itself, a Roman column and part of a road can be seen on the north side of the Place de la République. The late Roman walls enclosed a rectangular area of 8ha. Fragments, with coursed blockwork and triple tile courses, are visible at the base of the south tower of the cathedral in the Place Thiers and in the Boulevard Sainte-Anne, but they are mostly known from early nineteenth-century records.
Blanchet 39. *B.S.A.N.* 53 (1955-6), 169ff. Johnson (1983), 87-8 and plan.

## St Désir Hillfort
M55 13 IGN18 A6

At Malicorne, 2km SW of Lisieux, is the Camp de Castellier, a huge oppidum south of the Caen-Lisieux road, possibly the pre-Roman capital of the Lexovii and predecessor of Lisieux. Intermittent traces of a ploughed down but substantial rampart, said to be of *murus gallicus* type, enclose an area of some 160ha. The site is in hedged *bocage* country and the defences difficult to trace, though Wheeler's plan (largely from air photographs) is the essential starting point.
Wheeler and Richardson (1957), 118-19 and fig 33.

## Vieux (Aregenua)
M55 11 IGN18 A2

This small Roman town, SW of Caen, was the capital of the Viducassi, from whom its modern name derives. It is most famous for the 'Thorigny marble', a statue base of red marble with a lengthy inscription recording the career and influential friends of a local magnate, Titus Sennius Sollemnus. The stone has had an eventful history. First recorded in the sixteenth century at the Château of Matignons at Torigny-sur-Vire (hence 'Thorigny'), it perhaps originally stood in the forum at Vieux. Long preserved at St Lô, it was damaged by fire and reduced to fragments in the heavy fighting of July 1944. Taken to the University of Caen for restoration and safe keeping, it was returned to St Lô in 1989.

Sollemnus had held most of the magistracies that his small town could offer, and was a member of the Viducassian delegation to the annual Council of the Gauls at Lyon, where in 220 he was elected to the office of Chief Priest, one of the last to hold that office. Later, he finished the public baths at Vieux begun by his father. In 238 his statue was erected by decree of the Council of the Gauls, on land donated by the Viducassi. The inscription on the front face records his various offices, the side faces the texts of two letters sent to Sollemnus by important friends (*C.I.L.* XIII, 3162). Tiberius Claudius Paulinus had been commander of the Second Augustan Legion at Caerleon in south Wales (at nearby Caerwent the inscribed base of a statue erected in his honour by the tribal council of the Silures survives, a neat pendant to the Thorigny marble). He had then gone on to be Governor of Gallia Narbonensis and then Gallia Lugdunensis. When accusations were made against him at the Council of the Gauls, Sollemnus pulled strings to get the charges dismissed, and was rewarded with various presents and the promise of a job at York, where Paulinus was now Governor, with a salary paid in gold. The inscription illustrates both the levels at which different grades of Gallic aristocrat might operate, in local government or Imperial service, and the ways in which the system of *patrocinium* or patronage worked. It is difficult to imagine a modern politician having a similar transaction inscribed on his statue base.

The town possessed the usual civic amenities, though on a modest scale. Recent excavation showed that it already had stone buildings in AD 25-50 and produced fragments of the limestone figure of the town's protecting goddess or *Tutela*, with a towered crown. The baths were excavated by Foucault in 1703 and their plan published by Montfaucon, though this is sometimes ascribed to Valonges (Manche) in error. Possibly they are those built by Sollemnus and his father. The theatre-amphitheatre east of the village was excavated in 1852-4. The brick courses in its masonry suggested a second-/early third-century date (*C.A.F.* 1908, 504). In medieval times, Vieux was replaced as regional centre by Caen.

B. de Montfaucon, *L'Antiquité Expliquée* III, 2 (1723) p353 and pl CXXII; H.G. Pfaulm, *Le Marbre de Thorigny* (1948). East Deniaux *Récherches récentes autour du marbre de Thorigny* (Paris). Grenier III, 913-16 (theatre), IV, 350-55 (baths).
Ch Pilet, 'Vieux antique', *R.A.O.* 1 (1984), 63-84.
P. Vipard 'Une statue récemment découverte à Vieux' *Gallia* 47 (1990), 251-5.

## EURE

The present département corresponds closely to the Roman civitas of the Aulerici Eburovices, whose territory survived until 1792 as that of the diocese of Evreux. Other branches of the tribe were settled in Mayenne (Aulerici Diablintes) and Sarthe (Aulerici Cenomanni) to the south.

### Berthouville (Canetonum)

Rural sanctuary
M55 15 IGN7 D8
The shrine of Mercury Canetonensis, on the borders of the Lexovii, Eburovices and Veliocasses, shared the broad fertile plateau of the Lieuvin with a large Roman villa, possibly that of Q. Domitius Tutus, whose name appears on several items of silver from the temple treasure. It was whilst robbing building stone from the site in 1829 that the peasant proprietor found the 90+ silver vessels now in the Cabinet des Médailles in the Bibliothèque Nationale in Paris. Much of the site was then pulled apart by the owner in a frantic search for more treasure. The temple and theatre were excavated by various people later in the century, latterly by Camille de la Croix. The shrine comprised two large rectangular colonnaded courts, the west one containing the temple complex, the east a forum or market square. The published plan is not altogether clear, but the former contained two square conjoined temples (E and H) for Mercury and his consort Maia. Later, these were demolished and replaced by a line of three buildings — a Romano-

Celtic temple, a central tower-temple like that at Sanxay and a large hemicycle for gatherings or the display of offerings. The chronology is vague, but Augustan coins suggest an early start and la Croix thought that the rebuilding followed destruction in the third-century invasions, when the treasure was hidden. However, there is no need to associate the rebuilding with any violent destruction, and the treasure could have been hidden much later, from confiscation by Christian Emperors rather than from invaders. The theatre was of rather unusual plan, with a cavea of seven concentric walls and a pair of oblique walls flanking the stage building. *B.M.* 1862, 257-61 (temples), 1896, 312-40 (theatre). Babelon *Le Trésor d' argenterie de Berthouville près Bernay (Eure)* (Paris 1916). Grenier III, 956-8 and fig 316.

### Evreux (Mediolanum)
M55 16 IGN08 C1

The tribal capital of the Eburovices still retains impressive remains of its late Roman walls, of neatly coursed small blocks of stone (petit appareil) with levelling courses of brick at regular intervals. A number of public buildings were demolished to provide stone for their foundations, as can be seen in the archaeology gallery of the city museum, where the rear of the foundations are exposed *in situ* — a striking and unusual museum exhibit. The exposed section contains several reused columns. A collection of Corinthian and Tuscan capitals, fragments of columns and sections of entablature now in the gardens of the municipal library (9, Rue de l' Horloge) are from the same source. A ruin E of the city, known as the *Châtel des Sarrizins* (castle of the Saracens) was a theatre of classical type. It was destroyed in the nineteenth century, and only a plan survives. An inscription to Claudius by a priest of Rome and Augustus (*C.I.L.*

XIII, 3200) shows that it was of the same date as the amphitheatres at Saintes and Feurs, and was likewise paid for by a local magnate.

The museum collections are particularly fine, with some good Roman bronze statues and other finds from Vieil Evreux, and much other local archaeological material of all periods. Grenier III, 950-54 (theatre).

### Les Andelys Rural cult sanctuary
M55 17 IGN8 B1

Les Andelys is most famous for Richard I's great castle of Château Gaillard, but a Roman theatre at Noyers-sur-Andelys was probably part of a rural cult centre like Berthouville.

### Quillebeuf-sur-Seine Hillfort
M55 4 IGN7 C7

Four km east of the Tancarville bridge, overlooking the estuary of the Seine, is a promontory fort of some 95ha with a massive single rampart of 'Fécamp' type known as 'Le Camp aux Anglais'. Nearby is the smaller hillfort of 'Les Câtelets' at Bouquelon.
Wheeler and Richardson 1957, 120, Fichtl 1994, 156, 174.

### St Samson de la Roque
Early monastery
M55 4 IGN7 C6

St Sampson of Dol was a Welshman, educated, according to his early Life, at Llantwit Major in Glamorgan. His monastery at Dol in Brittany is marked by a cathedral, but there is less to see of his other monastery here at Pental, though a number of early sarcophagi are known from around the old parish church of St Sampson-sur-Risle in the valley and there are relief-decorated bricks like the seventh-century series from Nantes (though with different designs) in Evreux Museum.

### Vernon Hillfort
M55 18 IGN8 B2

Promontory fort of over 20ha on a long

*4 Vieil-Evreux (Eure) — plan of temple complex. After Grenier*

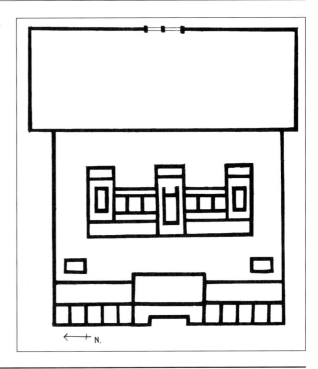

steep-sided hill on the NE bank of the Seine, bounded on the north by the road to Gasny. 'Fécamp' style rampart 7.5m high above the flat bottomed ditch, with two interned entrances and a third with overlapping rampart ends. Wheeler described it as 'a large and notable example of the Fécamp series'.

Wheeler and Richardson 1957, 121.

## Vieil-Evreux (Gisacum) Rural cult sanctuary

M55 17 IGN8 C1

Five km east of Evreux, Vieil-Evrux is a characteristic rural cult sanctuary. The name 'Old Evreux' is one of several ('Vieux Poitiers', 'Vieux Reims' etc) where antiquarian folk tradition has explained a Roman or Iron Age site as the predecessor of a later city. In the present case, not only is this clearly wrong, but the proximity of the two emphasises that towns and rural cult centres fulfilled different functions, and were not simply different grades of settlement.

The site was excavated by Esperandieu early this century. Parts of the baths are still visible (signposted from the D67), and have been conserved. The remains included a triple temple complex within a rectangular temenos; public baths; a theatre in the centre of the modern village and a building sometimes called a 'basilica'. The baths are of unusual plan, with two bath suites (for men and women?) set end to end, served by a central furnace block, and with a circular dry hot room next to the frigidarium (cold room) at each end. The line of the aqueduct serving the baths is still partly visible. The 'basilica' produced a series of bronze figures of high quality now in Evreux Museum, including statues of Jupiter, Minerva, Apollo, Bacchus, Silenus, Abundance and two Victories, a bronze mask, figures of animals, and pipe clay figurines of Venus and a horse and rider. Presumably they were votive

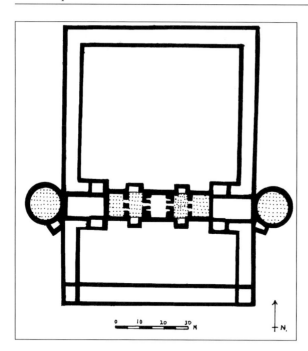

5   *Viel-Evreux — plan of bath building. Hypocausted rooms stippled. After Grenier*

gifts, and the 'basilica' must have been rather like a modern museum. The coins ended under Constantine at a time when many rural cult centres were becoming disused.

Two km away at Cracouville, near a spring, are the excavated remains of two successive Romano-Celtic temples. Finds included doctor's instruments, known from other similar sites, suggesting that medical help may have been available at such shrines.

Baudot 'Le problème des Ruines du Vieil-Evreux' *Gallia* 1, part 2 (1943), 191-206. Grenier III 950-54.

## MANCHE

Manche was within the territory of the Baiocasses of Bayeux (Calvados). A smaller tribe, the Venelli, is also known in the area, but they were probably absorbed by their larger neighbour in Roman times. Wheeler records a number of small promontory forts, in the 2-8ha range, very like those of Calvados. The only major sites are the heavily overgrown Mont-Castre and the Camp de Châtellier, which he excavated. Though Coutances (Constantia) and Avranches (Ingena) both appear as civitates in the *Notitia Galliarum*, neither has late Roman walls and significantly both appear in the list under their own names (e.g. *Civitas Constantia*) not as the caput of a tribal territory (e.g. *Civitas Baiocassium* for Bayeux). The entries may refer to their later ecclesiastical status, not to any late Roman civitates.

## Le Châtellier:
## Le Petit Celland Hillfort
M59 8 IGN16 C4

One of Wheeler's research aims in his survey of northern French hillforts was to seek evidence for the origins of the multivallate hillforts so characteristic of the British Iron Age (similar examples are almost unknown in France). He was therefore drawn to Le Petit Celland, 8km east of Avranches, where the southern defences of the 19ha contour fort are partly double. His excavations in 1938 showed that the main rampart was of *murus gallicus* type, with the outer bank on the south unfinished, and that the site had been destroyed by fire. Occupation at the time of Caesar's Gallic Wars suggested an historical context.

Wheeler thought that the fort had been built by Viridovix, chief of the Venelli, during the war of 56 BC and was only briefly occupied. The eastern entrance however may be of more than one period. The rampart ends overlap, like those on the smaller gates of the Camp de Canada at Fécamp, but the end of the overlap is sealed off with a hornwork, forming an oblique entry, with an interned entrance tacked on to the inner rampart. An original simple overlap entrance could have been strengthened with a hornwork and inturns, perhaps contemporary with the unfinished outer rampart.

Wheeler and Richardson 1957, 38-54.

### Mont-Castre Hillfort
M54 12 ICG6 C4

On the summit of the steep-sided ridge of Mont-Castre south of Lithaire is the 45ha hillfort of Grand Moncastre with a single rampart and inturned entrance. The site is heavily overgrown.

Wheeler and Richardson 1957, 115

### Port Bail Early Christian baptistery
M54 11 IGN6 C2

A paved hexagonal structure centring on a square pool or tank, 150m from the church. Excavated by Michel de Bouard in 1956 and identified as an Early Christian baptistery, the only one in France north of the Loire. To visit, ask at Mairie.

M. de Bouard *Cahiers Archéologique* 9 (1957), 1-22.

### Valonges (Alauna) Rural cult centre
M54 2 IGN6 B4

One km east of the town, at Alleaume, are the ruins of a rural cult centre. The Roman baths, first planned in 1765, are still standing to a respectable height, with a sequence of five cold and hot rooms, including a circular hot room. 800m away is the site of a Roman theatre, excavated by Foucault as long ago as 1691. The published plan suggests a typical Romano Gallic theatre-amphitheatre with a near circular orchestra/arena. There was also a temple.

B. de Montfaucon *L'Antiquité Expliquée* III, 2 (1723) pl. CXLV. Grenier III, 959-66.

# ORNE

The small département of Orne is on the southern edge of Normandy, on the border with Maine. Though the territory of the Esuvii was quite large, the area does not contain any major Roman sites.

### Alençon Museum
M60 3 IGN19 B1

The Musée de la Maison d'Oze (Place Lamagdeleine) contains local collections of prehistoric, Roman and merovingian material.

### Merri Hillfort
M55 12 IGN18 B4-5

Orne has few hillforts, save for a few small promontory forts, which begin in late Bronze Age and Hallstatt times. The Camp de Bierre, S of the hamlet of that name, is included since it features on maps (as 'Camp Celtique') and is an odd but impressive site. An oval promontory of 1.6ha is enclosed by a substantial drystone rampart, and two widely-spaced defences on the S. Radiocarbon dates indicate late Bronze Age beginnings, but the site must be multi-period (there was Gallo-Roman occupation).

Wheeler and Richardson 1957, 119-20; Bender 1986 200-201 (with plan).

**Sées** (Sagii, Civitas Saiorum)
M60 3 IGN19 A2

Though Sées appears in the *Notitia Galliarum*, and was presumably a late Roman civitas, it has produced no evidence of any late Roman walls and there is little evidence of Roman occupation. The thirteenth-century cathedral is however well worth a visit.

## SEINE-MARITIME

The present département of Seine-Maritime (once Seine-Inférieure) corresponds to the territories of the Caleti around Juliobona (Lillebonne) at the mouth of the Seine and the Veliocasses whose capital was Rotomagus (Rouen). By the late empire, the Caleti had been absorbed by their neighbours, and the civitas must now have corresponded broadly to the present area.

### Caudebec-en-Caux Hillfort
M55 5 IGN7 C6

Immediately W of Caudebec, two widely-spaced ramparts cut off a spur of high ground above the cliffs of the Seine and a river crossing. Rescue excavation in 1985-7 found extensive burning around the rampart, suggesting a timbered *murus gallicus*, though the defences were not sectioned. Inside was a rectangular late first-century BC structure used for cremations and a Gallo-Roman building. There is a second small promontory fort at Vignette, on the opposite (E) side of Caudebec.

M.-C. Lequoy 'Le camp retranche du Calidu' in Clicquet *Celtes en Normandie* 45-54.

### Dieppe-Braquemont Cité des Limes Hillfort
M52 4 IGN7 A11

The Cité des Limes, on the coast NE of Dieppe, is a triangular cliff-edge hillfort of 55ha, protected by chalk sea cliffs on the N and a broad valley on the S. On the E a massive earth rampart, stands over 9m high above the ditch bottom, with a broad shallow ditch and a sharply inturned entrance. To the S, the rampart turns and continues, at reduced scale, above the valley scarp. Towards the W the bank of an earlier and smaller enclosure is visible. In 1822-7 a Romano-Celtic temple was found inside the hillfort, with coins to Valens (364-78), but it has now tumbled into the sea. Later fortification is represented by German bunkers from the Second World War 'Atlantic Wall'.

Wheeler and Richardson (1957), 123-5. M. Mangard 'Etat des recherches sur la Cité des Limes' *Ogam* 21(1969), 31-56.

### Eu (Augusta)
M52 5 IGN03 A4

The temple and theatre of this 30ha rural cult centre were originally excavated by the Abbé Cochet in the nineteenth century. In 1975, fresh excavation of the theatre recovered 40 fragments of a monumental inscription which had fallen from the stage front. This recorded how Lucius Cerialius Rectus, priest of Rome and Augustus, had built the proscenium, with its decoration, at his own cost for the *Pagus Catuslugi* and dedicated it to the divine spirit of the Emperor and to Mars. The latest coins pre-dating the *frons scenae* were unworn issues of Lucius Verus (164) and Marcus Aurelius (166-8). Among the posts held by Cerialius Rectus was that of 'Prefect for the suppression of bandits', a reminder of how endemic this problem was in the ancient world.

The Catuslugi (the name means 'Army of Battle') were one of the smaller tribes of N Gaul, mentioned by Pliny (*N.H.* IV, 106). Eu was evidently their pre-Roman cult centre, for its early levels produced many Gallic coins, one from the British tribe of the Dobunni, as well as La Tène brooches and iron

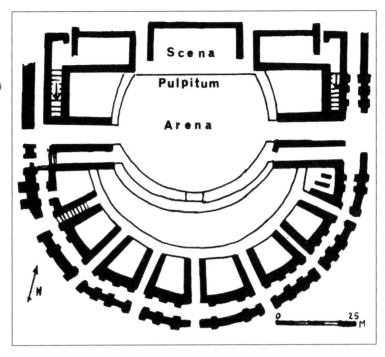

6   Lillebonne —
    plan of Roman
    theatre (after
    Gallia
    Informations)

weapons. The site was evidently re-founded under Augustus, and may for a while served as the tribal capital, but was later included in the territory of the Ambiani of Amiens.

Cochet *La Seine Inférieure Archéologique* (2nd ed., 1866), 331-2. *Gallia* 32 (1974), 330-1; 36 (1978), 308-9. Mangard 'L'Inscription dédicatoire du théâtre du Bois l' Abbée à Eu', *Gallia* 40 (1982), 35-51.

## Fécamp Camp de Canada
Hillfort

M52 12 ICG7 B6

The 20ha Camp de Canada east of Toussaint is the type specimen of Wheeler's 'Fécamp' style of hillfort defence, characteristic of the conquest period in northern and central Gaul. The level S approach is protected by a massive earth rampart standing 12m above the bottom of the broad shallow ditch, with its vertical outer face. The main entrance, sharply inturned, in the

centre of this, has a slighter outwork or barbican in front of it. The rest of the perimeter is defended by steep natural scarps, and a much slighter defensive bank. Two lesser entrances on the N and W have the rampart ends offset to form oblique entrances. In the centre of the site, a pond and area of paving within a rectangular enclosure might mark a Gallo-Roman cult site, if it is not more recent. The name 'Camp de Canada' (or des Canadas) is an old one, 'Canada' probably meaning 'sheep run'.

Wheeler and Richardson 1957, 62-75.

## Lillebonne (Juliobona)
M55 4 ICG7 C7

Lillebonne was the chief city of the Caletes, and a port on the Seine. The Roman theatre (key at Café de Hôtel de Ville opposite) is a 'theatre-amphitheatre' characteristic of Celtic Gaul. Known since the eighteenth century, recent rescue excavation under the adjacent roadway has revealed details

39

7   *Lillebonne — the Roman theatre. Photo J.K.K.*

8   *Lillebonne — the masonry of the theatre, with small squared blocks of* petit appareil *and brick bonding courses. The horizontal rows of square holes are for the timber scaffolding. Photo J.K.K.*

of the stage structures. The masonry is of *opus mixtum*, with brick courses at intervals. The curving seats on the *cavea* were flanked by two ceremonial entrances and a pair of rectangular rooms which may have been stage buildings. The recess in the middle of the *cavea* wall was a shrine, perhaps to Nemesis, the goddess of just retribution, as in other amphitheatres.

At some stage, the theatre was converted into a fortified strongpoint. The S gate was dismantled, and its voussoirs used to block the entrance passage, as can be seen on site. Walls faced in blockwork have been noted around a rectangular enclosure of 1.5ha on the N (stage) side and the theatre may have been incorporated in the line of late Roman defences, as at Tours, Périgueux and elsewhere. The museum (Hôtel de Ville, closed Tuesdays and Saturday-Sunday in winter) contains a good collection of Roman material from the excavations. There is more in Rouen museum.

The baths (Grenier IV, 345-9) lay opposite the theatre, under the present museum and at the foot of the rising ground. They were probably late first- to early second-century in date. On the hill above is a castle with one of the round keeps characteristic of the castle building of Philip Augustus (1180-1223) and found in northern and central France, e.g. Laval, Gisors or Villeneuve-sur-Yonne, with close copies in Britain, as at Pembroke and elsewhere.

De Vesly *Le Castrum de Juliobona* (1915). Johnson (1983), 88. *Gallia Informations* 1989-2, 209.

## Quiévrecourt Hillfort
M52 15 IGN03 C4

In 1989, archaeological survey on the line of the new N28 road west of Neufchâtel-en-Bray revealed a previously unknown hillfort enclosing 63ha on an irregular spur of high ground within a river loop. Late Bronze Age occupation included moulds for bronze casting, but the first defences were of *murus gallicus* type. After a period of disuse, they were remodelled with a massive earth rampart of 'Fécamp' type, perhaps at a time of emergency. This is one of a number of cases where these two types of defences have proved to be successive.

C. Beurion 'Le site protohistorique de Quiévrecourt' in Cliquet, *Celtes en Normandie* 23-34.

## Rouen (Rotomagus)
M52 14 IGN7 C11

The capital of the Veliocassi was a flourishing town of about 100ha at its peak, with quays and warehouses along the Seine, baths, and an amphitheatre for 20,000 spectators. The line of the late Roman walls, known from excavations, enclosed a rectangular area at its core, but nothing of the Roman town is visible. The Musée des Antiquites de la Seine-Maritime (198, Rue Beauvoisine, closed Thursdays) contains a wholly outstanding collection of regional archaeology of all periods.

## St-Martin-de-Boscherville
Romano-Celtic temple and early church
M52 14 ICG7 C10

Excavation under the Abbey church of St-Georges-de-Boscherville, in the village of St Martin de Boscherville, has shown that for once the story of a church built over the site of a Roman temple was true. A first-century Romano-Celtic temple in wood was replaced in the second century by one in stone, whose shell was still standing in the seventh century, when the ambulatory was taken down and the central cella converted into a church (compare Langon, Ille-et-Vilaine and Mont Beuvray, Saône-et-Loire). The existing abbey, a fine example of early twelfth-century

Norman Romanesque, was founded by Raoul de Tancarville, tutor of William the Conqueror. This was not however an example of 'continuity'. As in other cases, the church did not immediately replace the pagan cult, but reoccupied a convenient building disused for perhaps 300 years.

One of the Romanesque capitals in the church is of interest for other reasons. It depicts a man (the Merovingian goldsmith St Eligius or Eloi) holding a large mallet. He is a moneyer, who is striking coins. The rectangular block housing the lower die is in front of him, and he is holding the cylindrical bottle-shaped upper die. The mallet is raised, and he is about to strike a coin.

# 2 Brittany
## (Lugdunensis Tertia)

The late Roman province of Lugdunenis III covered a wider area than present day Brittany. It stretched south to the Loire, and included Touraine (the provincial capital was at Tours), Maine and Anjou. These are dealt with in chapter 3. Brittany includes the territories of five Iron Age tribes, corresponding to the five modern départements — the Osismes, Coriosolites, Riedones, Namnetes and Veneti. However, much of its present culture, as part of Celtic western Europe, stems from immigrations from S Wales and SW England in the period after the break up of the Roman Empire. A glance at a Breton calendar in a shop or bank will show the feasts of Welsh and Cornish saints like Cadoc, Illtyd or Petrock, and the Breton language is close to Welsh or Cornish rather than to ancient Gaulish.

Eastern Brittany, around Rennes, has much in common with the hedged *bocage* country of Normandy and Maine. Further west is an interior plateau — the *Argoat* — with poor granite soils covered with gorse and heather and a coastal strip — the *Armor* — with small fishing ports set on a coast of headlands, reefs and islands.

## CÔTES D'ARMOR (formerly Côtes du Nord)

The Côtes d'Armor, along the north coast of Brittany, was the territory of the pre-Roman Coriosolites.

**Corseul** (Fanum Martis)
M59 5 IGN16 E1
The capital of the Coriosolites, probably successor of the pre-Roman oppidum at Alet, was a town of 130ha at its greatest extent. Excavation of the public baths suggests that it still flourished in the late Empire, for after a late third-century fire they were twice rebuilt, lasting into the fourth century. However, there were no late Roman town walls, and Alet may have resumed its role as local capital. There are traces of the Roman town at Le Champ Mulon, 200m from the town centre near a sports field. The museum in the Mairie, and the adjacent public gardens have Gallo-Roman architectural fragments and other material.

1.5km towards Dinan is the high multi-angular D-shaped tower of the Temple of Mars or Haut Bécherel, first- or early second-century in date, of neatly coursed *Petit appareil* with putlog holes for the timber scaffolding used in its construction at regular intervals. Scars at the angles show where ashlar quoins have been robbed out, and a broad horizontal groove near the top of the walling marks where the roof of the surrounding ambulatory was tied to the tower. The flat face of the tower may have carried a pedimented classical facade, and faced a large temple enclosure, recorded in the nineteenth century.
R. Sanquer *Gallia* 31 (1973), 351-77 (baths); Galliou 1983, 64-6; Bender 1986, 65-7.

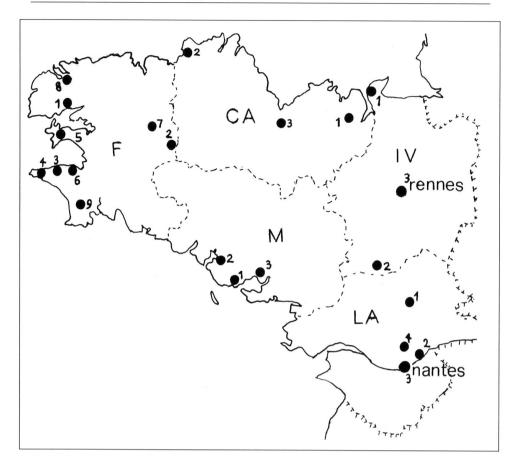

9   Brittany (Lugdunensis Tertia)
   **CA** Côte d'Armor *1 Corseul 2 Le Yaudet 3 Pléderan*
   **F** Finistère *1 Brest 2 Carhaix 3 Castel Coz 4 Castel Meur 5 Crozon 6 Douarnenez 7 Huelgoat 8 Lannilis 9 Plonéur-Lanvern*
   **IV** Ille-et-Vilaine *1 Alet 2 Langon 3 Rennes*
   **LA** Loire Atlantique *1 Abbaretz 2 Mauves 3 Nantes 4 Petit Mars*
   **M** Morbihan *1 Locmariaquer 2 Locoal-Mendon 3 Vannes*

**Le Yaudet** Iron Age and Roman fort
M59 1 IGN14 A3
This granite coastal headland W of Lannion has been occupied since prehistoric times. Around the time of Caesar, a *murus gallicus* rampart, now altered by late medieval fields and field walls, was built across the neck of the promontory, on an existing Iron Age site, and the rampart continued around the rest of the perimeter. Occupation continued in Roman times, and in the late third century a masonry wall was built around the headland, on the line of the Iron Age rampart. A gateway led down to a landing place and parts of the Roman wall have been conserved and left on display.

B. Cunliffe and P. Galliou, 'Le Yaudet, Ploulec'h, Côtes d'Armor, Brittany: an interim report on the excavations of 1991-4', *Antiq. J.* 75 (1995), 43-70.

## Louannec Iron Age stela with early medieval inscription
M59 1 IGN14 A4

A reused Iron age stela preserved in the transept of the nineteenth-century parish church E of Perros-Guirec has a secondary vertical inscription which closely parallels the fifth- to seventh-century Latin inscribed post-Roman memorial stones of Cornwall, Wales and southern Scotland. It reads DISIDERI FILI BODOGNOVS — '(the stone) of Desiderius son of Bodognous'. The mixture of Latin and Celtic personal names is characteristic and the stone provides important first-hand evidence for the historically attested migration from western Britain to Brittany in early Christian times.

Davies et al 2000, 137-144.

## Pléderan-Camp de Péran
Vitrified fort M59 3-13 IGN14 A5-6
Timbered 'murus gallicus' ramparts were sometimes set on fire, accidentally or by enemy action. The timbers served as fuel, their beam holes as flues. Often the rampart was vitrified into a solid mass. The two ramparts of this 1ha fort show the result. Good exposures of the vitrified wall are visible, with beam holes at 1m intervals.

Bender 1986, 73.

# FINISTÈRE
Finistère ('Land's End') in the western coasts of Brittany was the territory of the Osismes. The area offers a wealth of archaeological sites in fine coastal scenery, with megaliths, standing stones and Iron Age 'cliff castles' like those of Cornwall or western Ireland.

## Brest
M58 4 IGN13 B4
The superb natural harbour here is still a major naval port and dockyard. The Roman fort under the later castle was occupied by a unit of Moors, part of the command of the Duke of the Armorican and Nerviian Shore, equivalent to the Saxon Shore across the Channel. What may have been the other half of the same unit was stationed down the coast at Vannes. Part of the fort wall is visible, of small blockwork with tile courses. Its circular hollow projecting towers, like those of Cologne or Tongres, were removed in post-medieval times to improve access to the defences, but their scars are visible on the wall face and the foundations of one tower can be seen.

Johnson (1976), 79-80.

## Carhaix (Vorgium)
M58 17 IGN14 C3
The capital of the Osismes had the usual street grid and buildings of a Roman town, including a Romano-Celtic temple, public baths, and the only aqueduct in Brittany, but there is not much to be seen, save for columns, stone sarcophagi and a drain in the Jardin du Chapeau Rouge near the town centre.

## Castel Coz Promontory fort
M58 14 IGN13 A5-6
Castel Coz, on the coast N of Beuzec Cap-Sizun, is one of the Breton cliff castles that gave Caesar so much trouble, and which he describes. The site has Neolithic and Bell-Beaker occupation, triple Iron Age banks and ditches enclosing about 1ha and medieval refortification. Hut floors are visible in the interior, and excavation in 1869 revealed prehistoric, Iron Age and early medieval occupation.

Wheeler and Richardson 1957 109-10; Bender 1986 84-6.

## Castel Meur Promontory fort
M58 13 IGN13 A3-4
On the Pointe de Brézellec, N of Cléden-Cap-Sizun, the site had Neolithic and Beaker occupation before the building of the triple ramparts. 95

rectangular hut depressions are visible in the interior. Excavation in 1889 found much Iron Age material, now in the museum of St-Germain-en-Laye in Paris. The site had been destroyed by fire, perhaps by Caesar, but some early medieval pottery was found.
Wheeler and Richardson 1957 109, Bender 1986, 87-9.

## Crozon, Lostmarc'h
Promontory fort
M58 13-14 IGN13 B6
The Crozon peninsular is rich in prehistoric sites. W of the hamlet of Lostmarc'h on its west coast, two banks and ditches cut off a small headland. There are two possible ruined megalithic tombs in the interior.
Wheeler and Richardson 1957 110, Bender 1986, 90.

## Douarnenez Roman port
M58 14 IGN13 B7
Still a major commercial fishing port for sardines, tuna and mackerel, Douarnenez was in Roman times the centre of an industry producing *garum*, fish sauce, from the offshore shoals of young sardines that occur here in late spring. The Roman fish sauce industry spread from the west Mediterranean coasts of Spain and Morocco to the Atlantic coastlands of Iberia. By the time of Hadrian, it had arrived in Armorica. Though known at other places on the Breton coast, its main concentration was along the shores of the Bay of Douarnenez.

The catch was brought to roofed rectangular masonry tanks, carefully sealed with waterproof cement. These were filled with layers of sardines, alternated with layers of salt, and then left for five or six weeks, during which time the digestive juices of the sardines marinated the whole, whilst the salt prevented any decay. At the end of this time, the fish sauce was decanted into containers (possibly wooden barrels, for no amphorae or other pottery containers are known) for sale. Some 19 batteries of these rectangular masonry tanks are known around the shores of the bay, 2-4m deep, sunk into the ground, and cement-lined with a quarter-round moulding at the bottom in the manner of a Roman swimming bath. The probable destinations for this large scale commercial industry were the Roman frontiers in Britain and the Rhineland, for *garum* was a part of the standard military diet.

Though there is no direct evidence, it would be quite in keeping with Hadrian's way of doing things if the industry had begun with official encouragement, so that the Army could be assured of adequate supplies of *garum* without the trouble and expense of bringing it from Spain or Morocco. Some support for this is provided by an altar to the Divinity of the Emperor and to Neptune (an appropriate pair of dedicatees) set up at Douarnenez by C. Varenius Varus, *curator* (chairman) of a club of Roman citizens domiciled there (*I.L.T.G.* 338). This is now in the museum at Quimper. Douaranenez retained its role as an Atlantic seaport with links to Britain in late Roman times, when a lady was buried here in a lead coffin wearing hairpins of Yorkshire jet.
Galliou and Jones 95-100. R. Sanquer and P. Galliou 'Garum, sel et salaisons en Armorique romaine' *Gallia* 30, 1 (1972), 199-223.

## Huelgoat Hillfort
M58 6 IGN14 C2
Le Camp d'Artus stands on a heavily forested granite hill, littered with enormous granite boulders 'like herds of elephants' as Wheeler put it. The 30ha hillfort is enclosed by a *murus gallicus* with inturned entrances, a smaller kite shaped enclosure at its northern end,

and a medieval motte at the tip of the spur, originally with a stone keep. Wheeler excavated here in 1938 as part of his northern French hillforts project. Heavy burning in the entrances suggested violent destruction, probably during the Caesarian campaigns of 56 or 51 BC

Wheeler and Richardson 1957, 23-38.

## Lannilis Iron Age stela
M58 3 IGN13 B2

A plain four-sided granite pillar standing on a green in the centre of the village. There are several hundred Iron Age standing stones (stelae) in Brittany, and these are particularly widespread in Finistère. Unlike the unshaped standing stones of earlier prehistory, they are carefully shaped, often circular, square-sectioned or multangular tapering pillars, sometimes with vertical fluting, and at times given a distinctively phallic form by a cone-shaped finial. Morbihan has a variant type, lower and hemispherical. This and the next are simply included as typical examples.

Giot et al 1995, 239-52, with distribution map.

## Plonéour-Lanvern Iron Age stela
M58 14 IGN13 C9

Near the church, in the centre of the village, is a 4m high Iron Age menhir, a tapering granite pillar with vertical fluting and a knobbed finial. Not quite as obviously phallic as the pillar at Locoal-Mendon (Morbihan), but the general effect is clear enough. However, the stone is said locally to have been the mast of a boat in which a Welsh saint sailed to Brittany.

## ILLE-ET-VILAINE

Archaeological evidence suggests that the Coriosolites along the north coast of Brittany were at least as active in pre-Roman trade with Britain as the better documented Veneti of the south. Under

Roman rule, their capital was at Corseul (Côtes d'Armor), whilst Rennes was that of the Riedones.

A. Provost and G. Leroux *Carte Archéologique de la Gaule* 35 (1990).

## Alet — St Servan sur Mer
M59 6 IGN16 B3

Excavation by Luc Langoüet at this promontory fort in the estuary of the Rance outside St Malo has revealed a densely occupied political and trading centre occupied from about 80 BC until its destruction in the rising under Julius Sacrovir in AD 21. It was replaced as Cantonal capital by Corseul (Fanum Martis), but in the late third century the headland was surrounded by an irregular stone curtain wall with a series of square towers, resembling Le Yaudet. About 365-75 a large building like a military *principia* (headquarters building) was added in the interior. The site was garrisoned by a late Roman army unit, the *Martenses*. By the ninth century it was the seat of a Breton bishop.

## Langon
M63 6 IGN24 A5

Until it was rededicated to the Sicilian martyr St Agatha, the standing Roman building, now a church, in the middle of the village of Langon, bore a dedication which was surely unique in the history of the Christian Church: the *Ecclesia Sancti Veneris* — the church of St Venus. Various roles have been suggested for the Roman building, as a funerary monument, a temple or part of a baths complex. The mixed sandstone and brick courses suggest a second- or third-century date. The rectangular chamber which is now the nave is separated by 4m from an apsidal structure, now the chancel, which retains in the crown of the apse a Roman wall painting of Venus rising from the waves surrounded by fishes. The 'nave' was presumably once linked to the apse by an ambulatory of

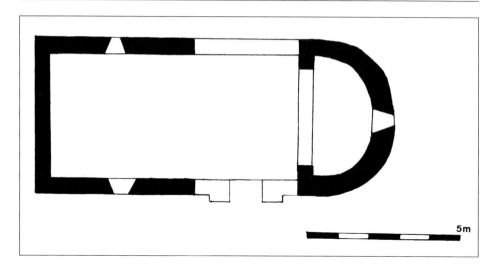

*10 Langon (Ille-et-Vilaine) — Roman mausoleum or temple (in black) and medieval church. After Royer*

*11 Langon (Ille-et-Vilaine) — 'The church of St Venus'. A Gallo-Roman shrine converted into a Christian church*

some sort, in the manner of the cella and ambulatory of a Romano-Celtic temple.

Langon was already the *Ecclesia sancti Veneris* by 838. In Romanesque times the two parts were joined to form the present church, and a wall painting of a kneeling figure adoring a seated saint replaced Venus. The Roman wall painting remained hidden until the nineteenth century, though oddly the figure of Venus must have been known at the time of the rededication, since this was based on the naked Venus and the fact that Agatha was allegedly martyred by having her breasts cut off. There may have been some cult connected with nursing mothers or the like, which formed a link. The Roman wall paintings were eventually recognised under their Romanesque successor by the antiquary Charles Langlois in 1842, and carefully exposed.

R. Royer, 'Un monument Gallo-Romain en Armorique: La chapelle de Langon', *Archéologia* 157 (August 1981), 16-21.

## Rennes (Condate)
M59 17 IGN16 C8

Inscriptions from the capital of the Riedones refer to a basilica, and possibly a temple of Mars Mullus. It had an active pottery industry, which in addition to the usual coarse wares produced *terra nigra*, mortaria and pipeclay statuettes.

The late Roman walls enclosed a pentagonal area of about 9ha, and were of somewhat unusual construction. Above a mortared foundation of blocks of schist was a base of granite blocks and reused architectural fragments. The main body of the wall was of alternate triple bands of small squared stone blocks and bricks, the latter giving the city its medieval name of 'ville rouge'. Five milestones, the latest of Tetricus (270-73), built into the foundations of a postern gate give a *terminus post quem* for

its building. The Musée de Bretagne (20, Quai Emile Zola, closed Tuesdays) is an excellent modern museum, which provides a lucid and detailed introduction to all periods of Brittany's past.

Blanchet 50-53 *T.C.C.G.* V, 57-66.

# LOIRE ATLANTIQUE

Loire Atlantique (previously Loire Inférieure or Loire Maritime) is around the estuary of the Loire, a river which is not only a major communications route, but marks the geographical boundary between northern and central Gaul. In pre-Roman times it was the boundary between the Namnetes north of the river and the Pictones to its south. Nantes has been an Atlantic seaport since at least Roman times, a major interface between Gaul and the Atlantic world, even if the prehistoric trading centre of *Corbilo,* sometimes identified with Nantes, seems to have been a myth. Provost *Carte Archéologique de la Gaule* 44 (1988).

## Abbaretz and Nozay
Early medieval tin mines
M63 17 IGN24 B6/7

Cassiterite (tin ore) has been exploited in quantity in Brittany since the later Bronze Age (Giot *Bull Soc Préhistorique Française* 95 (1998), 4, 599-600), and mining continued in later times. In this area N of Nantes, deep linear trenches have been dug into deposits of tin bearing schist. A radiocarbon date of AD 650±100 was obtained from associated material and two Merovingian Frankish coins are known from the site.

## Mauves-sur-Loire
Rural cult centre
M67 4 IGN24 C8

This 35ha vicus-sanctuary on the N bank of the Loire has a theatre-amphitheatre, baths and a rectangular

temple, which may have been of classical type, with a pronaos and columns. A first-century villa-like building associated with the sanctuary, excavated in 1967-75, was enlarged under Trajan, but abandoned at the end of the second century.
Grenier II, 2, 713; III 970-971. Provost *C.A.G.* 44, 67/

**Nantes** (Condivincum)
M67 3 IGN24 D7
Inscriptions refer to a tribunal, temple and vaulted portico and show that Nantes was already a busy Atlantic seaport, with a *vicus portensis*, a maritime port suburb with its own magistrates, along the quays of the now vanished Erdre, a tributary of the Loire. The late Roman walls enclosed an area of some 16ha on the north bank of the Loire, between the castle and the Hôtel de Ville. The early Roman city may not have been much larger. The walls were demolished piecemeal in the eighteenth and nineteenth centuries, producing much reused material, including two milestones of the Emperor Tacitus, showing that they must be later than AD 275. The Musée Archéologique (Place Jean V) contains important local Gallo-Roman and Merovingian collections, including architectural material from the sixth-century cathedral.

Christianity came to Nantes relatively early. Two men, Donatien and Rogatien, are said to have been martyred under Maximian around 286-304, and the rather hazardous process of counting back from bishops whose approximate date is known from church councils and the like puts the first bishop, Clarus, in the time of Constantine around 310-30. Both the martyrium of Donatien and Rogatien and the grave-church of the third bishop Similinus were long established by the time of Gregory of Tours in the sixth century.

Blanchet 56-60. D. Costa, *Nantes, Musée Th. Dobree, Art Mérovingienne* Paris 1964. Knight 1999. 96-100,158-9.

**Petit-Mars** Rural cult centre
M63 17 IGN24 C7
A vicus-sanctuary, excavated in the 1890s, with a large temenos or sacred enclosure which presumably contained a temple. To the E was a theatre-amphitheatre, aligned on the temenos.
Provost *C.A.G.* 44 111 and 1993, 149-50.

# MORBIHAN
Morbihan, along the S Breton coast, is most famous archaeologically for the great megalithic complex of Carnac and the megalithic tombs associated with it. In Roman times it was the territory of the Veneti, a maritime people with a fleet of stoutly built ocean-going ships, with which they traded with Britain. They had, as Caesar tells us, not a central oppidum, but a large number of 'cliff castles', defended promontories set on the edge of the sea, like those of Cornwall, SW Wales and western Ireland.

**Locmariaquer** Rural cult centre
M63 12 IGN 15 C7
The area around Locmariaquer on the Gulf of Morbihan contains some of the most spectacular prehistoric sites in western Europe, including standing stones and chambered tombs like the famous Gavrinis. Roman remains are less impressive. A theatre-amphitheatre was excavated in 1893 under the modern cemetery. The remains comprised a horseshoe of three concentric walls.
Grenier III, 972-3.

**Locoal-Mendon** Iron Age pillar-stone with early medieval inscription
M63 2 IGN15 C6
On the right-hand side of the road leading from the village to the tidal island of Ile Locoal, near a calvary, is a cylindrical Iron Age pillar stone of

phallic form. On the upper part is a later vertical inscription reading CROUX PROSTLON in half-uncial letters, with a long-stemmed cross and flanking vertical bands of key pattern. The island may have housed an early monastery, and it is possible that the inscription, probably of ninth- or tenth-century date, commemorates Prostlon, wife of a ninth-century Breton Count, Pascwethen.

Davies et al 2000, 221-224.

## Vannes (Darioritum)
M63 3 IGN15 C8

Despite Julius Caesar's ethnic cleansing of the Veneti, their new capital was in being by the time of the birth of Christ as a small coastal port. Augustan-Tiberian occupation is known, including Arretine ware, rare this far north, and early amphorae. Later, the normal planned town developed on the hill around the present church of St Paternus. A theatre was found here in the nineteenth century, and the site of a large public building is known, though excavation is difficult under the modern town. The late Roman defences lay W of the early town, across a stream, in the area of the medieval cathedral and town walls. Fragments of the late Roman walls are known, with the usual tile levelling courses and coursed blockwork set in pink mortar with crushed tile, though much was incorporated in the fine thirteenth-century town walls, themselves now partly demolished. The late Roman garrison of *Mauri Veneti* ('Moors of Vannes') was probably part of the same unit as the *Mauri Osismiaci* at Brest. By coincidence, a medieval document refers to the Roman walls as the '*murs Sarazins*' — a not uncommon name in western France for Roman work. The town was Christian by the mid-fifth century, and when a church council met here in 462-8, the preamble explained that 'The necessity of ordaining a new bishop has caused us to meet in the church of Vannes' (probably the later cathedral of St Pierre), so that there had been at least one previous bishop.

Galliou *L'Armorique Romaine* 71-2 *T.C.C.G.* V (Ecclesiastical Province of Tours), 95-100.

# 3 Maine, Anjou and Touraine
## (Lugdunensis Tertia)

Between Normandy and the Loire, four modern French départements can still be equated with major Gallic tribes of the time of Caesar, and with Gallo-Roman civitates. In Mayenne, the Aulerici Diablintes had their capital at Jublains, the only civitas capital of the four which has failed to develop into a modern city. The Cenomanni of Le Mans (Sarthe), the Andecavi of Angers (Maine-et-Loire) and the Turones of Tours (Indre-et-Loire) developed into the medieval Counties of Maine, Anjou and Touraine. These belonged to the Angevin kings of England, who took their name from Anjou, through Geoffrey Plantagenet, Count of Anjou, father of Henry II. Most was lost to the French king Philip Augustus by King John in 1204, though the English hung on to Tours until 1242.

The area is rich in standing Roman masonry, perhaps because the abundance of good building material made stone robbing less needful. The late Roman walls of Le Mans and Tours are among the best in France.

## Maine-Mayenne and Sarthe

Maine lay between Normandy to the north and the Loire to the south. The medieval County included the départements of Mayenne and Sarthe and the N part of Eure-et-Loire. In Roman times it was the territory of the Aulerici, divided between the Aulerici Diablintes on the W and the Aulerici Cenomanni of Le Mans to the E.

## MAYENNE
### Jublains (Noviodunum)
M60 11 IGN17 H3

The capital of the Aulerci Diablintes figures in the Notitia Galliarum as a civitas capital, but the remains, save for the remarkable fortified complex, are those of a vicus or a rural cult centre. In alignment SW, they comprise a rectangular temple, a circular shrine or tholos ('La tonnelle'), baths and a theatre.

The fortified complex was excavated in 1843, the first full illustrated description in English being by Charles Roach Smith. It was re-studied from 1975 on and has now been laid out and displayed. Its first phase, in the later third century, consisted of the central stone fortlet, surrounded by a double ditch with a stone built gateway and a minuscule Roman bathhouse to provide essential facilities for the small detachment of troops stationed here (both this and the later baths are protected by modern roofs). A very similar small bath existed e.g. within the Roman fort at Brecon in S Wales, for similar reasons. The distinctive plan of the fortlet may have been borrowed from some Roman frontier region elsewhere, though no close parallel has yet been found. It has four squarish tower-like projections, probably for accommodation rather than defence, for they only cover two faces of the tower. Inside were roofed timber structures around a central courtyard, and various tanks for collecting rainwater. Later

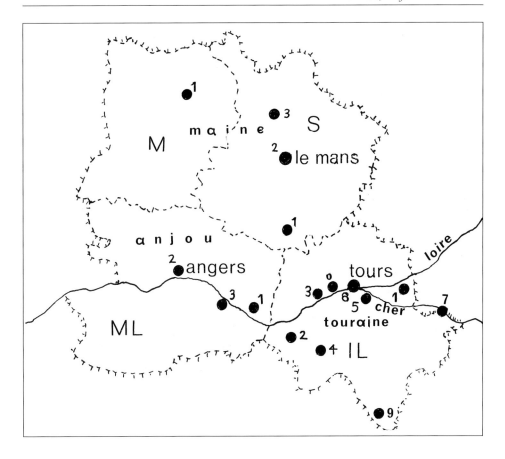

12 Maine, Anjou and Touraine (Lugdunensis Tertia)

**M** Mayenne *1 Jublains*

**S** Sarthe *1 Aubigné-Racan 2 Le Mans 3 Oisseau-le-Petit*

**ML** Maine et Loire *1 Allonnes 2 Angers 3 Gennes*

**IL** Indre et Loire *1 Amboise 2 Chinon 3 Cinq Mars 4 Crouzilles 5 Larcay 6 Luynes 7 Thesée 8 Tours 9 Yzeures*

three other small external turrets, one a latrine, were added.

In its second period, the double ditches were filled in, sealing coins of Tetricus (270-3), including some of the crude copies which passed for currency at this time, and continued to do so for some decades after his death. These included a small hoard. The ditches have now been re-excavated and, with their accompanying mounds, are visible on site. After their levelling, the earlier works were surrounded by a larger fort 110m square, with two opposed entrances and a series of semicircular towers. There was also a second replacement bath building, partly overlying one of the infilled ditches. Rebuffat thought that the fort served as a centre for the collection of the *annona* (a tax in produce and kind) and that the walls of the second phase were the work of the same gangs of masons who built the late Roman walls of Le Mans.

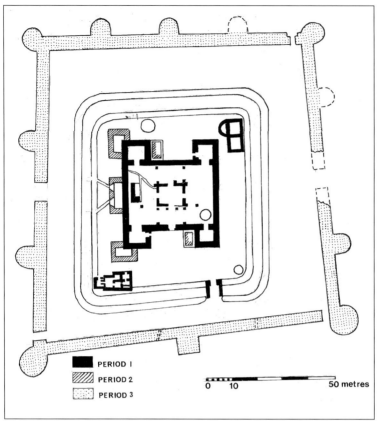

*13 Jublains (Mayenne) — plan of fortified complex*

PERIOD 1
PERIOD 2
PERIOD 3

0    10                    50 metres

C. Roach Smith *Collectanea Antiqua* III (1854), 103-8; R. Rebuffat 'Jublains, un complex fortifié dans l'ouest de la Gaule' *Rev. Archéol* 1985,37-256; J. Naveau 'Le Plan antique du Jublains (Mayenne)' *R.A.O.* 3, 1986 107-17. Grenier IV, 777-86.

## SARTHE

### Aubigné-Racan Rural cult centre
M64 3 IGN25 B9

Aubigné (or Cherré) lay on the frontier of the Turones of Tours and the Cenomanni of Le Mans, corresponding to the modern départements of Sarthe and Indre-et-Loire. Nearby is the promontory fort of Vaux. A Hallstatt cemetery under the Gallo-Roman theatre, apparently associated with a Megalithic tomb, suggests that the religious cult centre went back to prehistoric times. The complex includes a theatre, excavated in the 1870s, and still visible, a temple, baths, an aqueduct, and a large rectangular forum. There were fresh excavations from 1977 onwards. Grenier III, 872-3. *Gallia* 39 (1981), 343-5; 41 (1983), 302-4. *Gallia Prehistoire* 20 (1977), 442; 22 (1979), 576-7.

### Le Mans (Suindunum)
M60 13 IGN19 D2

The Roman walls of Le Mans are the finest and best preserved in France. The capital of the Aulerici Cenomanni, on a long narrow ridge between the Sarthe and the marshy valley of a now vanished tributary, began as a hillfort (*dunum*) whose broad ditch crossed the neck of the ridge north of the cathedral. The Roman town enjoyed the usual

14  *Le Mans (Sarthe), La Tour Magdeleine in 1883 — engraving by G. Bouet. Blanchet pl XI*

15 *Le Mans (Sarthe) Window opening in La Tour Magdeleine — engraving of 1878 by G. Bouet. The smaller upper window may be a secondary replacement The thicker brick courses at sill level mark the wall walk of the curtain. Blanchet pl. XII*

amenities. Public baths have been excavated on the flat ground between the walls and the Sarthe, in the area of the École Claude Chappe. Built in the mid-first century AD, they were reconstructed in the late second and demolished in the late third to provide material for the town walls (*Gallia* 41 (1983), 306-7; 43 (1985), 459-61). A theatre-amphitheatre like the Arènes de Lutèce in Paris was found in 1792 in the Parc des Jacobins SE of the cathedral, but only a plan survives. The forum lay around the Place St Pierre and there were two aqueducts.

The late Roman walls, 4m thick, and originally about 18m high, have a rubble core faced with small square blocks of stone, with triple tile bonding courses at roughly metre intervals and a broader band 5-6 tiles thick at wall walk level. The foundations are of massive blocks, many reused from earlier buildings, including sculptured stones and inscriptions, faced on the outside with three courses of large tufa and granite blocks. Above, the facing blocks, of white limestone and dark ironstone, are sometimes arranged in decorative geometric patterns of triangles, lozenges, hourglass shapes and flower patterns. Ten of the semicircular mural towers survive of an original 35. An average of 24-25m apart, they are solid to parapet level, with two stories above this, lit by round headed windows, as can be seen on the two best preserved, the Tour du Vivier and the Tour Magdeleine.

The really impressive remains of the walls are on the W, where the natural hillslope above the river was cut back to accommodate them. Elsewhere they are more fragmentary, and often hidden by later houses. The best starting point for a visit is the cathedral, which lies just inside their NE angle. When a new choir (finished in 1254) was added to the Romanesque nave, a section of the walls, including a tower, was demolished and the E end extended out beyond their line. One oddity worth noting is the sandstone menhir near the SW angle of the cathedral. Can this really be a prehistoric standing stone? A few fragments, including a tower, survive N of the cathedral, and the upper floors of two now vanished towers near the cathedral were turned into chapels in the early Middle Ages. The Roman N gate was probably near the end of the Place du Château. From their NW angle, the walls return parallel to the Rue de Gourdaine. Near the angle, one jamb of a postern gate, like those seen elsewhere on the walls, survives.

A flight of steps SW of the cathedral leads directly down to the W walls, parallel to the Rue St Hilaire and Rue de Gourdaine. The Tour des Pans de Gorron on the left differs from its fellows in being pentagonal rather than rounded, but is bonded in with the rest of the walls. Beyond is the well-preserved Tour de Magdaleine, which still retains the original windows on its two upper floors, though the smaller upper ones may have been altered in Roman times. Beyond the Tour du Tunnel, the walls are bisected by the Rue Wilbur Wright, cut through them in 1851-7. In the flank of the tower, a small brick postern gate survives, the collapsed part of its vault restored in concrete. On all this stretch, the polychrome patterning of the walls is particularly striking.

Beyond the Rue Wilbur Wright is another fine stretch, with two more towers. A flight of steps then runs uphill to the town centre through another postern gate, the Grand Pôterne. This has ashlar jambs and a round-headed outer arch of edge-set brick, but a pointed medieval arch has been inserted below, concealing the Roman brick vaulting. The Tour du Vivier beyond the steps again preserves its round-headed upper windows. The tile roof is perhaps not unlike the Roman original. Two further towers and a Roman drain opening, the so-called Petit Pôterne, with a medieval arch cut through its tile head, lead to the SW angle. The walls return just beyond this, though not a great deal is visible of this S face. The Roman S gate probably stood at the bottom of the Grand Rue. From the SE angle a few fragments of walling parallel to the Rue St Flaceau lead up to the Place St Pierre, where the wall described a dog-leg turn under the church of St Pierre in Curia to accommodate the wall of the Roman forum, which lay W of the Hôtel de Ville. The possible remains of a Roman gateway, with guard chambers flanking a central passage, are SW of the church, imbedded in houses and inaccessible, but the plan, and most of the surviving work, suggest that it is medieval. From the Hôtel de Ville, the line of the wall crosses the Rue Wilbur Wright and the Place des Jacobins back to the cathedral.

R.M. Butler 'The Roman Walls of Le Mans' *J.R.S.* 48 (1958), 33-9. J. Biarne and J. Guilleux, 'Le Mans, la plus belle enceinte gallo-romaine du Bas Empire en Gaul' *Archéologia* 145 (1980), 6-19.

**Oisseau-le-Petit** Rural cult centre
M60 13 ICG19 B1

Beside the main road from Le Mans to Alençon, and at the junction of Roman roads from Le Mans, Rouen and

Jublains, this 100ha site includes a theatre, three temples, baths and a huge monumental precinct. It may have begun in pre-Roman times, for 2000m E is the 3ha promontory fort of St-Evroult, with a massive stone rampart 8-10m high on the N, and a smaller rampart around the rest of the perimeter. There is a chapel of St-Evroult within it (for plan see *Gallia* 43, 1985, 458). The cult centre stood at the boundary of the tribes of the Aulerici and Esuvii. Excavations in 1984 revealed a Romano-Celtic temple built in the first century AD and continuing to the late third.
*Gallia* 43 (1985), 461-3.

## ANJOU AND TOURAINE

Angers and Tours are on the Loire, with their territories south of the river, between Maine to the north and Poitou to the south. Tours retains impressive remains of its late Roman town walls and early records show what we have lost at Angers, though the splendid castle and other medieval buildings there are some compensation.

## ANJOU — MAINE-ET-LOIRE
M. Provost *Carte Archéologique de la Gaule* 49 (1988)
### Allonnes Vicus
M64 12 IGN19 D2
A rural vicus, beginning in the late Iron Age. The baths have been excavated (Grenier IV, 325-plan) and sarcophagi, one with a seventh-century shield brooch, show that occupation continued into Merovingian times.
*C.A.G.* 49. 116. J. Biarne, *Allonnes dans l'antiquité* (Le Mans 1974); P. Terouanne 'Allonnes: vicus ou emporium?', *Caesarodunum* 11 (1976), 185-94.
### Angers (Juliomagus)
M63 20 IGN25 C4
The capital of the Andecavi 'the market

of Julius (Caesar)' was probably founded under Augustus, and there is no evidence of pre-Roman occupation. The late Roman name, Civitas Andecavorum, gave rise to the medieval name of Anjou, a twelfth-century possession of the Angevin kings of England. A theatre-amphitheatre and large bath building were still visible in the early nineteenth century, and medieval references to the *vetus mercatum* 'old market' suggest the forum still survived. The bath building has now been excavated (*Gallia* 41 (1983), 310-12).

The late Roman town walls enclosed an oval area of high ground between the medieval castle of 1228-38 and the cathedral and bishop's palace. They had the usual massive foundations with much reused material, in places founded on the natural rock. At one point the wall of an earlier building had been incorporated in the fabric. Above was coursed stonework with tile bonding courses and semicircular projecting towers. The plan of one gate, with two similar towers, is known from excavation. The walls enclosed 9ha, and whilst the city at its peak covered 60ha, this cannot be taken as an accurate measure of the town's shrinkage. Late third-/fourth-century extramural occupation is known and the size of late Roman defences may have been standardized around 9ha in Lugdunensis III, whatever the size of the town (see my *End of Antiquity* p16). The date of the walls is uncertain, but if they were as late as those of their neighbour Tours, the extramural occupation could pre-date them.

Nothing of the walls is now visible, but in medieval times they served as a strongpoint of the Counts of Anjou, including Fulk Nerra (972-1040), pioneer castle builder and progenitor of the Plantagenets. Part of the English Angevin Empire, Angers was captured in

1204 by Philip Augustus, king of France. A number of fine buildings of the Angevin period survive, including the hall of the Hospital of St John, founded by Henry II in 1175, which is now the archaeological museum.

M. Provost, *Angers Gallo-Romain: naissance d'une cité* (Angers 1978); Provost, 'Une tour de l'enceinte gallo-romaine d'Angers', *Gallia* 38 (1980), 97-116; J. Mallet ' L'enceinte gallo-romaine d'Angers', *Annales de Bretagne* 71 (1964), 85-100.

## Gennes Rural cult centre
M64 12 IGN25 C6

On the Loire SE of Angers, Gennes was possibly the capital of the small tribe of the Ambitarvi mentioned by Pliny (*Natural History* IV, 33). It had, among other buildings, baths, an aqueduct, and a theatre-amphitheatre. There is a concentration of megalithic tombs in the area, and Merovingian sarcophagi suggest that occupation continued to post-Roman times.

de Caumont, *Congres Archéol de France* 1862, 128-134 and plan p229. Grenier III, 925-6. IV, 327.

# TOURAINE — INDRE-ET-LOIRE
J. Boussard, *Carte Archéologique de la Gaule Romaine* Forma orbis romani XIII 1960; M. Provost, *Carte Archéologique de la Gaule* 37 (1988).

## Amboise (Ambatiacus)
M64 16 IGN26 C4

The oppidum of Châtelliers under the present castle has a single rampart across the neck of a spur above the Loire. Excavation by A. Peyrard has shown that its first defence was a timbered rampart of La Tène I date, about 400 BC. There were several rebuildings before the final massive 'Fécamp type' rampart. This phase produced much final La Tène material, including coin moulds and large quantities of Italian Dressel 1 amphorae.

In the late first century AD a vicus developed with timber buildings which housed bronze-smiths, potters, cloth-workers and bone-workers. Later, major stone quarries developed. The vicus was occupied to the early third century and there was also a religious sanctuary with monumental stone structures. When Martin of Tours came here in the late fourth century, he demolished what sounds like one of the circular tower-temples of western Gaul, built of large ashlar blocks, 'domed and of great height'.

*Gallia* 38 (1980), 328; 43 (1985), 297-301. *Bull Soc Archéol Touraine* 39 (1980), 345-50. Provost *C.A.G.* 37. 73.

## Chinon
M64 13 IGN25 D9

There may have been a late Roman fortified site under the medieval castle on its dominating rock ridge, for a substantial Roman wall, sculptures and inscriptions were found in the nineteenth century, and the Roman general Aegidius besieged it shortly before 464. A hoard of gold coins (trientes) of the eastern Emperors Zeno, Anastasius and Justin of *c*.AD 500 is also known. In the tenth century it was known as the *Castrum Kaionense*. Bishop Bricius of Tours, immediate successor of St Martin, built a church here and Maximus, a disciple of Martin, founded the minster (*collegiale*) of St Mexme below the castle. Burials from the fifth century onwards have been found below the Romanesque minster, which has now been excavated and restored.

*C.A.G.R.* XIII, 35-6. *C.A.G.* 37. 80. Y. Esquieu *Arch. Med* 21 (1991), 441-2.

## Cinq-Mars-la-Pile
Funerary monument
M64 16 IGN25 C10

'La Pile', alongside the Loire and the

Roman road from Tours to Angers, has been known and studied since the eighteenth century. It is a funerary monument of white limestone and brick 29.4m high, with a 2m high base and two upper stages, crowned by a pyramid and 4 tall brick pillars. The uppermost stage, on the side facing the Loire, is decorated with patterned panels of polychrome brick — stars, diamonds and triangles — recalling the similar decoration of the late Roman walls of Le Mans. Perhaps third- or early fourth-century in date, the type derives from the Toulouse area of SW France. It has been suggested that it may have been the memorial of a wealthy merchant.

P. Audin 'La pile de Cinq-Mars et les piles gallo-romaines', *Annales de Bretagne* 84. 3 (1977), 351-67. *C.A.G.* 37 156.

## Crouzilles, Mougon

Vicus and pottery kilns
M68 4 IGN25 D11

A major pottery making centre in the first and second centuries, with a wide range of products including coarse wares, pipeclay statuettes of Venus, horses and nursing mothers and amphorae (Dressel 2-4 and Gauloise 4). Provost *C.A.G.* 37, 73 and 1993, 159.

**Larçay** Late Roman castellum
M64 15 IGN26 C3

Excavation by Jason Wood has done much to put this enigmatic site on the south bank of the Cher E of Tours into context, but its exact date and purpose remain obscure. An early Roman monumental building, circular and with columns, was demolished to provide building material, and many column sections and sculptured fragments were reused in the wall foundations. There was no dating evidence for the castellum, and it would seem to have been unfinished, the N wall never having been completed above its foundations, though the others survive

to a considerable height. In the later Middle Ages, the site may have been used for agricultural purposes.

In some respects, Larçay recalls the first phase of Jublains (Mayenne) and it could have been a similar centre for the control and taxation in kind of the surrounding area in the period between the Gallic Empire and Diocletian, though in the absence of hard dating evidence, this must remain speculation. The late dating of the town walls of Tours (see below) may at least explain why the *castellum* was thought necessary so near the city, which may not have then been walled.

Interim reports in *Archaeol J.* 144 (1987), 444; 145 (1988), 398.

**Luynes** Aqueduct
M64 14 IGN26 C1

From near the Roman *vicus* of Luynes, an aqueduct carried the water of the la Pinnoire to Tours, 10km E, where it supplied the baths. Most of this is in an underground channel, but between Luynes and Fondettes it crossed a small valley on an aqueduct bridge. Many of the original piers are still visible.

*C.A.G* 37, 154.

**Thésée** (Tasciata) Possible mansio
M64 17 IGN26 C6

Mozelles, at the confluence of the Cher and the Renne, has the ruins of three Roman buildings, identified by Provost as a possible mansio or roadside posting station within an enclosure. The largest is a basilica-like hall 40 x 13.5m with an E annexe and a S gallery flanked by two pavilions, in the manner of some Roman villas. There are traces of 27 windows and 7 doors. Excavation suggests a Hadrianic date.

*C.A.G.* 41, 42 and Provost 1993, 160.

## Tours

(Caesarodunum, Civitas Turonorum)
M64 15 IGN26 C2

The key to understanding the geography

of Tours lies in the life and death of its fourth-century bishop, Martin. Tours began as a settlement on a slight hill commanding an important crossing of the Loire. Galinié's extensive excavations found no trace of Gaulish origins. There is a cluster of Iron Age *oppida* along the Loire here (at Amboise, Rochecorbon, Fondettes and Montlouis) and Tours may have arisen as a replacement, in some sense, for one or more of these. The early Roman town was around the present cathedral, and along the road running west from Orleans towards Angers. Houses and baths of the early first century AD onwards were excavated below the medieval castle, and the site of a temple is known. A building inscription of Hadrian (*C.I.L.* XIII, 3078) and two mentioning the *Civitas Turonor(um)* were found reused in the foundations of the town walls. The town may have covered some 70ha at its peak. Its main memorial is its amphitheatre, whose oval line can be followed from the Place Grégoire de Tours east of the cathedral around the curve of the Rue General Meusnier. The amphitheatre was embedded in the late Roman walls, the eastern half of which is largely intact, rather like a fossil shell in a rock.

Martin was an ex-soldier, born at Szombathely (Steinamanger) in Hungary, and brought up in the military cantonment at Ticinum outside Milan. He became bishop here in 371/2 and died in 397. His predecessor Litorius (337-70) had been given the house of a local magnate for the site of a church. This lay some 1000m W of the amphitheatre on the road to Angers, though as the town walls were probably not yet built, it cannot be described either as intramural or extramural. Litorius was buried in his *Basilica Litorii,* but about the time of his death the Church acquired a new city-centre location within the newly built town walls. The area to the W around the *Basilica Litorii* remained the main Christian cemetery area, and it was here that Martin was buried. A church built over his remains by his successor Bricius developed into one of the greatest Abbeys of medieval France.

The amphitheatre was first identified in 1853. It is built of limestone from Joué-les-Tours, south of the city across the Cher, but the amount of brick used suggested to Grenier that it was Hadrianic or Antonine. The town walls, in which the amphitheatre was encased, enclosed a trapezoid area. They are of a mixture of stone types, because of the reuse of material. From the curving section around the amphitheatre they can be followed almost as far as the Loire, where they returned along the riverbank parallel to the present Quai D'Orléans. They then returned parallel to the Rue Lavoisier to the west end of the cathedral. Their remains have now been photogrammetrically recorded, and their construction studied in detail. Once the massive un-mortared foundations, including much reused material from a range of earlier buildings, had been laid, the facings were raised a few courses at a time, set in pink mortar. When this had set, the rubble core was added, using white mortar, and the process then repeated. The greatest surprise of the excavations was the evidence for the date of the wall. A series of stratified coins were associated with its construction, and these end abruptly in 370-80. A connection with Tours becoming the capital of the new province of Lugdunensis III about this time has been suggested, but the date raises other problems, not least the chronology of other town walls in the province, at Angers, Nantes, Le Mans and Rennes.

There is now similar evidence however from Orleans (see below).

Tours also has rare evidence for the buildings that lay inside these walls. Sulpicius Severus refers to a *praetorium* or governor's residence and a prison within the walls in the time of Martin, and a memory of the former may survive in the street name Rue de la Bazoche, NE of the cathedral. The church of *S. Martini de Basilica* (de la Bazoche) was used to house Martin's body when it was brought within the walls during Viking raids. A charter of 903 calls it 'An open area with the hall adjoining, once called the accursed (*Maledicta*) . . . within the walls of Tours, with its wall and postern . . . from the Orleans Gate (*Porta Aurelienensi*) round to the amphitheatre, 96 perches'.

The Abbey of St Martin of Tours was demolished in 1802 to make way for the Rue des Halles. Two towers of the Old Basilica survive, the Tour d'Horloge and the Tour Charlemagne. Despite the name of the latter, they were late twelfth- or thirteenth-century additions to the Romanesque church of 1175. The New Basilica, on the left of the Rue des Halles, dates from 1887-1924. Below the choir is a crypt containing the tomb of St Martin, discovered in 1860. One walk of the early sixteenth-century cloister of the Old Basilica also survives in the convent of Petit-St-Martin (3, Rue Descartes).

Grenier III, 682-4 (amphitheatre) *C.I.L.* XIII, 3076-7. L. Pietri, *T.C.C.G.* V, 19-39. J. Wood, 1983 'Le castrum de Tours; étude architecturale du rampart du Bas Empire', *Recherches sur Tours* 2, (Tours) 11-60.

## Yzeures-sur-Creuse (Iciodurum)
M68 5 IGN34 B7

*Iciodorum Vicus* was a small market town serving a pagus or rural district in the surrounding countryside. A local magnate, M. Petronius . . .milius (the last name is incomplete) set up an altar and column with sculptures of the seven gods of the days of the week, and a battle of gods and giants. This was dedicated to Mercury, and to the divinities of two emperors, either Marcus Aurelius and Lucius Verus (161-9) or Severus and Caracalla (198-211). 300 years later, bishop Eusochius built a church here, one of a series built by the bishops of Tours to spread the Christian message from town to country. The altar and column were demolished, and their fragments were found reused in the foundations of the church, or an early successor. Bishops relied on local magnates for the resources with which to build country churches, and here Petronius's successors could have been involved. Yzeures is a classic example of the way in which the Church replaced the social structures of the pagan countryside with its own.

*C.I.L.* XIII, 3075. Grenier III, 414-16. *Carte Archéologique de la Gaule Romaine* 13, 5-6.

# 4 The Ile-de-France
## (Lugdunensis IV)

According to Julius Caesar, the territory of the Carnutes around Chartres contained a consecrated place said to be the centre of Gaul, where the Druids met for an annual assembly. Though it has never been identified, this religious importance may be reflected in the number of sacred cult sites known in the area. The late Roman province of Lugdunensis IV or Lugdunensis Senona (after its capital at Sens) first appears in the *Notitia Galliarum*. An inscription (*C.I.L.* XII, 921) honouring its *consularis* or governor shows that its original name was Maxima Senonia, and the provinces of Lugdunensis III and IV could have been creations of Magnus Maximus (383-8).

The name Ile-de-France uses 'Island' in the medieval sense of an area surrounded by rivers or the like, in this case the Seine, Oise and Marne, though as Marc Bloch explains, the name was also used in a geographically looser sense. In an area with such superb medieval cathedrals as Chartres and Notre-Dame de Paris, Roman sites naturally take second place. The Cluny Baths in Paris are however an outstanding survival, and the seventh-century crypt at Jouarre shows, with unique clarity, the turning point between the art of late antiquity and that of the Middle Ages.

M. Bloch *The Ile-de-France: The Country around Paris*, 1913 (trans. J.E. Anderson 1971).

## EURE-ET-LOIRE
### Chartres (Autricum)
M60 7/8 IGN19 B11

Chartres was, in Roman times, the capital of the Carnutes, and part of the Roman forum has been excavated. The late Roman town was presumably walled, though no certain trace has been found.

### Mienne-Marboué Villa
M60 17 IGN19 C10

Though there is nothing to be seen on site, this remarkable villa on the banks of the Loire, excavated in the 1830s, merits inclusion not only for its size and layout but for its apparent fifth-century date. The main residential block was a vast rectangle measuring 150 x 240m, comprising three long narrow ranges of buildings with a colonnade-like entrance range on the E. Further E was an even larger block of agricultural buildings ('villa rustica') and a temple. The complex has been compared to the British villas at Bignor and Woodchester.

The most remarkable features were the mosaics, known (apart from a tiny fragment preserved in the modern hamlet) only from nineteenth-century engravings. One showed two cupids holding a shield inscribed in crude style, *Ex Oficina Ferroni Felix Uti Ste Leco* — 'From the workshop of Ferronius, (?) use this and be happy Steleco'. If this interpretation is correct, Steleco (presumably the owner of the villa) had a Germanic name akin to that of the late

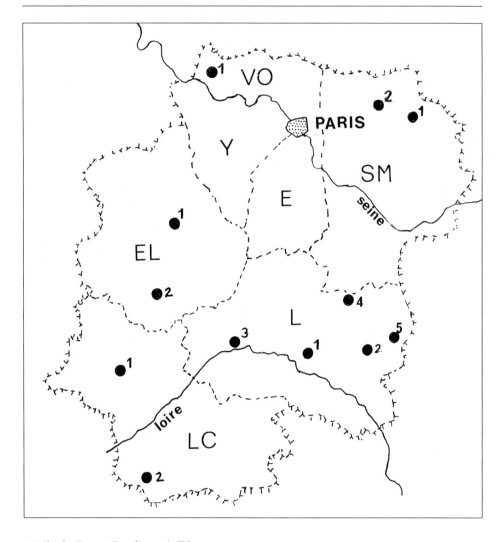

16 Ile-de-France (Lugdunensis IV)
   **EL** Eure et Loire *1 Chartres 2 Mienne-Marboué*
   **L** Loiret *1 Bouzy-le-Forêt 2 Montbuoy 3 Orléans 4 Sceaux-en-Gatinais 5 Triguéres*
   **LC** Loir et Cher *1 Areines 2 Thesée*
   **SM** Seine-et-Marne *1 Jouarre 2 Meaux*
   **VO** Val d'Oise *1 Genainville*

Roman general Stilicho. The forms of lettering and general crude style suggest a date no earlier than the very end of the fourth century, and more probably in the fifth. There have been no modern excavations to confirm this, but a now demolished chapel of St Martin and a sixth- or seventh-century sarcophagus cemetery are known near the villa temple.

M. Blanchard-Lemée, 'La villa à mosaiques de Mienne-Marboué', *Gallia* 39 1981, 63-83.

## LOIRET

Provost, *Carté Archéologique de la Gaule* 45 (1988)

### Bouzy-le-Forêt Rural shrine
M65 1 IGN27 A5

A cult centre on the boundary of the territories of Orleans and Sens, close to a marsh, the Etang des Planches, which might itself have been a place of cult. Of the very small theatre associated with it, only the foundations survived.

Grenier III, 876-7.

### Montbuoy Rural shrine
M65 2 IGN27 A8

The well-preserved theatre-amphi-theatre N of the village was of an unusual plan, described by Grenier as a 'third of an amphitheatre'. The cavea, on one side of an oval arena, was like a section of an amphitheatre, including a small square chamber under its centre, opening on to the arena, to support the 'president's box' and perhaps serve as a shrine (a bronze statuette of Mercury was found just outside it). Nearby, a spring empties into a series of tanks, suggesting a water cult, and a wooden cult figure like those from the Sources of the Seine is known. Coins run from Augustus to Constantine, suggesting that, like other rural cult sites, Montbuoy fell into disuse soon after 300. A huge hoard of third-century coins ending under Tetricus (270-73) found here in 1938 led to the suggestion that the site was destroyed in the third-century 'great invasions', but other hoards have since come to light, one going down to about 310.

*Bulletin Monumental* 1863, 191-7. Grenier III, 921-4 (Chennevières).

### Orléans
(Cenabum, Civitas Aurelianorum)
M64 9 IGN26 A10

Cenabum lay in the southern part of the territory of the Carnutes of Chartres and, despite its later importance, only

became a civitas capital in the late Empire, when it was renamed in honour of the Emperor Aurelian. Occupation began in around AD 1-25 and a theatre was found E of the walled area in 1821, but nothing is now visible. Brick courses in its masonry suggested that it was no earlier than the second century.

The late Roman walls enclosed a rectangular area between the Loire and the cathedral, and between the Rue Royale on the W and the Rue Bourdon Blanc on the E. Rebuilt several times in the Middle Ages and now demolished, nothing Roman remains above ground. The only surviving fragment is the medieval SW corner tower, the Tour Blanche. Two excavated stretches, by the N transept of the cathedral (Mail Pothier site) and at Place Louis XI showed the usual coursed blockwork and triple tile courses, with medieval rebuilding above. Mail Pothier included one of the solid half-round projecting towers known to have existed from early plans and records. It also produced important dating evidence. Late third-century coins (Postumus and Tetricus) in demolition layers preceding the wall initially suggested a possible date, but further work produced material of the mid-fourth century or later in similar contexts on both sites. This brings Orléans into line with Tours, where similar dating evidence is known.

The Musée Historique de l'Orléanais (Place de la République) contains a collection of Roman bronze animals and other figures from a temple treasure found in a sand pit at Neuvy-en-Sullias (M64 10) in 1861. The splendid cast bronze horse with a dedicatory inscription has four rings on its base to enable it to be carried in procession in pagan ceremonies, exactly as described by Sulpicius Severus in one of the miracles of Martin of Tours.

There are also a stag, several boars, human figures, including a dancing girl, and a trumpet.

Blanchet 73-6. Grenier III, 840. *Gallia* 43 (1985), 344-50. *Neuvy* Grenier III, 727-9, *C.I.L.* XIII, 3071.

## Sceaux-en-Gatinais

(Aquae Segestae) M61 12 IGN21 H1

A bathing establishment on the road between Sens and Orléans with a large theatre, baths, the terrace of a temple temenos, and a bath or water tank served from the springs, much of the site being still visible. The coin list runs down to 320-30, suggesting that it may have been disused by the mid-fourth century.

Grenier III, 874-6, IV, 726.

## Triguères Rural cult centre

M65 3 IGN21 J3

4km E of Châteaurenard, on the borders of the Carnutes and the Senones, Triguères included a Romano-Celtic temple in a rectangular colonnaded temenos, baths, and an unexcavated theatre-amphitheatre. The central *cella* of the temple was built around a prehistoric standing stone, 'la Roche du Vieux Garçon'. As at Vieux Poitiers (Vienne), this suggests a pre-Roman sacred site. Most of the temple complex was probably second-century. Little is now visible. The hillfort of 'Le Donjon' here was possibly *Vellaunodunum*, an oppidum of the Senones attacked by Caesar in 52 BC. It surrendered on the third day of the siege (*B.G.* VII, 11).

Grenier III, 331 (baths); 944-946 (theatre); IV, 733-7 (temple).

## LOIR-ET-CHER

Provost, *Carte Archéologique de la Gaule Romaine* 41 (1988).

## Areines Rural cult centre

M64 6 IGN26 A5

Areines lay on the road from Orléans to Le Mans, just across the Loir from Vendôme. Discovered in the 1860s, it included a theatre- amphitheatre, baths and a Romano-Celtic temple. The theatre is still visible.

Grenier III, 947-9.

## Thesée Rural shrine

M64 17 IGN26 C6

The ruins of Mozelles are on the banks of the Cher (and sometimes known as Pouillé from the village on the opposite bank). The first timber shrine was replaced under Tiberius by a square stone temple with two altars or offering tables. There is an inscription of AD 82-102, but the site was abandoned in Antonine times, perhaps because of flooding from the river. A large rectangular pool may have been for medicinal bathing and oculists' stamps and representations of eyes suggest that the shrine specialised in eye troubles. The economic aspect of such shrines is shown by four buildings with storage cellars and a series of second-century pottery kilns.

Provost *C.A.G.* 41 and 1993, 145-6.

## PARIS, YVELINES

### PARIS (Lutetia)

The original pre-Roman oppidum of the Parisii was on the Ile-de-la-Cité, as Caesar tells us. Pre-Roman levels and coins were found in the excavations under the Parvis of the cathedral of Notre Dame in 1969, but nothing else is known. The left bank town of Lutetia S of the river was founded in the first century AD, with no earlier Gaulish settlement. The remains of Roman Paris thus fall into two distinct topographical groups. On the Ile de la Cité, remains of Roman buildings and of the late Roman defensive wall are on display in the archaeological crypt below the Parvis. On the left bank are impressive remains of a major Roman bath building (Cluny Baths) and of an amphitheatre (the Arènes de Lutèce).

Under the late Empire, the Ile-de-la-Cité was surrounded by a defensive wall, like many other French cities. It was here that the army of Julian mutinied in 360 over a demand from the Emperor Constantius II that the pick of the army should be transferred to the eastern front, and proclaimed Julian Emperor. However, despite these Imperial connections, and its later fame, Paris was not capital of the province of Lugdunensis IV. That distinction belonging to Sens; indeed the Bishop of Paris was a mere diocesan bishop of the Archbishop of Sens until 1622. By the sixth century though, Paris had become one of the major seats of the Merovingian kings. Gregory of Tours describes a great fire here in 585, and it would seem that it was already, like a medieval city, crammed with timber buildings amid surviving Roman masonry structures and had defences with a timber gate. Elsewhere he describes a Merovingian magnate and his wife touring the luxury jewellery shops on the Ile (near the present Quai des Orfèvres ('Quay of the goldsmiths'), though their shopping expedition came to an unpleasant end.

## The Left Bank

Roman *Lutetia* south of the river lay along two north-south streets represented today by the Rue Saint Jacques and the Boulevard Saint Michel ('Boul Mich'). At right angles to these were two other roads, represented by the Rue des Ecoles and the Rue Cujas. The Musée de Cluny (Metro station St-Michel), with impressive standing remains of a major Severan bath building (the *North Baths*) and its still vaulted Frigidarium incorporated within the museum buildings, makes a useful starting point. Just across the Boulevard Saint Michel, at its junction with the Rue Racine, stood a small *Classical*

*Theatre*, second-century in date, excavated in 1861 when the Lycée Saint-Louis was built. In the opposite direction, under the E end of the College de France, was a larger second-century bath building, usually called the *Greater Baths* or the Thermes de l'Est. Partially excavated at various dates between 1894 and 1935, its complex and incomplete plan is not easy to understand. However, it seems to have included the usual range of three cold, warm and hot rooms running west-east. East of the rectangular frigidarium were two large circular rotundas, probably a tepidarium and a hot dry room (sudarium). Beyond was a caldarium, with flanking hot baths. Further S, at the top of the Rue Gay Lussac, next to the forum, was a third bathhouse, the *Lesser Baths*. Except for the Cluny Baths, none of these are now visible.

The *Forum* of Roman Paris was built in the late first century under the Flavian Emperors and occupied an area stretching between the Boulevard St Michel on the E and the Rue Saint Jacques on the W in the area of the present Rue Soufflot, S of the Sorbonne. It consisted of the usual three elements. There was a temple of the Imperial cult on the E, a central forum and a basilica at the W end, the whole being surrounded by rows of shops. Nothing is now visible.

## The Cluny Baths

The *Musée de Cluny* (Musée du Moyen Age), with its magnificent collections of medieval art and artefacts, was once the Hotel de Cluny, one of only two late medieval Hotels (aristocratic town residences) surviving from medieval Paris. The Roman baths, known as the 'Palais des Thermes' since the twelfth century, survive because they were bought about 1330 by the Abbot of the Burgundian monastery of Cluny and converted into a town house, with his garden sited above the vault of the frigidarium. A later clerical owner, Jacques of Amboise, bishop of Clermont, rebuilt the house in its present form between 1485 and 1500. In the eighteenth century the frigidarium was used as a barrel factory before being cleared of its later internal fittings in the 1820s. The museum was created in 1844 and the remains of the baths excavated in 1946-57.

The baths date from the Severan period, around AD 200. Approaching from what is now the Boulevard St Germain, to the rear of the present museum, the Roman visitor would have found an impressive N facade over 80m in length, and walls of *opus mixtum*, with the small neat masonry divided up by regular brick banding, still stand to an impressive height. A square vestibule at its centre was flanked by a pair of long rectangular vaulted exercise halls or *apodyteria* (Q and R), part of one of which remains. From these, the bather would have passed into the *frigidarium* (A). This is not only still intact, with its vault at a height of 13.85m, but the vault itself rests on eight projecting corbels in the shape of ships prows, emphasising the importance of Roman Paris as a river port. There was a rectangular cold bath in the N wall.

Another bath and an oval lobby separated the frigidarium from the *tepidarium* or warm room (K) now in the museum garden next to the Boulevard St Michel. This had a series of rounded and rectangular niches originally housing pedestalled washing basins (looking rather like bird baths) in which the bather could have swilled himself down, as in a modern shower. Remains of a hypocaust have been found beneath its floor. Next door, also in the garden, is the *caldarium* hot bath (L), heated by

three parallel furnaces in the W wall. The three large semicircular niches would have held hot baths. There are traces of the hypocaust and fragments of the fallen vault still lie on the floor. From here, a series of three other heated rooms (O, P and G/H) led back, through a small vestibule B, to the frigidarium, forming an overall circular route through two parallel ranges of rooms. At the present moment (September 2000), the baths are in course of a major conservation programme.

The Cluny Baths also house an important collection of sculptures from Roman Paris. Pre-eminent among these are the sculptured fragments of a Jupiter column, of a type not uncommon in northern Gaul and the Rhineland (and sometimes in England). They consisted of a large column whose base carried sculptured figures of the gods and whose top was crowned with a figure of Jupiter fighting a giant. This, the earliest known example, was found under the choir of Notre Dame in 1711, its blocks reused in the foundations of the late Roman city wall. It was erected in honour of the Emperor Tiberius (AD 14-37) by the corporation of Paris boatmen (*nautae Parisiaci*), as the inscription tells us: '(under) Tiberius Caesar / Augustus (to) Jupiter, the Best / and Greatest / the boatmen of Paris / out of their public corporate funds built this'. The column is also extremely important for the understanding of Celtic religion, for it carries a series of labelled sculptures of gods, including the horned god *Cernunnos*; the three horned bull *Tarvos Trigaranus* (complete with cranes picking the ticks from its back); the god with a serpent *Smert(rios)*; various Roman gods, and three bearded men labelled *Evrises*. A sculptured frieze from a different monument shows three hunting dogs with collars chasing hares into a large net.

17  Paris — Arènes de Lutèce (photograph Stefan Levi)

## Arènes de Lutèce

Some distance east of the main urban complex, the *Arènes de Lutèce*, in the Rue Monge near the Jussieu Metro station, is one of the theatre-amphitheatres popular in 'Celtic' Gaul. Excavated in 1869 (after being saved from destruction to make way for an omnibus depot by the protests of Victor Hugo and others), it has been rather heavily restored and laid out on display. There are tiers of seating around an oval arena, and a stage front with a series of alternate rectangular and semicircular niches, with three entrances leading from the stage building behind. To the rear of the front seating was a horseshoe-shaped cavea or access tunnel, with radiating passages for access. The Arènes were probably late first-century in date. There was some evidence of later repairs, and it may have been the 'circus' which,

according to Gregory of Tours, the Merovingian king Chiperic restored in Paris.

## Ile-de-la-Cité

The regiments of tourists visiting Notre Dame are mostly unaware that beneath their feet, under the Parvis or Square W of the cathedral, is a remarkable display telling of the history of Paris from its origins until the demolitions which created the present square in the nineteenth century. In 1965-72 a large rescue excavation was directed by Michel Fleury before the construction of an underground car park. Eventually, the scheme was changed to allow the preservation of the archaeological remains. If the visitor avoids the roller skaters and columns of tourists (who give a wholly new meaning to the phrase 'following the flag') he or she will find at the W end of the Parvis, at the far end

18  Paris — Arènes de Lutèce. 'It was here, in the second century of our era that the municipal life of Paris was born . . . where naval contests were followed by the fights of gladiators and by comedies and dramas . . . In passing, reflect before this first monument of Paris, that the town of the past is also the city of the future, and that of our hopes.' Plaque erected by the Syndicats d'Inititiative to mark the bi-millennium of Paris in 1951. Photograph Stefan Levi

from the cathedral (and next to the Prefecture of Police familiar to readers of Inspector Maigret), some stairs down, and an inscription 'Crypte Archéologique'. At the top of the stairs is a cast of the inscription to Tiberius by the Paris boatmen, now in the Musée de Cluny.

The complex of archaeological foundations are well labelled, but can be confusing at first glance, particularly since only parts are Roman, and they include substantial work of more recent times, up to the foundations of the eighteenth-century foundling hospital. It is perhaps best to begin with a chronological overview, helped by the series of dioramas beyond the ticket desk. The first gives an excellent picture of what it calls 'the predestined site' — Paris before Paris. The Ile-de-la-Cité lies in the middle of the Seine, with two smaller islands in its wake and a larger area, the Ile Saint Martin, enclosed by an ancient arm of the Seine, to the N. Around it are marshes ('Marais' —

hence the name of a now fashionable Paris quarter) and low surrounding hills, some with familiar names like Montparnasse and Montmartre. The next diorama shows the Roman city, with its forum, bath buildings and theatre ranged along its two parallel streets. The third shows the medieval city of Paris, with the early thirteenth-century walls of Philip Augustus.

The Parvis (created in its present form by the town planner Haussmann under Napoleon III) occupied an area along the southern edge of the Ile-de-la-Cité, originally bounded on the S by the first-century Roman riverside quays. Parts of these can be seen at the E end of the crypt below the foundations of the late Roman city wall (the entry stairs to the crypt are on the S side, so E is to the right, beyond the dioramas). Their smaller coursed rubble masonry can easily be distinguished from the large reused blocks of the late Roman city walls. A large late second-century public building of unknown function, possibly a forum, occupied the W part of the crypt. It had a massive buttressed wall facing the river, but this is in a sector of the crypt not normally open to the public.

The late third- or fourth-century city wall followed the line of the quays on this side. Its S gate lay just outside the W end of the crypt, and was found in 1986 in building an access tunnel to the Metro. Its massive squared blocks, some with cramp holes, were recycled from earlier building. The Merovingian king Childebert I (511-58) built a large cathedral dedicated to St Stephen (Saint-Etienne), its S wall on the line of the presumably demolished Roman city wall. The W part of its nave was found in excavation and is marked out on the surface of the Parvis above. It was a five-aisled structure (i.e. with two rows of columns on each side, not the more usual one), perhaps modelled on Old St Peters in Rome. Only the W facade wall lies within the area of the crypt, again in an area not open to the public.

P.M. Duval, *Paris antique, des Origines au Troisième Siècle* (Paris 1961); M. Fleury and V. Kruta, *La crypte archéologique du Parvis Notre-Dame* (Paris 1990). A useful small leaflet guide *Lutetia: Roman Paris* in the series *Media Cartes* is available in the Archaeological crypt at Notre Dame and elsewhere.

## St Denis Early church

Now in a working class suburb north of Paris, St Denis was the Westminster Abbey of France. Founded over the tomb of the third-century martyr St Denis (Dionysius) in the Roman vicus of Catolacus, it was in the Middle Ages an immensely wealthy abbey, the burial place of the kings and queens of France from Merovingian times until the French Revolution. Their tombs were then destroyed, though fortunately the effigies and memorials had already been

removed to a museum, and were returned later. After a period of serious neglect (at one stage it was used to store gunpowder, with disastrous results), the church was eventually restored by Viollet le Duc in 1847-79.

The existing church combines the west end and apse of Abbot Suger's church of 1136-44 with the nave of 1247-81. Below the latter is a large Carolingian church of about 750 and, below again, several earlier churches. The earliest, a simple rectangular structure, may be late Roman. It was succeeded by a Merovingian church with long rectangular nave, ambulatory and W porch; a crossing; and an eastern apse of the same width. Suggested dates have ranged from the late fifth century to the time of Dagobert I (629-39), but it bears a striking resemblance to St Wilfred's seventh-century church at Hexham in Northumberland. A large oval monastic enclosure (the *castellum sancti Dionysii*) is known from excavation (*Gallia Informations* 1989. 2, 50 for plan), and N of the basilica were an extensive late Roman and medieval cemetery, and a row of early churches, including a circular baptistery.

*Saint-Denis* ('Patrimoine au présent', Caisse Nationale des Monuments Historiques et des sites).

## St Germain-en-Laye Museum
(Metro — St Germain-en-Laye)

The National Museum of Antiquities is housed in a former royal palace whose occupants have ranged from Mary Queen of Scots and the Stuart exiles Henrietta Maria and James II to Field Marshal von Rundstedt. The archaeological collections cover the period from the Palaeolithic to Charlemagne. Even to list the highlights of the Iron Age and Roman galleries would take up far more space than is available here. The prehistoric and

Roman galleries of the British Museum are the only equivalent.

## SEINE-ET-MARNE

**Jouarre** Early monastery
M56 13 IGN09 D6

About 630, Adon, a Merovingian nobleman, was treasurer to King Dagobert I, whose court has been described as a 'nursery of bishops'. Adon's family had been friends and supporters of the Irishman St Columbanus, and he left the court to found a double monastery for nuns and monks at Jouarre. His cousin Theodechilde was the first abbess. Later, Agilbert, bishop of Paris, retired to Jouarre, where he died about 680. Agilbert had studied in Ireland and been bishop of Dorchester in Oxfordshire before returning to France soon after 664. Like many of the greater Merovingian monasteries, Jouarre had three churches, dedicated to St Mary, St Peter, and St Paul — an Abbey church, parish church and funerary church respectively. It is still a Benedictine nunnery. Two of the churches survive in a later form and the remarkable funerary crypts of the third church make Jouarre one of the most important places in France for the study of early medieval art. The Abbey church of Notre Dame was demolished, save for its W tower, at the Revolution. Its successor dates from 1837. The late medieval parish church of St Pierre is to the N. East of it once stood the church of St Paul, with the crypts of St Paul and St Ebregesile.

The church of St Paul, excavated in 1869-72, had a rectangular nave with the crypt of St Paul to the E. It was extended S when the crypt of St Ebregesile was added early in the eighth century. The crypt of St Paul (conducted tours by the nuns) has two rows of three reused Roman marble columns, of cipollino, porphyry and a black and white marble, with crisply carved early medieval capitals of white Pyrennean marble, variations on a classical Corinthian form. The fluted column against the tomb of St Theodechilde (but not its capital) is a modern replacement. The crypt has undergone changes since it was built towards the end of the seventh century, and to get some idea of its original appearance, it is necessary to bear these in mind. The groin-vaulted roof is Romanesque, and the rough masonry plinths on which the tombs now stand was a continuous platform until 1884, when it was cut through to 'improve' visitor access to their sculptures. Worst of all, the tombs were vandalised in 1627, when they were literally broken into by Queen Marie de Medici (mother-in-law of King Charles I) in search of relics, which were then translated to shrines and reliquaries. The severe damage which is still evident upon them dates from that time.

The row of six house-shaped tombs are along the E wall, with a seventh in the NW corner. Starting at the N end, the tomb of Adon is in the niche behind the sculptured effigy of St Ozanne, a twelfth-century Cistercian nun, said to have been the daughter of an Irish king. Her late thirteenth-century figure is from the same workshop as some of the royal tombs at St Denis. Next to her is the tomb of St Balde, aunt of Adon and Theodechilde, and third Abbess of Jouarre. The sculpture above shows two angels, holding a book and a censer. Its date is uncertain.

Three of the tombs have sculptured decoration of high quality, each in a different style. That of Theodechilde, the first abbess, in the centre, has rows of formalised scallop shells alternating with inscribed bands recording in monumental capitals her name and merits. The lid has worn vine scroll decoration. An altar once stood in front of the modern fluted column. The plain tomb next to it (a reconstruction of 1843) is that of her aunt, the Venerable Mode, sister of St Balde. Beyond is the sarcophagus of Theodechilde's cousin, Aguilberte, the second abbess. Its roof slabs have an overall abstract pattern of circles and lozenges, the body a diamond pattern with trefoil foliage and a border of Greek fret. This panel was smashed in 1627 and replaced wrongly. The present left half belongs on the right (the now central fret border was the right-hand edge) and what is now the right-hand half is not only in the wrong place, but upside down (as the inverted trefoils show).

The third decorated sarcophagus is the only one with figure sculpture. The tomb of Agilbert, sometime bishop of Wessex and of Paris, it has been broken and reconstructed from fragments. Most of the lid, decorated with vine scroll like that on the tomb of Theodechilde, is now missing. The side shows a Resurrection scene, with the saved standing with raised arms in the orante position of early Christian prayer. Some have loin cloths and sash-like grave clothes. The sculpture at the head of the sarcophagus is not visible, but a cast is shown above. It shows Christ in Majesty holding the Book of Judgement and surrounded by symbols of the Evangelists.

Much of the fascination of Jouarre lies in the way it stands at the hinge of late Roman and medieval art, and the range of artistic influences it blends into a unique synthesis. Alongside the late antique capitals and the influence of late Roman sculptured sarcophagi (see also the Roman style *opus reticulatum* masonry on the W wall) are Carolingian features like the decorative bands of lettering and some of the figure sculpture, whilst the figure of Christ in Majesty could easily have served as the model for the tympanum of a Romanesque church doorway. Insular influences are perhaps less easy to pin down, but the neoclassical figure sculpture and inscribed bands recall the Ruthwell and Bewcastle crosses in Northumbria, whilst the pattered slabs from the tomb of Aguilebert, otherwise hard to parallel, can be matched on a decorated slab from an altar or shrine at the Saxon church of Bradford on Avon (Wiltshire), in Agilbert's old diocese.

The crypt of St Ebregesil was originally separate, the two doorways through being later insertions. Ebregesil was bishop of Meaux, brother of Aguilbert and cousin of Theodechilde. Jouarre is very much a family mausoleum. The crypt was largely rebuilt in the eleventh century, and though a number of reset Merovingian marble columns and capitals survive. The remainder, of local limestone, and the vaulting, are Romanesque. It was originally twice its present length, but in 1640 the W half was demolished and the remainder linked to the Crypt of St Paul by the inserted doorways. The tomb of St Ebregesil is in a niche N of the altar. Marquise de Maillé, *Les crypts de Jouarre* (Paris 1971).

## Meaux (Iatinum)
M56 12 IGN09 D4

Meaux was capital of the Meldi. Parts of the late Roman walls, altered and refaced in the Middle Ages, can be seen on the N of the gardens of the bishop's palace and in adjacent gardens. They enclosed a long narrow rectangle with the shorter S side resting on the Marne, a similar arrangement to Sens. Presumably the Roman town was a ribbon development running N along the road from the bridge and river crossing.
Blanchet (1907), 82-3.

## VAL D'OISE
### Genainville Temple complex
M55 18 IGN08 C7

The rural temple complex, with theatre and baths, sited next to a spring, was excavated as a long-term research programme by P.-H. Mitard and the Centre de Recherches Archéologiques du Vexin Français and is now a national monument. The drystone foundations of a small rectangular shrine of the early first century AD were found below the temple, and Gallic coins and a sculpture of a cross-legged god holding an animal belong to the same period. The rich finds include sculpture; a bronze statuette of Mercury and a caduceus showing the dedication of the temple; fragments of bronze letters from votive inscriptions and masks in sheet bronze appliqué. These, with material from other excavations in the Vexin, are now in the society's excellent museum at Guiry-en-Vexin. The complex dates to the mid- to late second century, but the theatre may never have been finished.

P.H. Mitard, 1983 *Le Site Gallo-Romain de Vaux de la Celle à Genainville* (Centre de Recherches Archéologique du Vexin Français). *Gallia Informations* 1993, 1-2, 126-31.

# 5 Flanders, Artois and Picardy
## (Belgica Secunda)

Picardy comprises the départements of Aisne, Oise and Somme. This is an area with a strong sense of regional identity in its culture and its language or dialect (it is now possible in some towns to get married in Picard). Nord is the southern fringe of Flanders, the remainder of which is in Belgium. The Franco-Belgian frontier hereabouts dates only to the time of Louis XIV, and the Congress of Vienna in 1815. Artois, between Flanders and Picardy, corresponds broadly to the Pas-de-Calais. In the time of Caesar, the Belgic tribes of this area were said to have their own language. Quite what this means has been much argued about, but presumably there was sufficient regional variation in manners and dialect to give the claim some credibility. Caesar also puts the tribes into at least ranking order with his statement that the Bellovaci were able to put 100,000 men into the field, the Suessiones 50,000 and the Ambiani and the Remi 10,000 each, though it was the Suessiones under their king Galba who provided the military leadership, and the main gold coinage of the region was struck by the Ambiani.

*Guide-Répetoire* 8 (1965) Nord, Pas de Calais; 16 (1968) Aisne and Somme.

## AISNE

The département corresponds with the territories of the Suessiones of Soissons and the Viromandui of Vermand. It contains a number of important Gaulish *oppida*, usually with the modern name Le Châtel or Le Châtelet. Only the major ones are included here. According to Caesar (*Gallic War* II, 4), the Suessiones possessed 12. Under Augustus, new capitals for the two tribes were established at *Augusta Suessionum* (Soissons) and *Augusta Viromanduorum* (St Quentin).

One modern curiosity is Hitler's intended underground headquarters for Operation Sealion — the invasion of Britain in 1940 — at Margival, NE of Soissons. He paid only one brief visit, in circumstances very different from those intended, in June 1944.

### Arlaines Auxiliary fort
M56 3 IGN09 A6

Roman forts of classic 'playing card' shape are rare in France, so that this stone built 5ha fort, 11km W of Soissons, close to the Gaulish *oppida* of Ambleny and Pommiers, is worthy of note, though there is nothing to see on the ground. The tombstone of a trooper of a cavalry regiment, the *Ala Vocontiorum* is known, and the Headquarters Building and Commandant's House have been excavated. To the front and rear of these, nineteenth-century excavations produced what in plan look like large store buildings, but are probably no more than several superimposed sets of barracks (the excavator thought the site was a villa). The N Gate has also been excavated. Occupied from the time of Claudius to the late 70s, the fort's two phases may be connected with local revolts in AD 21 and 69.

M. Reddé, 'Le camp militaire romain d'Arlaines et l'aile des Vocontes', *Gallia* 43 (1985), 49- 79 and do. 1996, 189-90.

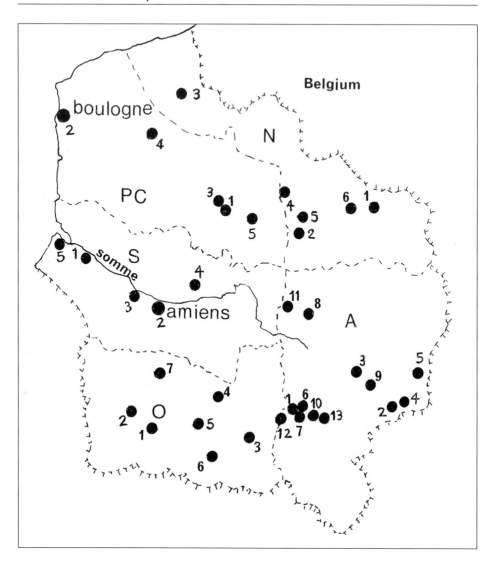

*19* Flanders, Artois and Picardy (Belgica Secunda)

**A** Aisne *1 Arlaines 2 Mauchamps 3 Laon 4 Neufchâtel-sur-Aisne 5 Nizy-le-Comte 6 Pasly 7 Pommiers 8 St Quentin 9 Vieux-Laon 10 Soissons 11 Vermand 12 Vic-sur-Aisne 13 Villeneuve St Germain*

**N** Nord *1 Bavay 2 Cambrai 3 Cassel 4 Douai 5 Etrun 6 Famars*

**O** Oise *1 Bailleul 2 Beauvais 3 Champlieu 4 Gournay-sur-Aronde 5 Nointel 6 Senlis 7 Vendeuil-Caply*

**PC** Pas de Calais *1 Arras 2 Boulogne 3 Etrun 4 Thérouanne 5 Vis-en-Artois*

**S** Somme *1 Abbeville 2 Amiens 3 Chausée-Tirancourt 4 Ribemont-sur-Ancre 5 St Valery*

## Berry-le-Bac-Mauchamps

Campaigning fort M56 6 IGN09 A11
North of Berry le Bac, a ridge between
the Aisne and its tributary the Miette,
followed by the D925 road, is the site of
a 43ha Roman camp. This was excavated
by Napoleon III in 1862, who thought it
to have been built by Caesar during his
campaign of 57 BC for his six legions.
However, the near rectangular fort,
bisected by the modern road, has
*claviculae* — hook shaped inturns — at
the entrances, and these, and surface
finds of sherds of Dressel IB amphorae,
suggest a date later than Caesar. There
could though have been more than one
period of occupation, and fresh
excavation is needed to determine its
chronology. Little is visible on the
ground, since the area is intensely
cultivated and later military works —
First World War trench systems and a
German airfield heavily bombed in 1944
add to the problems.
Peyre, *Revue Etudes Latines* 66 (1978),
175-215. Haselgrove (1990), 63.

## Laon Museum and library

M56 5 IGN09 A9
The Bibliothèque Municipal (9, Rue du
Bourg) contains, apart from an
important collection of sixth- to ninth-
century manuscripts, a Roman Orpheus
mosaic from the villa of Pont St Mard.
There is also a regional collection of
Gallo-Roman material in the Musée
Municipal (32, Rue Georges Ermant).

## Neufchâtel-sur-Aisne

Vieux Reims Hillfort M56 6 IGN09 A11
The oppidum of Variscourt, at the
junction of the Aisne and Suippe, 20km
N of Reims, covers 170ha within a
rectangle of defences. Excavated from
the 1970s onwards, the site shows clear
signs of urbanization, with streets of
houses and separate specialist metal
working quarters. The amphorae
(Dressel IA), other pottery and

metalwork suggest a brief period of
occupation just before the Roman
conquest.
Fichtl (1994) 177-8. Constantin and Ilett
Fleury 1982 'Les installations de La Tène
III de Condé-sur-Suippe-Variscourt ('Le
Vieux Reims') deux campaigns de
fouilles *Vallée de l'Aisne*' (*Rev Archéol de
Picardie* special number) 265-76. *Gallia*
37 (1979), 303-5; 39 (1981), 264-6; 41
(1983), 236-8.

## Nizy-le-Comte Rural cult centre

M56 6 IGN10 A1
Gallo-Roman cult centre N. of Reims. A
theatre and temple, poorly excavated in
the nineteenth century. Large reused
Roman masonry in walls of the medieval
castle. Finds include two sculptured
tricephalic (triple) heads and a
milestone. An inscription (*C.I.L.* XIII, 2,
1, 3450) from the theatre records that
Lucius Magius Secundus dedicated a
proscenium for the pagus (rural district)
of the Vennecti to Apollo and the numen
of Augustus. This is one of several cases
where the generosity of a magnate to his
local community, and his loyalty to the
Imperial house, is signalled in this way.
Ben Redjeb 1987 'Une agglomération
secondaire des Rèmes: Nizy-le-Comte'
*Rev. Archéol Picardie* 1-2, 33-60.

## Pasly Hillfort M56 4 IGN09 A7

Promontory fort on hill NW of
Soissons, dominating the village from
the W. Three sides protected by steep
natural scarps, the fourth by a massive
single rampart 200m long and 10m high
cutting off the neck of the plateau.

## Pommiers Noviodunum

M56 4 IGN09 A7
Gaulish oppidum 40ha in extent, with
massive single rampart 300m long.
Probably the capital of the Suessiones
besieged by Julius Caesar in 57 BC and
replaced after the conquest by Soissons.
The scale of the bank and ditch defeated
Caesar's initial assault, whereupon he

built a camp and siege towers, and began filling a section of the ditch. The next day, the Suessiones surrendered. The wealth and importance of the site is shown by its coins and pottery, from pre-Caesarian issues to the time of Augustus and at least 100 Republican wine amphorae of Dressel 1B type.

A major problem is the relationship of Pommiers to the large open settlement at Villeneuve-Saint-Germain on the other side of Soissons, and which of them was Caesar's *Noviodunum*. Since -dunum implies a fortified site, Pommiers is the obvious choice, but Villeneuve was the newer ('Novio') of the two. Despite the usual idea that Villeneuve was transitional between Pommiers and Soissons, it is now clear that there is a distinct chronological overlap between the former two. Haselgrove (1990, 63-4) hints at one possible solution by citing evidence from recent excavation for two periods of occupation at Pommiers and suggesting the second period could have been an example of the Roman use of hillforts as military camps. More evidence is needed however.

Julius Caesar, *De Bello Gallico* Book 2, 4. Vauvillé 'Le Camp de Pommiers', *Congrès Archéol de France* LIV (1887).

## Saint-Quentin

(Augusta Viromanduorum)
M53 14 IGN04 C8
The capital of the Viromandui moved here from the hillfort of Vermand in Augustan times. By the late Empire it had returned there. The basilica dominates the surrounding countryside, and in its crypt is the sarcophagus of the martyr St Quentin, cut from a Roman column. Little else is visible of the Roman town.

## Saint Thomas — Vieux Laon

Iron Age hillfort M56 5 IGN09 A10
Possibly Bibrax, an oppidum of the Remi described by Julius Caesar. The Remi were consistent allies of Rome, and Bibrax was attacked in 57 BC by the Belgic coalition army, who tried to storm its walls. Its commander, the Remic nobleman Iccius, appealed for help to Caesar. He sent reinforcements, who had surprisingly little trouble getting through the Belgic siege lines. These included Balearic slingers and Cretan archers, and with their arrival, the Belgae abandoned the siege (*B.G.* II, 6-7).

This 32ha oppidum has been the site of important excavations. The main rampart is of *Murus Gallicus* type, with a timber framework held in place by iron nails. The interior is divided in two by a later 'Fécamp type' earth rampart, one of many cases where the two types have proved to be successive.

Lobjois, 'L'oppidum du Vieux-Laon à St Thomas', *Revue du Nord* 46 (1964); 'Les fouilles de l'oppidum gaulois du "Vieux Laon" á St Thomas', *Celticum* 15 (1966), 1-26.

## Soissons (Augusta Suessionum)

M56 4 IGN09 B7
Successor of the oppidum at Pommiers or of the open pre-conquest site at Villeneuve-Saint-Germain, the name suggests an Augustan foundation. There are remains of a large Roman theatre in the grounds of a girls school, and a site known as the 'Château d'Albâtre' ('Alabaster Castle'), which has produced second- and third-century mosaics, wall paintings and statues, maybe the main baths. A few fragments of the late Roman walls, enclosing some 12ha are visible. The cathedral contains a reliquary with the bones of the Roman shoemaker-martyr St Crispin, on whose joint feast day with St Crispian the battle of Agincourt was fought. The Municipal Museum, in the former Abbey of St Leger, has Roman material from the town.

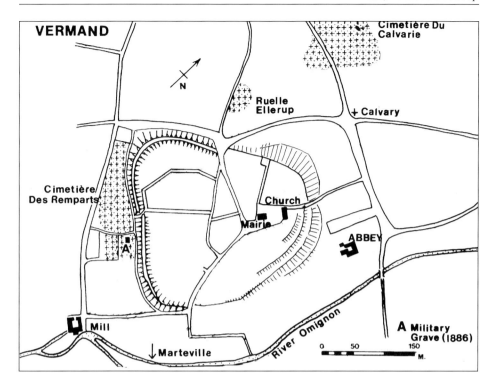

*20  Vermand (Aisne) — plan of hillfort and cemeteries*

In the fifth century, Soissons was the centre of a remarkable postscript to Roman Gaul. When the Emperor Majorian was murdered in 461, his *magister militum* (general) Afranius Syagrius Aegidius, member of a dynasty of Lyon aristocrats, refused to recognise his successor Libius Severus. Severus was a puppet of the de facto Italian ruler Ricimer, and unrecognised by the eastern Emperor Leo, so that Aegidius was both rebel and loyalist. He moved his power base to western and northern Gaul and on his death in 465 his sub-Roman realm, the so-called 'kingdom of Soissons ', passed to his son Syagrius, who was eventually defeated and killed by the Frankish king Clovis in 486, having outlived the western Empire by a decade.

Grenier III, 841-3. B. Ancien and M.

Tuffreau-Libre 1980, *Soissons gallo-romain, découverts anciennes et récentes* (Soissons).

## Vermand

Hillfort and late Roman cemeteries
M53 13 IGN04 C7

The Iron Age hillfort around the present village of Vermand was presumably the pre-conquest capital of the Viromandui. A massive single rampart rising 6m above the interior covers the S and SW approach where the ground is flat, but elsewhere is largely replaced by natural slopes. The ditch is largely infilled, but may have been of the broad 'Fécamp type'. In Augustan times the administrative centre moved to a new town at Augusta Viromanduorum (St Quentin), but by the late Empire had shifted back to this defended crossing of the Omignon. Whether the hillfort was re-fortified at this time is unknown, but excavations in the last century revealed four large late Roman cemeteries outside the ramparts, with some 700 N-S inhumations, richly equipped with pottery, glass, metalwork and coins, and a number of military graves with weapons and the fittings of military belts. Much of this work was done by agents of the American magnate J. Pierpont Morgan, and most of the material is now in the Metropolitan Museum in New York.

The most spectacular grave was that of a late fourth-century Roman army commander, almost certainly of Germanic origin, found in 1886. He lay in a large chalk-cut grave pit under a vanished barrow, with an array of weapons and equipment, including the richly decorated silver-gilt fittings of a ceremonial baton, though sadly most of his personal equipment had fallen prey to grave robbers. He may have commanded troops in personal attendance on the Emperor. The material is now in New York. In medieval times, Vermand gave its name to the County of Vermandois, an important corn growing area, and its territory survived until 1792 as the diocese of Noyon.

Wheeler and Richardson 1957, 131-2. Knight 1999 37-8.

## Vic-sur-Aisne Hillfort
M56 3 IGN09 A6

Gaulish oppidum of Le Châtel, 9ha with single large rampart, presumably the predecessor of the Roman vicus attested in the place name.

## Villeneuve-St-Germain
Iron Age settlement M56 4 IGN09 A/B7

A large semi-urban Iron Age settlement. A bank and double ditch cut across the neck of a meander of the river Aisne, enclosing an area divided into four sectors by ditches meeting at right angles. These were flanked by rows of heavy posts. There may have been some sort of wooden structure above the ditches. They defined residential and industrial areas of the site, but their precise nature and function remain obscure, though rather similar timber roadways are known from Roman forts. Some 2ha of the residential area has been excavated, revealing square or rectangular timber houses set in yards and aligned along a street. The other areas contained many pits filled with industrial debris, including much bronze and iron slag, debris from a mint, and various craft tools. The site was occupied from about 50-15 BC. There was no early Roman pottery or coins, and the inhabitants were probably resettled in the newly founded Soissons in Augustan times.

C. Constantin et al 1982, 'Villeneuve-St-Germain, les Grands Grèves, les bâtiments de La Tène III' in *Vallée de l'Aisne: cinq années des fouilles protohistoriques* (special number of *Rev. Archéol de Picardie*) 195-205. J. Debord 1982, 'Premier bilan de huit années des fouilees à Villeneuve St Germain' in *Vallée de l' Aisne* (see above), 213-64. J. Debord 1984, 'Les origines gauloises de Soissons: oscillation d'un site urbain', *Rev. Archéol de Picardie* 3-4, 27-40. Roymans 1990, 202-6.

## NORD
Nord is the southern fringe of Flanders, the present Franco-Belgian frontier dating only from the time of Louis XIV. In Roman times, its northern parts belonged to the Morini of Cassel, the southern to the Nervii, whose capital was at Bavai. Under the late Empire, faced by insecurity (and a rising sea level), Cassel was replaced by Tournai and Bavai became a fortified military depot, the civil power falling back on Cambrai.

## Bavai (Bagacum Nerviorum)
M53 5 IGN04 A11

Capital of the Nervii, on the strategic Amiens-Cologne trunk road, founded under Augustus. An inscription (*C.I.L.* XIII, 3570), now in Douai museum, records Tiberius passing through Bavai in AD 11, en route to the Rhine frontier. A street grid covering 15ha was laid out under Claudius. By the late first century a second, less regular grid was constructed east of this, the town eventually reaching a size of 40ha. One source of its prosperity may have been its role as a supply and manufacturing depot for the troops of the Rhineland.

By the late first century Bavai was a prosperous town, some houses already with mosaics, and with a growing pottery industry, including tile and mortaria kilns. Some mortaria manufacturers like Q. Valerius Veranius and Summacus exported their products widely, including to Britain and may even have relocated their workshops to Kent. Its commercial prosperity may be reflected in the forum complex, much of which has been excavated and is on display. This may date from the early second century and is similar to that of Trier in size and layout. It is tripartite. To the W is a colonnaded court and temple, surrounded on three sides by a *cryptoporticus*, a series of pillared semi-underground chambers. A rectangular *curia* or council chamber projects on the N. The central part was a forum flanked by ranges of shops, and a civic basilica (town hall) is set laterally to the E. The complex makes extensive and striking use of *opus mixtum* — coursed masonry interspersed with tile courses at regular intervals, a technique widely used in Trier.

Similar *cryptoportici* occur in other Gallic fora, most notably at Arles. Traces of painted wall plaster and other decoration show that they are not simply store chambers (nor would these have been appropriate around the main municipal temple). Their purpose may have been largely architectural — to provide foundations for a suitably lofty surround to the temple on a levelled site — and the underground chambers might have served as meeting rooms for guilds and other organizations.

Under the late Empire, the capital of the Nervii was moved to Cambrai, and the forum complex converted into a defensible military stores depot on the Amiens-Cologne highway. At first only the forum was fortified (about 2ha). Later the whole complex was converted into a bastioned fort double this size. The two periods can be distinguished by their types of mortar. That of the first period is hard and white, the second period uses red mortar with crushed brick, like that of the second period at Famars.

H. Bievelet, 'L'exploration archéologique de Bavai, 1942-7', *Gallia* 25 (1967), 195; J.C. Carmalez, *Septrention* 10 (1980), 20-4; E. Will, 'Les enceintes du Bas-Empire à Bavay', *Revue du Nord* 44 (1962), 391-401; B. Hartley in J. Dore and K. Greene (eds), *Roman Pottery Studies in Britain and Beyond*, B.A.R.S. 30 (1977), 5-18; R. Delamaire, *Septrention* 2 (1972), 46-54.

## Cambrai (Camaracum)
M53 3-4 IGN04 B7

A vicus of the Nervii, at a road junction on the navigable Scheldt, where the Cologne-Amiens highway was crossed by the N-S Soissons-Arras road, Cambrai became their civitas capital in the late Empire, replacing Bavai.

## Cassel (Castellum Morinorum)
M51 4 IGN02 B4

On a hill rising above the Flanders plain is the civitas capital of the Morini. Early plans show rectangular late Roman

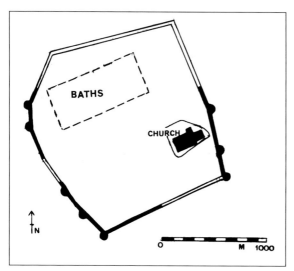

21 *Famars (Nord) — late Roman defences. After Bersu and Unverzagt*

defences rather like those of Boulogne, and excavations have shown these to be of late third-century date with brick levelling courses and pinkish mortar. All that is visible today is a rather pleasant public garden, with a memorial to the First World War general Marshal Foch, and a few traces of medieval walls and post-medieval bastioned defences.

Roger Hanoune and Arthur Muller, 'Recherches archéologiques à Cassel (Nord)', *Revue du Nord* 66 (Jan-March 1984), 155-68. *Gallia Informations* 1989-2, 153.

### Douai Museum

M53 3 IGN02 D7/8

The excellent Musée des Sciences Naturelles et d'Archéologie contains important Roman and Merovingian collections from local sites, including Bavai, Hordain etc.

### Etrun-sur-Escault

Iron Age hillfort M53 4 IGN04 A9
'Camp de César' of 20ha north of Cambrai with 'Fécamp type' rampart. Fichtl (1994), 161.

### Famars (Fanum Martis)

M53 4-5 IGN02 D10

A vicus in the territory of the Nervii, with pottery kilns producing grey wares for local distribution. It had early Roman baths with mosaics, and, from the name, a temple of Mars. In late Roman times, part was requisitioned for a quadrangular fort with projecting semicircular towers, enclosing about a hectare, and the baths adapted as a corn mill for official grain supplies. Parts of the walls survive on the NW edge of the present village. They are of two periods, the first with yellow mortar and fairly shallow hollow towers. The second, encasing them on the outside, has harder red mortar with brick fragments and heavier deeper towers. Their chronology is still to be worked out. A late Roman army unit of Nervian Laeti was stationed here, unusually within their own tribal territory. A coin of Valentinian III and pottery show that occupation continued well into the fifth century, and the rich grave of a young Merovingian nobleman is known from near the church within the walls. At this time, the area was known as the *Pagus Fanomartensis*.

The excavation of the Roman fort was a remarkable story. The baths had already been excavated in the 1820s, but in 1917 two young German officers, Gerhard Bersu and Wilhelm Unverzagt, undertook official rescue excavations here when there was a danger that the village might be engulfed within the western front. The excavation records were destroyed in a Berlin air raid in 1943, but luckily the proofs of the completed report survived, and the excavations were published in 1961. In the meantime, Bersu, a refugee from Nazi Germany, had played a central role in the development of modern excavation techniques in Britain, and spent the war interned on the Isle of Man, where he conducted several important excavations. There were fresh excavations in 1959-62.

Bersu and W. Unverzagt, 'Le castellum de Fanum Martis (Famars, Nord)', *Gallia* 19 (1961), 159-90; P. Leman, 'Une riche tombe mérovingienne à Famars', *Archeologia* 81 (April 1975), 34-40; J.K. Knight 1999, 41-2.

## OISE

The département of Oise corresponds with the territories of the Bellovaci and Silvanectes, with their Roman capitals at Beauvais and Senlis. The hillfort at Bailleul-sur-Therain may have been the pre-Roman predecessor of Beauvais.

### Bailleul-sur-Therain — Mont César Hillfort
M55 10 IGN08 A8

Contour fort of 35ha on an isolated hill SE of Beauvais. Occupied from Neolithic times onwards, the Iron Age rampart has been much damaged by quarrying. The only hillfort in the territory of the Bellovaci, it may have been their capital before the foundation of Beauvais. A Gallo-Roman temple in the interior continued to the late Empire.

Wheeler and Richardson 1957, 128. Fichtl 1994, 154-5.

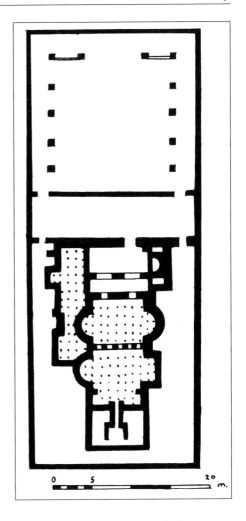

*22 Champlieu (Oise) — plan of baths. Rooms with hypocausts stippled. Grenier IV, 335*

### Beauvais (Caesaromagus)
M52 17 IGN08 A7

In 1636, when fortifications were being made on the little hill of Mont Capron N of the town, ruins of a Roman temple complex came to light. The surviving plan shows a rectangular classical temple of Antonine date with southern apse, set in a sequence of rectangular courtyards, the northern one, which gave access to the temple, being colonnaded. The rich sculptural and architectural decoration

*23 Champlieu (Oise) — the Roman theatre-amphitheatre. Photo Dini Hardy*

includes vine scrolls and fragments of Corinthian columns. Similar pieces reused in the town walls suggest that it was demolished in the late third or early fourth century to provide material for them.

The late Roman walls enclosed a rectangular area of 10ha on the E bank of the little river Frète, in the heart of the modern city, between the Rue Racine N of the cathedral, the Rue de la Taillerie on the E, and the rue Dr Gérard on the S. Sculptures and huge masonry blocks were recorded in its foundations from the seventeenth century onwards, and fragments with brick levelling courses and projecting towers still survive. In medieval times, it was known as the *mur sarrazin* (Gallia 9 (1951), 82, 12 (1954), 144).

Leblond, *Bull Archéol du Comité* 1914, 3-39 (Mont Capron); Grenier III, 416-19; Blanchet 116-120.

**Champlieu** Rural cult centre
M56 2 IGN09 B 4

The ruins here, known since the eighteenth century, were first explored by the architectural historian Viollet le Duc (*Revue Archéologique* 1860, 44-54). They include a temple, forum, theatre and baths. New excavations in 1977-8 produced Iron Age timber structures, possibly a shrine, with iron weapons and Gallic coins. The first stone buildings were of the early first century AD. By the end of the century a Romano-Celtic temple of monumental masonry with fluted columns had been built. This was succeeded by an even grander temple in the mid-second century, with a podium, Corinthian columns and sculpture.

The baths behind the theatre are of simple linear type, within a rectangular enclosure wall. On the N, a modest-sized *palaestra* or courtyard 20m square leads to an undressing room, followed

*24  Champlieu (Oise) — the Roman baths. Rear wall of theatre in background. Photo Dini Hardy*

by the usual sequence of cold, tepid and hot rooms, with hot and cold plunge baths to the E. The three apses would have held stone basins on pillars (rather like bird-baths) for bathers to wash down, and one such basin was found in the *calderium*.

Grenier IV, 335. G.P. Woimart, *Rev Archéol de Picardie*, 1:2 (1993), 63-198.

## Gournay-sur-Aronde Hillfort
M56 2 IGN09 A3

Oppidum of 100ha,with 'Fécamp style' rampart and two *muri gallici*, occupied from 300 BC to Augustan times, and again in the late Empire. Excavation inside the hillfort revealed a remarkable Iron Age cult centre, with a rectangular ditch and palisade enclosing a sequence of timber shrines. The ditch had been used for the deposition of offerings in La Tene II times, including a mass of human remains, minus heads (these were presumably exhibited elsewhere), sacrificed animals and large quantities of shields, spears and scabbarded swords.

Caesar described how the Gauls sacrificed prisoners of war and battle booty to their gods. Gournay and similar finds elsewhere are graphic illustration of the practice.

J.-L. Brunaux et al, *Gournay I: les fouilles sur le sanctuaire et l'oppidum 1975-84* (*Rev. Archéol de Picardie* special no, 1985); J.-L. Brunaux and A. Rapin, *Gournay II Boucliers et lances, dépôts et trophées* (*Rev. Archéol de Picardie* 1988); T. Lejars, *Gournay III Les Fourreaux d' Épée* (1994).

## Nointel Roman siege works
M56 1 IGN09 B2

In the posthumous final Book of Caesar's *Gallic War*, Aulus Hirtius described Caesar's elaborate siege works against the Gallic alliance led by the Bellovaci in his final campaign of 51 BC. They are now also known from Matharet's excavations on the Montagne de Nointel. Caesar encamped on one side of the broad marshy valley of the Brèche, facing the Gauls, who were on high ground on the other side. He initially had four legions with him, plus Gallic auxiliary cavalry. His army was encamped within an enclosure 100ha in size, its back against the steep slopes of the hill. Within this were two large camps, each of 22ha, which presumably held two legions apiece, and a smaller fort of 1. 6ha, the normal average size of an auxiliary fort. This probably held Caesar's headquarters and bodyguard of Praetorian Guards. Other camps outside the main defences probably held the Gallic cavalry. Towards the foot of the hill, facing the Gauls, was a linear earthwork with a series of regularly spaced fortlets each 61 x 41m. After careful preparation, two log and brushwood causeways 600m long were rapidly laid across the marshy valley to permit a rapid flank march by a now much augmented Roman army for the final battle.

G. Matherat, 'La technique des retranchements de César d'après l'ensignement des fouilles de Nointel', *Gallia* 1 (1943), 81-127.

**Senlis** (Augustomagus Silvanectum) M56 11 IGN09 B2

The name suggests an Augustan foundation for the capital of the Silvanectes. A well-preserved oval of late Roman walls enclose an area of 6ha in the higher part of the old town around the cathedral. There were originally 28 projecting semicircular towers, some 27m apart, of which 16 survive. At this time, Senlis seems to have shared a unit of laeti and gentiles (?mixed infantry and cavalry) with Reims. There are impressive remains of an amphitheatre 500m W of the town, using a small natural valley for the contours of the arena.

Blanchet, 112-116.

**Vendeuil-Caply** 'Mont Catelet' M52 18 IGN03 D11

This Roman rural shrine S of Breteuil sur Noye, on the Roman road from Amiens to Senlis, began as a major La Tène II site, later a 12ha Roman fort of Augustan date with double ditches. The ditches of an early cult centre are known, with a stone Romano-Celtic temple of the time of Nero or Vespasian. The theatre was built at the end of the first century, and enlarged under Commodus. Air photographs suggest a forum, a second theatre and temples. Like many such cult centres it was built on a tribal boundary, in this case between the Bellovaci and the Ambiani.

Agache Piton and G. Dilly, 'Le fanum de "Châtelets" de Vendeuil-Caply', *Rev Archéol de Picardie* 1985, 1-2, 25-64.

## PAS-DE-CALAIS

The County of Artois was in Roman times the territory of the Atrebates and Morini, with their civitas capitals at Arras and Thérouanne. The département is rich in mottes and other earthwork castles, and though a number of small earthworks are called 'Camp de César', it is not always clear whether these are Iron Age or medieval.

R. Delamaire, *Carte Archéologique de la Gaule* 62 (1994).

### Arras

(Nemetacum, Civitas Atrebatum) M51 16/52 10 IGN02 D6

Civitas capital of the Atrebates, who also settled in southern England, where their oppidum was at Silchester (*Calleva Atrebatum*). The earliest occupation was Augustan, and the large hillfort at Etrun, 5km away, could be its predecessor. There is another link with England in the Musée Municipal (Place de la Madeleine), where the Beaurains treasure includes the famous and frequently reproduced gold medal showing the entry of Constantius Chlorus within the walls of London in 296. Recent excavation has found the late Roman wall, with a pair of Theodosian barracks separated from it by an intervallum road. Associated weapons and horse gear suggest a cavalry unit. Batavian laeti are recorded here in the Notitia Dignitatum.

Alain Jacques, 'Le présence militaire à Arras au Bas Empire' in Vallet and Kazanski 1993 (eds), 195-207.

## Boulogne (Gesoriacum)
M51 1 IGN01 C2

Boulogne was the departure point for Britain from Gaul even before Claudius's invasion in AD 43. Early roads linked the estuary of the Liane with Lyon, and through Cologne with the armies of the Rhine frontier. Julius Caesar may have sailed from here on his second British expedition in 54 BC. By AD 39 the cross-channel route was sufficiently important for Caligula to build a lighthouse. The polygonal Tour d'Odre, very like the Roman lighthouse inside Dover Castle, but which fell into the sea in 1644, may have been a later rebuild. By AD 70-100, Boulogne was the naval base for the Channel Fleet, the *Classis Britannica*, many of whose stamped tiles have been found here.

Then as now, Roman Boulogne was divided between the Ville Haute, on the promontory above the city, and the Ville Basse around the port. The 12ha *Classis Britannica* fort was in the Ville Haute. Its characteristic rectangular form can be followed in the line of the medieval walls. The Headquarters Building stood on the site of the Place Godefroy de Bouillon, from whence the Rue du Puits d'Amour led down to the *Porta Praetoria* or front (SW) gate. As with many Roman forts and medieval castles, the corners of the fort were angled towards the cardinal points. Excavations in 1967-84 by Claude Seillier uncovered a stretch of its defences, and a series of barrack blocks at its rear. After an initial timber

period in the late first century, the buildings were rebuilt in stone under Trajan and again in Severan times, the overall chronology being similar to that of the twin fort at Dover. The Boulogne fort continued in occupation until the time of the Gallic Empire. Under the late Empire, Boulogne, previously a mere vicus or small town within the civitas of Thérouanne, was promoted to an independent civitas.

Claude Seillier in *C.A.G.* 62, parts 1-2, 214-301; do. in Reddé 1996, 212-19.

## Etrun — Camp de César
Hillfort M53 1 IGN02 D5

This 20ha hillfort 5km NW of Arras, the only one in the territory of the Atrebates and in the present département, was probably the predecessor of Arras. It should not to be confused with the similarly named site outside Cambrai in Nord. The E defences lie under the present village, but on the W a massive 'Fécamp type' rampart survives.

Wheeler and Richardson 1957, 132; Fichtl 1994, 161.

## Thérouanne (Tarvenna)
M51 13 IGN02 C2

An inscription (*C.I.L.* XIII, I, 3560) confirms that this was the capital of the Morini, but the town, a French outpost on the border of Imperial territory, was demolished by order of the Emperor Charles V in 1553, after he had taken it by siege, and formally abandoned in 1559 under the Treaty of Cateau-Cambresis. Since, the site has been open fields, with the line of the medieval ramparts showing in field boundaries.

Excavation under the demolished cathedral has located a large second-century house and the line of late Roman defences has been suggested, in a rectangular area in the NW quadrant of the medieval walled town. Under the late Empire, its territory was divided when Boulogne, previously a vicus within its territory, was promoted to a civitas. The apse of an eighth-/ninth-century cathedral is known under its demolished Gothic successor.

H. Bernard, 'Thérouanne, ville morte', *Archéologia* 81 (April 1975), 41-63.

## Vis-en-Artois Vicus

M52 10 IGN04 A5

Roman vicus on the Arras-Cambrai road, at a crossing of the river Sensée. The possible site of the battle of *Vicus Helenae* where Aetius defeated the Franks about 428. They were enjoying a wedding feast in a village close to a wooden bridge when Aetius made a surprise attack. This was enough to make the Franks sue for peace. Merovingian pottery kilns are known east of the village.

## SOMME

For most British visitors, the word 'Somme' will mean not only an area of northern France, but also the battle, or series of battles, of July-November 1916. There are many guidebooks to the western front, but even the visitor with no particular interest in battles or battlefields may be glad of a brief account to put the numerous cemeteries and memorials which form such a poignant feature of the landscape hereabouts into historical perspective. The German invasion of France and Belgium in 1914 was intended as what would later be called a 'Blitz krieg' ('lightning war'), culminating in the capture of Paris. By the end of the year it had been halted in the battles of the Marne and First Ypres, and trenches, machine guns, barbed wire, massed artillery and mud had created a stalemate. The British sector of the front was basically a 50 mile N-S line (its actual length being about 80 miles). Its northern hinge was at Ypres in Belgium (to the N the Belgians were holding the line of the river Yser), its southern hinge on the Somme, S of which was the French army. The major battles on this front (Second Ypres and Loos in 1915; the Somme in 1916; Arras, Messines, Third Ypres (Passchendale) and Cambrai in 1917; the German 1918 spring offensive and the British victory at Amiens in June) were all attempts to break through that N-S line in one direction or the other.

The Somme offensive had two main objectives: to capture the commanding ridge of high ground north of the Somme between Thiepval and Combles, and to relieve the pressure on the French army at Verdun, where, after a long battle of attrition, the situation was critical. The results thus cannot wholly be judged in terms of ground won. The assault opened on 1 July on a 14 mile front between Serre and Maricourt, with a frontal attack uphill against deeply entrenched machine gun positions and belts of wire, with tactics that might have been effective against an eighteenth-century army equipped with muskets. On the first day 20,000 British troops were killed, many of them from the 'Pals' battalions drawn from a single industrial town, a particular occupation or group, or even a football club. The battle continued with a series of costly set piece assaults on individual features — a single wood could cost a division of between 12,000 and 16,000 men — until mid November, by which time Haig had advanced six miles at a cost of 499,476 men, of whom 150,000 were killed.

The present département of Somme corresponds fairly exactly to the territory of the pre-Roman Ambiani. It includes a number of major hillforts, and excavations in Amiens have revealed the history of the rise, growth and decline of this major Roman city, though there are no visible remains outside the museum.

In the surrounding countryside, the remarkable air photographs of Roger Agache have revealed the Gallo-Roman countryside in great detail, with large numbers of villas, temples and rural shrines set in their natural environment of woods, hills and streams. Roman forts are known from air photographs at Folleville (16ha) and Roye (6ha), but there is nothing to see on the ground.

**Abbeville** Musée Boucher de Perthes
M52 7 IGN03 A8
Named after the nineteenth-century local antiquarian who discovered Palaeolithic handaxes and the bones of extinct animals in glacial gravels, thereby demonstrating the antiquity of Man, the museum contains local archaeological collections and a display of the air photographs of Roger Agache.

**Amiens** (Samorobriva)
M52 8 IGN03 D4
Samorobriva, 'the ford on the river Somme', may have originated under Julius Caesar as a protected river crossing. The civilian town was founded under Augustus, and growth was rapid. An early grid of rectangular insulae next to the river proved too small, and a second grid pattern of larger square insulae had to be added to the S. By the reign of Claudius, Samorobriva covered 60ha. Under the Flavian Emperors, it acquired the usual civic amenities — an imposing double forum complex and public baths in what is now the Rue de Beauvais. By the early second century the city had grown to 150ha — rather larger than the walled area of Roman London — and acquired a large amphitheatre and a monumental entrance to the forum, though much of the city would be lightly built up with parks and gardens in the manner of most ancient cities.

The city withstood a serious fire in about 170-80. The forum complex was restored to the same plan, and the baths rebuilt in monumental style. Another fire about 250 may coincide with the onset of serious decline. Fires of this kind were endemic in ancient cities (Roman London had several), and there is no indication that either fire at Amiens was other than accidental. The city now began to shrink, and cemeteries to impinge on previously inhabited areas. The mid-third century city may have covered some 80ha. By the end of the century this had halved, and the late Roman walls enclose 20ha, though there were probably extramural suburbs.

Despite this shrinkage, Amiens remained an important city in the late Empire. The double forum and macellum (market) complex, together with the adjacent amphitheatre, were requisitioned and turned into a military supply depot and armament works, which continued to function until the mid-fifth century. The amphitheatre was demolished in 1117 by Louis VI, lest it be fortified by his enemies. This and the forum complex are known from excavations and chance discoveries, but nothing is visible.

The Musée de Picardie (48, Rue de la République) contains important regional archaeological collections. Of particular British interest is the 'Amiens patera', an enamelled skillet found in 1949 which was a souvenir from Hadrian's Wall. Its decoration shows the wall and its towers, with the names of a series of its forts.
D. Bayard and J. L. Massy, *Amiens Romain* (1983).

**La Chausée-Tirancourt**
Hillfort and archaeological park
M52 8 IGN03 B10
The Camp de César forms the centrepiece of the archaeological country park of Samara, NW of Amiens, opened in 1988. It encloses a triangular area of 35ha between the valley of the

Somme and that of the Acon, with a massive single rampart 450m in length along the third side. There are traces of a second (?earlier) rampart inside this, enclosing 12ha. Two Roman temporary camps, discovered from the air, lie outside it. Besides the hillfort, excavation of which is in progress, the park includes reconstructions of Neolithic, Bronze Age and Iron Age houses, the main gate of the hillfort, a wetland exhibit, botanical gardens and an arboretum.

Excavation in the main entrance of the hillfort in 1983-90 showed that both defences and entrance were of two periods. The first was a simple dump rampart of chalk 3.5m high, with a massive ditch. In the second phase, after a violent destruction, the rampart had a facing of sandstone reinforced with horizontal and vertical timber beams. A reconstruction of this can be seen on site. In both phases, there was a timber gate on 3 ranges of 6 postholes, with a guardroom above. Pottery and coins date the second phase to *c*.40-25 BC and finds of Roman military material in the gate-passage have led to the suggestion that it could represent occupation by the Roman army. The alternative is that the material could have been from a Roman demolition of the gateway.

J.L. Brunaux, S. Fichtl and Ch Marchand, 'Das "Camp César" bei la Chausée Tirancourt (Somme)', *Saalburg Jahrbuch* 45 (1990), 5-45; Agache plates 127 and 128 (air photographs) and fig 8, p228; Fichtl 45-8.

## Ribemont-sur-Ancre

Rural cult centre M52 9 IGN04 C2
This Gallo-Roman rural cult centre began as a Gaulish sanctuary of a surprising kind. The earliest levels are Middle and Late La Tène (La Tène II and III) and are associated with offerings of weapons and brooches and a charnel heap of 200

individuals, the defleshed bones neatly arranged in sorted heaps around a central feature. There are no skulls, which may have been displayed elsewhere. Similar charnel heaps are known elsewhere, as at Moeuvres (Pas-de-Calais) where a heap of 200 disarticulated human skeletons, again with no skulls, were found within a ditched enclosure in 1913, associated with La Tène II weapons and brooches (Déchelette *Manuel* II, 3) and at Gournay-sur-Aronde. Such finds, which must represent human sacrifice or the slaughter of prisoners of war, confirm Caesar's account of human sacrifice among the Druids.

After the Roman conquest, Ribemont developed as a rural cult centre. The earliest temple is late Augustan or Tiberian. A theatre to hold 3,000 spectators was added early in the reign of Nero. Public baths were built under Trajan and in Antonine times the temple was rebuilt with sculptured decoration on fine imported limestone. About 160 the theatre was remodelled as one of the theatre-amphitheatres characteristic of northern Gaul. At its peak the sanctuary covered 25ha. Burnt down in the later third century, it was restored under Constantine, but thereafter, like many of the rural cult centres, it fell rapidly into disuse.

J.L. Cadoux 1978, 'Un sanctuaire Gallo-Romaine isolé: Ribemont-sur-Ancre', *Latomus* 37, 325-60.

## Saint-Valery-sur-Somme

M52 6 IGN03 A7
St Valery may have been the base of the *Classis Samara*, the late Roman fleet stationed at the mouth of the Somme (the *Notitia Dignitatum* has *Classis Sambrica* 'of the River Sambre' in error). A late Roman fort may underlie the medieval walls and tiles stamped Cl(assis) Sam(ara) are known from Etaples, further up the coast.

# 6 Champagne and Alsace-Lorraine
## (Belgica Prima and Germania Prima)

Champagne is a name well known in Britain, if only as that of the products of the vineyards around its regional capital, Reims. It forms the eastern part of the Paris basin, and until France acquired Lorraine and Franche-Comte in the sixteenth century, was the eastern boundary of the kingdom of France. Despite the fame of its wine, it is not a naturally fertile agricultural area. Its chalky plains lack surface water and, unlike Picardy to the west, it was only with modern fertilisers that large-scale corn production became possible.

Alsace-Lorraine consists of two very different regions, separated by the forests of the Vosges. Lorraine has never been a rich area, save in its huge deposits of iron ore and coal. Its forested soils, poor and acid, are often heavy and difficult to work. Even this was turned to advantage by the Romans however, for the iron rich clays of the Lavoye area formed the basis for an important pottery industry. Today it is a major industrial area. Its central artery is the Moselle, and Metz, at an important crossing of the river, has been the fortified centre of Lorraine since Iron Age times. East of the Vosges is Alsace, rich farming land, whose vineyards, timbered farm houses and red sandstone buildings belong to the Rhineland and the beginnings of central Europe.

## CHAMPAGNE
### ARDENNES
The forested hills of the Ardennes, dissected by deeply cut stream valleys, extend across the border into the adjacent Belgian Ardennes. The area contains good quality iron ore and a number of small rural settlements, including Baalous and Château Porcien, both with shrines beginning in La Tène III. Several villas are known, but no major Roman sites. Much of the area may have been an Imperial estate, the property of the Emperor.

### AUBE
#### Pouan
M61 6 IGN22 B4
The early fifth-century treasure from a princely grave found beside the Aube W of Arcis-sur-Aube in 1842 belongs to the same world as Sutton Hoo. The gold and garnet metalwork includes a sword with pattern welded blade, gold encased grip and richly decorated scabbard; a similar scramasaxe or hunting knife; a gold ring inscribed HEVA; a gold torque and bracelet and a series of gold and garnet buckles. It is now in the museum at Troyes.
E. Salin and A. France-Lanord, 'Sur le trésor barbare de Pouan, Aube', *Gallia* 14 (1955), 65-75.

#### Troyes (Augustobona)
M61 16-17 IGN22 C4
The late Roman walls of Troyes enclosed 16ha, though the early Roman town extended over 80. Their line can be followed in a rectangle of streets between the cathedral and the site of the castle (Place de la Tour), a stream marking their outline to the N and W. Carolingian sources speak of the 'wall of the civitas

and its towers'. These were rebuilt about 1150, and nothing now remains. Troyes had a Christian bishop by 429, when Lupus of Troyes, a former monk of Lerins and a noted theologian, visited Britain with Germanus of Auxerre. The Musée des Beaux Arts (21, Rue Chrétien de Troyes) contains a major local collection of prehistoric and Roman material. Blanchet 71-3.

# MARNE
## Châlons-sur-Marne

(Durocatalaunum) M56 17 IGN10 D5
Sited at a an important crossing of the Marne at a point where it is still navigable, Châlons was the site of two decisive late Roman battles. The late Roman town was small, with defences enclosing around 5ha. Near here in 273-4, Tetricus, last of the Gallic Emperors, surrendered to Aurelian after losing a battle. Even more decisive was the Battle of the Catalaunian Fields in 451. Attila, leader of the Huns, frustrated in his ambitions for high office within the Roman Empire, invaded Gaul and advanced as far as Orleans, which he besieged. When his former ally, the Roman general Aetius, approached with his army of Franks, Burgundians and Visigoths, Attila fell back. The decisive battle took place at an estate named Mauriacum outside Châlons, and Attila was defeated. Ironically, Aetius's victory led to his downfall and death, for the support of the Huns had underwritten his power. In 454 he was murdered by Valentinian III.

## Reims

(Durocorturum, Civitas Remorum)
M56 6 IGN10 B1
The Remi were allies of Rome, and this may be reflected in the history of their city, which was also capital of Gallia Belgica, and, after Diocletian, of Belgica Secunda. Reims began soon after the time of Julius Caesar, and the fortified

settlement (*Duro*) indicated by the place-name was, in its first phase, an oval ditched enclosure of about 110ha. By the early first century AD there was a grid of metalled roads and a more substantial enclosure ditch, perhaps reflecting the town's status as a *civitas foederata* (Allied city). The first-century triumphal arch, the Porte de Mars, was incorporated in the late Roman and medieval ramparts, and so survives, somewhat restored. It is a three-arched structure, with fluted Corinthian columns and a series of pedimented niches that may once have held statues. In contrast, the amphitheatre and late Roman walls are known only from early records, the last traces of the amphitheatre being removed in 1853. The walls, incorporating the Porte de Mars and another early monumental arch in their line, enclosed 60ha, the third largest circuit in northern Gaul after Trier and Metz. The forum had a cryptoporicus like those at Arles and elsewhere, and a lost inscription recorded by a fifteenth-century bishop (*C.I.L.* XIII, 3255) told how Constantine (308-37) gave a bathhouse to the city of the Remi. Its location is not known.

One other vanished monument deserves mention. Flavius Jovinus was *magister militum* (army commander) to Valentinian I, and consul in 367. A devout Christian, he built a church, the *Basilica Joviana* in the cemetery area S of the city as a burial place for himself and as a home for some north Italian martyr relics he had acquired. Long demolished, early accounts tell how it had polychrome wall mosaics above its nave arcades, with figures set in a field of gold and an inscription (*C.I.L.* XIII, 3256) in letters of gold.

Grenier III, 696; R. Neiss 1984, 'La structure urbain de Reims antique et son évolution du Ier au IIIe siècle', *Rev. Archéol de Picardie* 3-4, 171-91.

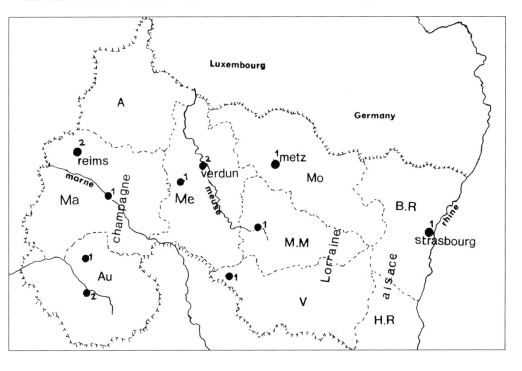

25 Champagne and Alsace-Lorraine (Belgica Prima and Germania Prima)
   *A* Ardennes
   *Au* Aube *1 Pouan 2 Troyes*
   *M* Marne *1 Châlons-sur-Marne 2 Reim*
   *MM* Meurthe et Moselle *1 Toul*
   *Me* Meuse *1 Lavoye 2 Verdun*
   *Mo* Moselle *Metz*
   *V* Vosges *Grand*
   *BR* Bas-Rhin *1 Strasbourg*
   *HR* Haute-Rhin

## LORRAINE

Useful for this area is the series M. Toussaint, *Répetoire archéologique du département de . . . (période gallo-romaine)*, hereafter Toussaint *Répetoire*.

## MEURTHE-ET-MOSELLE

Toussaint, *Répetoire . . . Meuthe et Moselle* (Nancy 1947).

Meurthe-et-Moselle and its western neighbour Meuse were the territory of the Leuci, one of three tribes (Treveri, Mediomatrici and Leuci) whose lands formed an eastern bulge of Gallia Belgica projecting into Germania Superior. There is a 50ha oppidum at Boviolles, Naix Void (Meuse), the predecessor of Roman Naix, where nineteenth-century excavations produced evidence of extensive occupation, and another of 20ha at Ste Geneviève NE of Nancy (Meurthe-et-Moselle). (Cotton 1957, 204; Collis 1975, 167).

**Toul** (Tullum) M62 4 IGN23 A6

Toul on the Moselle was the Cantonal

capital of the Leuci, but does not seem to have been highly urbanized, perhaps because of rivalry from Naix, which under the early Empire may have shared the role of Cantonal capital with it. The late Roman walls enclosed an area of about 12ha. A coin of Carinus in its core shows that they date from 284-5 or later.

# MEUSE
Toussaint, *Répetoire . . . Meuse* (Bar le Duc 1946).

The Forest of Argonne, W of Verdun on the boundary of the départements of Meuse and Marne, was the centre of a major pottery industry from the second century to Merovingian times.

**Lavoye** Pottery production centre
M56 20 IGN10 C10

From the time of Hadrian, Lavoye was one of the main production centres for east Gaulish samian. Some 60 kilns have been excavated, and there were branch factories at Les Allieux and Avocourt. After the demise of the samian industry in the third century, Lavoye and other centres in the Argonne continued to produce high quality red-slipped wares in forms from the samian repertoire, including bowls deriving from Dragendorf 37 (the hemispherical decorated bowls found in every museum with collections of Roman pottery). These were decorated with complex roulette patterns and close study of the individual roulettes has made it possible to identify a series of phases of the industry, going down to around AD 530. Far from ending (as was once thought) at the time of the 'Great invasions' of 407, one branch workshop of Argonne ware was actually opening at this time. For bibliography see pottery gazetteer (Appendix).

**Verdun** (Virodunum)
M57 11 IGN10 C11

A vicus of the Mediomatrici of Metz,

Verdun became capital of the western part of the civitas under the late Empire. In view of its recent history, it is hardly surprising that little of its Roman past is now visible. The late Roman walls enclosed an area of around 12ha.

# MOSELLE
Toussaint, *Répetoire . . . Moselle* (Nancy 1950).

**Metz** (Divodurum)
M57 13 IGN11 C7

Metz, capital of the Mediomatrici, on an important crossing of the Moselle, commands routes between northern France and the Rhineland. The first fortified settlement here was a hillfort with *murus gallicus* defences, dated by dendrochronology to between 114 and 110 BC. The Roman city had two large sets of baths, one with a circular swimming pool and courtyard paid for by a local man who had been Priest of Rome and Augustus at Lyon (*Gallia* 34, (1976), 363). Similarly the city aqueduct, bringing water from Gorize entered the city via a *nymphaeum* sponsored by a group of *Seviri Augustales* (priests of the local Imperial cult, *C.I.L.* XIII, 4325).

Nothing is visible of the 'Grand Amphitheatre', found in 1902-3 and now under the railway station, 600m SE of the walled town. An inscription gave the name of its principal donor, M. Vegisonius Marcellus, who probably lived in the late first or early second century. Two features of interest were a large cruciform sunken structure reinforced with oak beams, below the arena, for the management of the stage machinery, and a Christian chapel or martyrium built into the ruinous N entrance. This, of reused columns and stonework, with traces of mosaics and a tiled roof, may have been associated with the first bishop of Metz, Clement. It later became the church of *St Petri in Amphitheatro*. A chi-rho monogram and fragments of memorial inscriptions confirmed its Christian character. There was a second, much smaller amphitheatre of the theatre-amphitheatre type, later incorporated in the town walls. It may have been as late as the third or fourth century.

The late Roman walls enclosed an irregular polygon of 70ha next to Trier the largest walled city in north Gaul. They included the smaller amphitheatre and were finally demolished around 1561, when new bastioned fortifications were built. Several hundred architectural pieces were found in their foundations, and were promptly reinterred in those of the new. Nothing of the walls is now visible, but the rich Gallo-Roman collections of the museum (2, Rue du Haut-Poirier) are housed in part of a Roman bath building.

The ruined church of St Pierre-aux-Nonnains on the citadel is a late Roman brick basilica very similar to the better known one at Trier. It uses similar stamped bricks (dated by thermoluminescence to 400±15) and may have been a judicial basilica for the provincial governor. Research preparatory to opening to the public has placed the basilica in context. Built on the site of a demolished house, it was associated with a vast bath complex to the north (t. l. date of 370±15). After alterations in Merovingian times and in the twelfth century, it was converted into a Gothic church.

Grenier, 'Découverte d'un amphithéâtre romain à Metz', *Bull. Soc Antiq. de France* 1913, 256-261; Grenier III, 695-704; Blanchet 98-9; D. Heckenhenner et al, 'Le quartier de l'arsenal à Metz: topographie urbain et évolution architectural durant l'antiquité', *Gallia* 49 (1992), 9-36; St Pierre, *Gallia Informations* 1989, 2, 121-3; X. Delestre, *Saint-Pierre-aux Nonnains* (G.A.F.).

# VOSGES

Toussaint *Répetoire . . . Vosges* (Epinal 1948).

The forested hills of the Vosges, with their almost continuous cover of fir and beech, and their many glacial lakes, separate industrial Lorraine from the rich farming country of Alsace.

## Grand M62 2 IGN23 C3

The temple of Apollo-Grannus, probably the place where the still pagan Emperor Constantine had a vision of Apollo and Victory in 309 (Pelletier, *Panegyrics* 1952, III, 72), is marked by a flourishing Roman settlement with impressive remains of an amphitheatre, theatre, an apsed building with a large third-century mosaic, aqueduct, two public baths and houses with fine mosaics. The site of the temple lies under the present village.

Grenier III, 487-90; F. Braemer, *Caesarodunum* 8 (1973), 108-13; for a model of the theatre-amphitheatre see A. Olivier *R.A.E.* 43 (1992) 154-6.

# BAS-RHIN and HAUT-RHIN

## Strasbourg (Argentoratum)
M62 10 IGN12 C9

Strasbourg (Bas-Rhin), though within France, belongs with the other legionary fortresses of the Rhine frontier, at Xanten, Bonn, Neuss and Mainz. The fortress lies under the modern city, around the cathedral, and only a brief outline of what excavation has revealed is needed here. The earliest fort was built under Augustus, and an altar dedicated by a trooper of a cavalry regiment, the *Ala Petriana* (which was to end up, doubled in size, as part of the garrison of Hadrian's Wall) belongs to this early phase. From about AD 10-15 the Second Augustan Legion, *Legio II Augusta*, was here and the clay rampart and V-shaped ditches of its fortress are known. After it left for Britain in AD 43, the fortress may not have been fully occupied until about AD 90, when *Legio VIII Augusta* arrived from Mirabeau (Côte d'Or).

The known legionary fortress dates from this time. Originally with earth and timber defences, it later acquired a characteristic early Empire legionary rampart, with a stone curtain wall with internal rectangular towers fronting the clay bank. Under the late Empire, this was encased within a thicker curtain with semicircular towers projecting over the filled-in early ditch. A broad flat-bottomed ditch lay outside this new defence.

Reddé, 1996, 203-7.

# 7 Charentes and Poitou
## (Aquitania Secunda)

Aquitania Secunda, divided from Aquitania Prima to the east under Diocletian, included the territories of the Biturges of Bordeaux, whose city formed the provincial capital; the Petrocorii of the Dordogne (for these two see chapter 8); the Santones of the Saintonge; the Pictones of Poitiers, and the Nitobriges of Agen.

The medieval Saintonge, in Charente and Charente-Maritime, was the pre-Roman territory of the Santones. Agrippa drove a road westward from Lyon into their territory, and Saintes, at its termination, was probably the early capital of Gallia Aquitanica. Inland, the populous countryside needed other religious and market centres, and there are impressive remains at Bouchards NW of Angoulême, and at Chassenon in the Vienne valley.

To the N, the huge civitas of the Pictones, centred on Poitiers, occupied three modern départements — Vendée, Deux-Sèvres and Vienne. The ruins of the rural cult centres at Sanxay and Vieux-Poitiers have been excavated and laid out on display, whilst Civaux, with its vast early medieval sarcophagus cemetery, is one of the most striking sites of western France. Poitou is rich in Merovingian and early medieval sites, and Poitiers is one of the few cities with buildings of the period.

## CHARENTE
### Angoulême (Ecolisina)
M72 13 IGN40 D6
Angoulême stands on a high limestone hill above the Charente. Its late Roman walls have long vanished, but from the sixteenth century onwards were a rich source of Roman sculptures and inscriptions, which had been reused in their foundations. Some can be seen in the garden of the museum of the Archaeological Society of the Charente (44, Rue Montmoreau), which also contains finds from Bouchards and Chassenon. The medieval ramparts still form a pleasant walk, with good views, but the 1866 restoration of the cathedral by an architect called Abadie was perhaps unfortunate.

### Bouchards, St Cybardeaux
(Germanicomagus) M72 13 IGN40 C5
The theatre of this rural cult centre 'the market centre of Germanicus' is as large as those of Arles or Orange, and this small settlement was clearly important in the religious, social and economic life of the surrounding countryside. Excavated by the Jesuit priest Camille de la Croix in 1901-6, one significant feature was the bank of three semicircular rows of 'seats of honour' in the orchestra. This flat area between the stage and the seating, used in ancient Greece for the theatrical chorus, was in Gallo-Roman times reserved for dignitaries. Local magnates came to the theatre not only to see, but to be seen.
P. de la Croix 1908, *Etude sur le Théatre Gallo-Romain des Bouchards* (Angouleme); L. Maurin 1981, *Les Ruines gallo-romaines des Bouchards à Saint-Cybardaux* (Bordeaux).

### Chassenon (Cassinomagus)
M72 16 IGN40 C11
The impressive remains of this bathhouse, in places still standing 5m high, in masonry of *opus mixtum* with

*26  Chassenon (Charente) — the Roman baths. Photograph Linda Harris*

brick bonding courses, have long been known, and were once thought to be the palace of a Roman governor. Excavated and conserved in 1985, there are now guided tours and a museum, organized by a 'Society of the Friends of Chassenon'. They belonged to a rural sanctuary on the Roman road from Lyon to the early capital of Gallia Aquitania at Saintes. There may have been a pre-Roman water cult here. W of the baths was a characteristic tower-temple of western Gaul, like Périgueux or Talmont, surrounded by an octagonal ambulatory, like that at Civaux, with marble pavement and base for a cult statue. Flanking this was a grid of over 50 circular cisterns, probably of cult significance, but also designed to tap ground water for the complex. There was a theatre-amphitheatre to the N, a possible forum, two aqueducts and traces of a boundary wall enclosing the sacred temenos.

Entrance to the baths was on the E, where a courtyard contained the *apodyterium* (undressing area). Part of a *palaestra* (exercise hall) is visible on the S. Beyond are two parallel bath suites, with the usual sequence of cold, warm and hot rooms, set each side of an impressive central hall. After the building fell into disuse, it was quarried for the manufacture of Merovingian sarcophagi of 'Chassenon stone'.

P. Barrière, 'Une bourgade gallo-romaine: Chassenon, ses monuments et ses puits', *R.E.A.* 39, (1937) 241-55.

## CHARENTE-MARITIME
### Aulnay-de-Saintonge

(Aunedonnacum) Legionary fortress
M72 2 IGN40 B3

Aulnay is best known for its magnificent twelfth-century church, with its wealth of Romanesque sculpture. In the nineteenth century, three Roman tombstones were found here, of legionaries from *Legio XIV Gemina* and *Legio II Augusta*. These were pre-Claudian, since both legions were in

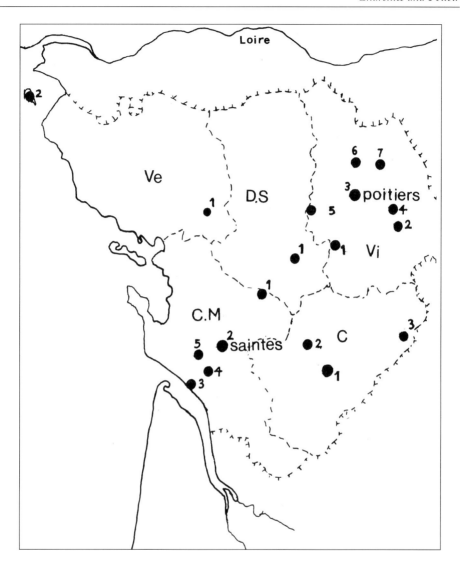

27  Charentes and Poitou (Aquitania Secunda)

*C* Charente *1 Angoulême 2 Bouchards 3 Chassenon*

*CM* Charente Maritime *1 Aulnay de Saintonge 2 Saintes 3 Talmont de Gironde 4 Thaims*
*5 Tour de Pirelonge*

*DS* Deux-Sèvres *1 Melle*

*Ve* Vendée *1 Noirmoutier*

*Vi* Vienne *1 Chatillon en Couhe 2 Civaux 3 Poitiers 4 St Pierre les Eglises 5 Sanxay 6 Vendoeuvres*
*7 Vieux Poitiers*

Britain from AD 43, but their context remained a mystery until 1976, when, during a drought, the ditches and internal buildings of a Roman fort of classic 'playing card' shape were seen from the air. The fort, which lay on the Roman Saintes-Poitiers road, covered 5.4ha, enough for a vexillation of 1,000 men (2 cohorts) from each legion.

Extensive excavation followed in 1976-92. A coin of AD 20 from the base of the massive posthole of a corner tower showed that the fort could not have been built before this, and the coins, of Augustus and Tiberius, ended with issues of about AD 30. The excavators linked the site with the revolt of the Turones (from around Tours) in AD 21, which Tacitus records (*Annals* III, 41) was put down by legionary detachments under Visellius Varro, Governor of Lower Germany. The excavations recovered the plans of timber internal buildings, including the Headquarters building, the Commanding Officer's house, other officers' houses and store buildings, as well as closely dated pottery and military metalwork. Since this is an air-photograph site, there is nothing to be seen on the ground.

D. and F. Tassaux et al, 'Aulnay de Saintonge: un camp Augusto-Tibérien en Aquitaine', *Aquitania* 1 (1983), 49-95, 2 (1984), 105-59; Reddé 1996, 177-88.

## Saintes (Mediolanum Santonum)
M72 11 IGN40 D1

Mediolanum was probably the early capital of Gallia Aquitanica, and contains a remarkable group of monuments from the time of Augustus and Claudius. The Triumphal Arch of Germanicus, now on the right bank of the Charente near the Archaeological Museum, once stood in the middle of the river bridge. In 1842, when it was in process of being removed for 'traffic improvements', the Inspector of Ancient Monuments, Prosper Mérimee (who also wrote the novel *Carmen*, source of the opera), had it moved stone by stone and re-erected on its present site. It dates from AD 19, as the votive inscription (*C.I.L.* XIII, 1036, *I.L.T.G.* 217) tells us. It was erected by a wealthy magnate, Caius Julius Rufus, in honour of the dead Germanicus, his adoptive father, the Emperor Tiberius and his father Drusus. It comprises two tall archways flanked, above a high plinth, by flat fluted pilasters with Corinthian capitals, like those on the Augustan gates of Autun. Above are three boldly moulded cornices. Rufus's grandfather was Caius Julius Gedomo, a Gaulish aristocrat awarded Roman citizenship under Julius Caesar, whose name and forename he took. Julius Gedomo's own father had the distinctly un-Roman name of Epotsorovidos. Julius Rufus was Priest of Rome and Augustus at Lyon, where he also paid for the building of the amphitheatre at the meeting place of the Council of the Gauls. A temple of the Divine Augustus stood adjacent to the bridge, on the site of the Post Office. The first street grid followed shortly after the building of these earliest monuments.

W of the town, off the Rue Lacurie, is the Roman amphitheatre (Arènes — ring for admission). An inscription (*C.I.L.* XIII, 1038) dates it from the reign of Claudius (41-54). Two vaulted passageways, W and E, formed ceremonial entrances for the processions of competitors which proceeded the games. Each side of the E entrance is a vaulted chamber within the *cavea*. That on the S, with access to the arena, may have been the shrine of Nemesis, the goddess of just retribution, usual in amphitheatres. The small square chamber on the N side of the arena supported the base for the president of the games, but also opens to the arena, and it may have served other functions.

The seating, for 20,000 spectators — an indication of the size of the first-century city — was supported on a series of 70 radiating vaulted passages, which also provided external access to the stairs. On the E the first tier of external arcading survives to full height. As at Poitiers and Bordeaux, the amphitheatre was known in the Middle Ages as the 'Palace of Gallienus', said to have been a mythical queen of Charlemagne. Why the third-century Emperor should be remembered in this way is not clear. There may also have been a circus. A nineteenth-century antiquary identified its site in a small valley N of the town, and some confirmation was recovered from German anti-tank ditches in 1944. An adjacent hamlet called Fourneaux 'lime kilns' might explain its disappearance. The site of the theatre is also known, but nothing is visible.

The line of the late Roman walls is known from sixteenth- and seventeenth-century plans. They enclosed a pentagonal area, with the present cathedral marking the approximate centre. The Roman road leading from the bridge skirted them on the north. In 1609, when some of the towers of the wall were demolished, sculptures and column drums were found, and such discoveries have continued periodically to the present day. Recent finds include a reused inscription of the early third century. An impressive collection of this material can be seen in the Archaeological Museum.
Maurin, *Saintes Antiques* (1978). Grenier III, 650-7, 835, 994-6; Bedon et al, 1988, 5-42.

## Talmont-sur-Gironde
The Moulin de Fâ (Tamnum)
M71 15 IGN46 B2
On a hill E of Royan, a windmill, the Moulin de Fâ, stands on a massive circular masonry platform 36m across.

This was the foundation of a high circular tower like that which still survives at the Temple of Vesuna at Périgueux. Roman *Tamnum* was both rural cult sanctuary and small coastal port, for the sea came much closer than it does today. Excavation around the temple has shown that it stood within a colonnaded precinct like that at Périgueux, and that this in turn was part of a larger complex, including a bath suite, a large forum N of the baths, and a temple to the E. The line of a 2m high rock-cut aqueduct channel is also known, bringing water from a source some 3km E.

Architectural fragments show that the temple made generous use of red, green and white marble, some of it richly sculptured. Like the Périgueux temple, it consisted of two circular concentric walls, opening out on the SE to a conventional temple facade with a series of columns and a pediment. The inner wall, within which the modern windmill stands, was the temple cella. Reinforced with a series of massive blocks set at intervals, it formed the foundation of the high circular tower-temple. The outer wall enclosed a roofed ambulatory for pilgrims and religious processions, as in a more conventional Romano-Celtic temple.
M.L. Basalo, 'Le temple du Moulin du Fe, Barzan, Talmont-sur-Gironde', *Gallia* 2 (1944), 141-65.

## Thaims
Roman villa and early church
M71 5 IGN46 A2
The Romanesque church was built on the site of a Roman villa, some of whose walls survive S of the tower. There are also parts of a heated bath suite. Inside the church are two Gallo-Roman marble sculptures, of Bacchus and Epona. There are several early medieval sarcophagi in a garden S of the church and the crossing contains a Carolingian sculpture of St

Peter and some associated architectural features. This seems to be another case where a Roman villa survived in some form to give rise to an early medieval church.

## Tour de Pirelonge
M71 9 IGN46 A2

Funerary monument S of N150 between Saintes and Saujon.

# DEUX-SEVRES

The huge tribal territory of the Pictones spread over three modern départements — Vienne in the east around Poitiers, Deux-Sèvres in the centre and the Vendée in the west. Deux-Sèvres is a land of open limestone plains and corn-land.

## Melle (Metellum) M72 2 IGN40 A4

In the ancient world, silver, essential for coinage, was produced by refining argentiferous lead. The lead mines of *Metellum*, worked in Roman times, continued in use after the end of Roman rule. They were still a source of silver in the seventh century, and there is a prolific series of Carolingian coins with their mint signature, some of which reached Britain in Viking times. A good collection of these is in the Musée du Pilori in Niort. One early mine was reopened a few years ago, and there are now guided tours. Melle also has three fine Poitevin Romanesque churches, and St Hilary's may have a link with the Roman Empire. The figure on horseback over the N front has been variously interpreted as Christ, Charlemagne, or the emperor Constantine.

# VENDÉE

The Vendée was the western part of the huge civitas territory of the Pictones of Poitiers. In many ways, including geologically, it is a southern extension of Brittany.

M. Provost, *Carte Archéologique de la Gaule: La Vendée* (1996).

## Fontenay-le-Comte Museum
M71 1 IGN33 D5/6

The Musée Vendéen (Rue Gaston-Guillemet) has a good display of the archaeology and history of the Vendée, including a fine collection of Roman glass.

## Noirmoutier Site of early monastery
M67 1 IGN32 A/B4

Though there are no visible remains of its early history, Noirmoutier is the equivalent of Lindisfarne or Mont Saint Michel. An early monastic settlement on a tidal island, cut off at high tide, it was founded by St Philibert, a Gascon of noble birth, after he had been expelled from Neustria, north of the Loire, by Ebroin, Mayor of the Palace, in 674. His *Life* contains much information about seventh-century trade in the Atlantic seaways, with British and Irish sailors trading footwear and clothing, probably in return for oil and salt. A shipload of Mediterranean olive oil arrived at Noirmoutier as a gift to Philibert from friends or relations in Bordeaux.

In the ninth century, the monks of Noirmoutier fled inland to St Philibert de Grandlieu S of Nantes, with the bones of their founder, to escape the Vikings, just as the monks of Lindisfarne fled to Chester le Street and ultimately to Durham with the bones of St Cuthbert. There is an important ninth-century church at St Philibert, but his relics are at Tournus in Burgundy, where the monks finally settled under Charles the Bald. The name Noirmoutier, 'monastery of the black monks', refers to the eleventh-century Benedictine abbey, whose crypt contains Philibert's empty tomb. The museum in the adjacent castle contains photographs of the nineteenth-century sailing ships which carried local salt to Britain and elsewhere, and a surprising collection of Sunderland lustreware, brought back on the sailing ships as wedding presents, the later equivalent of Philibert's shipload of olive oil.

## VIENNE
### Châtillon-en-Couhé Hillfort
M68 13 IGN40 A7

Off the N10 Poitiers-Angouleme road just north of Couhé, the rampart and broad ditch of a 'Fécamp style' hillfort cut off a spur of high ground within a loop of the Dive.

Hogg (1969), 262 with plan.

**Civaux** Roman vicus, early church and cemetery M68 15 IGN34 D5

Civaux is one of the most surprising archaeological sites in western Gaul. The enormous size of the territory of the Pictones, governed from Poitiers, meant that there was a need for subsidiary rural settlements. Some of these took the form of rural cult centres like Sanxay or Vieux Poitiers, with temples, theatres, baths and rural markets. Civaux started out in the same way. A theatre is known in the hamlet of La Croche on its outskirts and the cemetery begins with Roman cremation burials. However, it is the late Roman and post-Roman remains that make Civaux so remarkable. The church, whose apse of small squared blocks may be of reused Roman stone, is dedicated to the martyrs Gervasius and Protasius, whose relics were brought to Gaul from north Italy by St Martin of Tours. A Christian funerary inscription of late fourth- or very early fifth-century date reading *Aeternalis et Servilia Vivatis in Deo* ('Aeternalis and Servilia may you live in God'), with a chi-rho monogram above, was found built into its masonry in 1862 and is now displayed inside the church.

The settlement then was already Christian by the opening of the fifth century. The frequently repeated (and misunderstood) claim of his biographer Sulpicius Severus that Martin of Tours replaced pagan temples with churches takes on a new aspect here. Excavation immediately N of the church revealed two concentric squares of walling, like a Romano-Celtic temple. Inside one of the ambulatories was a small but unmistakable Christian baptistery. This was interpreted as a third-century temple, replaced by Martin or a follower with a Christian church, and reused as a baptistery. It might be possible to regard it though as a baptistery or annexe contemporary with the church. Happily however, the remains can be seen on site, and the visitor can make up his or her own mind.

A short distance away from the church is the huge cemetery, which begins in Roman times and is still in use. Its boundary hedge of reused sarcophagus lids set upright is a unique and extraordinary sight. Early Roman cremation burials are known, and the earliest phase of the inhumation cemetery was of simple earth graves. Only later did the readily available limestone of the Vienne valley lead to the production of stone sarcophagi on a huge scale (several quarry sites are known). An early excavator estimated their number at 16,000, and sixteenth-century tradition saw them as the graves of those who fell fighting the heretic Goths at the battle of Vouillé. In the nineteenth century, the village did a thriving trade selling them as horse troughs — no doubt to the future confusion of archaeologists. Large numbers can still be seen, a few with early chi-rho monograms and crosses cut on them. In the village, a museum displays material from the site.

F. Eygun, *Congrés Archéol de France, 109 e Session (Poitiers) 1951*, 179-91; *Gallia* 19

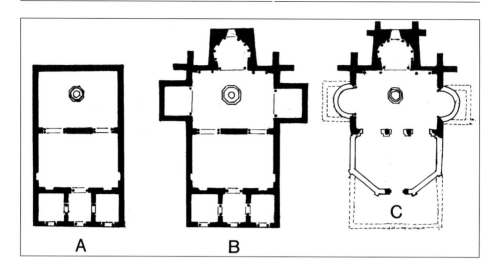

*28 Poitiers — period plan of baptistery of St Jean*

(1961), 402-8; 21 (1963), 453-61; E. James (1977), 174-6.

## Poitiers (Limonum)

M68 13 IGN34 C3

Seventeenth-century watercolours show impressive remains of a Roman amphitheatre outside the city walls around the Rue de Magenta and Rue des Arènes (*Congres Archaéol de France* 1912, 104-14). Its last vestiges were swept away in 1857, though some remains were found in 1951 (*Gallia* 9 (1951), 102-3). The late Roman walls, containing reused material, enclosed an irregular rounded area in the centre of the city. Notre-Dame la Grande lay just within the W wall, the cathedral complex and the baptistery of St Jean were near its E gate, with the monastery of St Radegunde to the east.

Whilst relatively little is known of the Roman city, Poitiers contains major monuments of the Merovingian period, in the fourth to seventh centuries. The modern nunnery of Holy Cross still preserves items sent by the Byzantine Emperor Justin II to Queen Radegund (518-87) with a portion of the True Cross. Part of the reliquary which contained this is still at Holy Cross, together with a carved wooden reading desk which once belonged to St Radegund. She was a Thuringian princess, orphaned by the Merovingian king Chlotar I, who educated her and made her his third wife. She eventually managed to obtain release from her marriage and retired to Poitiers, where she founded a house of nuns. In 567 the Italian poet and hymn writer Venantius Fortunatus became bishop there and several poems written by him to Radegunde survive; 'To the Lady Radegund with Violets' is a typical example, though he also wrote the Crusader Hymn *Vexilla regis prodeunt* to celebrate the arrival of the relic of the True Cross. The city also contains two important, if idiosyncratic buildings of the period: the Baptistery of St Jean, originally late Roman, but remodelled in Merovingian times, and a seventh-century semi-underground structure, perhaps modelled on the Holy Sepulchre in Jerusalem, usually known as the Hypogeum of Mellaubaudes.

*29  Poitiers — interior of Baptistery of St Jean. Photograph J.K.K.*

## The Baptistery of St Jean

This singular looking building has a long and complex history. In its first phase, as recovered in excavation by the archaeologist-priest Camille de la Croix in the 1890s, it was a late Roman baptistery of unusual type. Instead of the usual centrally planned octagonal rotunda and central baptismal pool, it was rectangular, with three successive rooms. A small square entrance hall fronted the street, flanked by two lobbies, possibly undressing rooms for male and female baptismal candidates. These led into a large rectangular central hall, beyond which was a second hall of similar size housing the octagonal baptismal pool. A conduit supplied water from a nearby aqueduct, and a tile drain took the used water away to a deep sump. Little of this first phase remains, due to later reconstruction, but its masonry of small coursed blocks can be seen externally in the lower part of the N and S facades (as far as the bases of the two partially blocked windows).

In the sixth century, the southern third of the building, around the baptismal pool, was remodelled. Two flanking annexes (on the sites of the present N and S apses) and a rectangular E apse like a miniature chancel gave a cruciform plan. This probably corresponded with the introduction of an altar and relics. The apse and its surrounding facades were richly decorated with columns of variously coloured marbles and freshly carved capitals of St Béat marble from the Pyrenees. Traces of now vanished mosaics, including a cross within a circle, were recorded in the nineteenth century and probably belong to this phase. Its masonry, seen for example in the upper parts of the N and S facades, was of large ashlar blocks which look suspiciously like reused early Roman masonry. The external decoration of this phase is even more remarkable.

The N and S facades each had two tall round-headed windows (now partly blocked). At springing level (the bottom of the arched heads), a cornice supports four flat pilasters with crude foliage capitals. Above is a second cornice on which perch three round or triangular headed gables. These, which in theory should be 'supported' by the pilasters do nothing of the sort — they are too short. Above in the pediment are three similar small triangular features. All six are decorated with marigold and flower patterns and crosses, sometimes inlaid with brick. The external decoration may be slightly later than the remodelling of the interior. Parallels can be found at Mazerolles, a church near Poitiers re-founded in the seventh century for an Irish *peregrinus*, Romanus, and at Vertou outside Nantes, an Abbey founded shortly before 601.

Later, probably in the tenth century, the N two thirds of the building were demolished, leaving only the area around the baptismal pool. A six-sided structure replaced the demolished portion, opening onto the baptismal area through three impressively tall arches. The flanking annexes to the baptismal area were also demolished, and replaced by apses. These in turn were demolished about 1820, the present apses being nineteenth-century restorations. The building now belongs to the Société des Antiquaries de l'Ouest, and houses a collection of sarcophagi and other material from local sites.

Fr. Eygun, 'La Baptistère Saint-Jean-de-Poitiers', *Gallia* 22 (1964), 137-71.

## The Hypogeum of Mellaubaudes

Sited in the area of a Roman and Merovingian cemetery outside Poitiers, on the road to Bourges via St-Pierre-les-Eglises. It was another of the discoveries of the Belgian Jesuit Camille de la Croix, who excavated it in 1878. A memorial to him stands in the garden outside the hypogeum, carrying, rather like the names on a war memorial, a list of his excavations — a monument that any archaeologist might envy.

Basically a rectangular semi-underground chapel, reached by a flight of steps down, and originally with a stone vaulted roof, it was the late seventh-century funerary chapel of an Abbot Mellabaudis, whose sarcophagus is set in an arched recess (*Arcosolitum*) one side of the altar. An inscription originally on the door lintel reads (Hic Mem)oria Mellebaudi Abb(at)i — 'Here is the *Memoria* of Abbot Mellabaudis'. Another long inscription on the door jamb begins 'Here I, Mellaubaudis, have built for myself this little crypt (*speluncula*) where my burial is'. *Spelunca* was often used at this time for the Holy Sepulchre at Jerusalem, and Mellebaudis may have intended his burial place to echo this. Another on the opposite jamb reads 'Alpha and Omega, the beginning and the end. Everything is each day worse and worse, since the end (of the world) approaches.'

The most striking aspect is the almost bewildering array of sculptures and inscriptions. The wall plaster was painted in coloured bands, there were red paint inscriptions around the arcolositum, recording the relics that Mellaubadis had deposited there, and a large painted cross on the rendering of the altar. Even the treads of the steps were carved with vine scrolls and interlaced serpents. There are engraved figures of apostles and archangels, in a style very like that of the coffin of St Cuthbert at Durham, and the lower part of a crucifixion, showing the two thieves. Some of the engravings had glass inlays, which would have glittered in the darkness of the crypt.

R.P. de la Croix, *Hypogée Martirium de*

*30  Poitiers — Hypogeum of Mellaubaudes. Photograph J.K.K.*

*Poitiers* (Paris 1883); Fr Eygun and L. Levillain, *Hypogée des Dunes á Poitiers* (Poitiers 1964).

## Saint-Pierre-les-Églises

(Calviniacum) M68 14 IGN34 C5

This village, near the fine Romanesque Abbey of Chauvigny, on the Roman road running east from Poitiers towards Argenton, has produced seven Roman milestones, one of which (of Commodus) is set up outside the apse of the church. A Merovingian sarcophagus cemetery, like that at Civaux, underlies the churchyard. Some sarcophagi can be seen near the entrance and a Merovingian tomb inscription is known. The church, with its apse of small squared blocks (probably reused Roman stonework), is partly Carolingian, and contains wall paintings of the same date, with New Testament scenes including the visitation, the three magi and the crucifixion. According to a twelfth-century source, it was built on the site of a Roman temple. The Roman name however is of the type common in western Gaul combining a Roman personal name (Calvinius) with '-acum' — a villa or estate.

R.P. de la Croix, 'Cimetières et sarcophagi mérovingiens de Poitou', *Bull. Archéol* 1886.

P. Deschamps, *Congrés Archéol de France 109ᵉ session (Poitiers) 1951* 164-78.

## Sanxay Rural cult centre
M68 12 IGN33 D11

The ruins of Sanxay or Herbord, in the countryside of Poitou 12km from Lusignan, are among the most complete examples of the rural cult centres of 'Celtic' Gaul. Excavated by Camille de la Croix in 1881-3 and then bought by the state for preservation, the site is managed by a local society, the 'Friends of Sanxay' for the Monuments Historiques. Only the main parts of the complex — the theatre, baths and main temple — are visible.

Set within a loop of the small river Vonne, the complex centres on a temple with an octagonal tower-like cella (only the foundations remain) of a kind characteristic of western France. This is surrounded by a cruciform ambulatory for the circulation of pilgrims. Set within a square colonnaded temenos E of this was a large piazza whose central feature (the 'Petit Temple') was a circular tholos or shrine of a kind traditionally associated with 'special' heroic graves, again with an elaborate bath suite. Grouped around the main complex were at least nine buildings interpreted by de la Croix as hotels for pilgrims, but which were probably residential. Across the Vonne to the S was a 'Romano-Celtic' theatre-amphitheatre. Outlying features included a second bath suite near the river, and a Romano-Celtic temple on rising ground across the Vonne, forming an E-W alignment with the main temple and tholos.

J. Formige, 'Le sanctuaire de Sanxay' *Gallia* 2 (1944), 44-120; Pillard, *Les Ruines d'Herbord, Commune de Sanxay* (Niort 1982); P. Aupert, *Sanxay, Sanctuaire Gallo-Romain* (G.A.F.).

## Vendoeuves Rural cult centre
M68 7 IGN34 B10

A circular tower-temple (Tour Mirande), built under Nero, stands at one end of a temenos containing a large artificial pool. A long colonnade in front of the temple gives access to baths and to a basilica with a hypocaust, perhaps for meetings of local magistrates. A second court, perhaps a forum, lies beyond the first. An inscription refers to the building of the basilica by a priest of Rome and Augustus who was Curator (administrator) of the vicus.

## Vieux-Poitiers Rural cult centre
M68 4 IGN34 B4

At the confluence of the Clain and the Vienne south of Châtellerault, a tall stump of masonry known as the 'Tour de Vieux Poitiers' points upwards above the flat farmland. It is a standing fragment of a Roman theatre, part of a 45ha rural cult centre with a theatre, temples, a grid of streets and pottery kilns. Occupation began in Neolithic times and a standing stone bears the inscription RATIN BRIVATIOM FRONTU TARBELSONIOS interpreted as 'Frontu son of Tarbelsonios has consecrated this stone to Brivatos'. Recent air photographs have revealed a circular tower-temple like that at Périgueux, and a Romano-Celtic temple, each within a temenos.
A. Ollivier and R. Fritsch, 'Le vicus de Vieux Poitiers' *Archéologia* 163 (1982), 52-61; C. Richard, 'Lieux cultuels gallo-romains du sud de la Vienne: Apport de la prospection aérienne' *Aquitania* 5 (1987), 133-47.

# 8 Aquitaine and Gascony
## (Aquitania Secunda and Novempopulanae)

The two southern cantons of Aquitania Secunda were the lands of the Biturges of Bordeaux and the Petrocorii of Périgord (the Dordogne). They are included here with their southern neighbours of Novempopulanae, between the Gironde and the Pyrenees.

Novempopulanae ('The nine peoples') was a later addition to the three Gallic provinces (Lugdunensis, Aquitania and Belgica) created by Augustus. When Novempopulanae was split off from Aquitania is uncertain. An inscription found in 1660 reused as a church altar at Hasparren near Dax refers to the establishment of the province, but is not closely datable. Suggested dates vary from the second century to the third. By late Roman times it could boast twelve 'cities', including a capital at Eauze. Some of these must have been very small, though Bayonne, despite its strategic importance and late Roman defences, was not included. Characteristic of this area are small hill towns with an oval circuit of walls. Excavation evidence, particularly from St Bertrand, suggests that these walls may be no earlier than the very late fourth century.

*C.I.L.* XIII, 412 and J.-P. Bost and G. Fabre, 'Aux origines de la province de Novempopulanie: nouvel examen de l'inscription de Hasparren' *Aquitania* 6 (1988), 167-78.

## DORDOGNE
### Coulouniex, Camp de César
Hillfort M75 5 IGN47 C11
This hillfort near Périgueux is said to have *murus gallicus* ramparts, but details are few.
Collis 1975, 191.

### Montcaret Villa
M75 13 IGN47 D6
The large villa with its impressive mosaics excavated by Jules Formigé between the wars is typical of many in the region in that following its destruction early in the fifth century, a large cemetery of sarcophagi and long cists was cut into its ruins, many through walls or mosaics. Explanations of this phenomenon have ranged from use of land not fit for the plough to the survival of a late Roman villa church. One grave contained a Byzantine bronze pectoral cross and two sixth-/seventh-century buckles. The choir of the church has seven carved marble capitals of Pyrenean marble of the same date, and there are fragments of others in the site museum. J. Formigé, 'Fouilles de Montcaret de 1921 a 1938' *Cong. Archéol de France* 102 (Bordeaux-Bayonne 1939), 182-95; Percival 1976 188-90.

### Périgueux (Vesunna)
M75 5 IGN47 C11
The capital of the Petrocorii was named after the goddess Vesunna, the ruins of whose temple are still very impressive. It occupied an entire insula north of the forum. Its central cella is a massive circular tower, originally clad in marble, 21m in diameter and still standing 27m high. Originally this was the inner of two concentric walls, with a classical temple facade projecting on the E. The present breach in the wall is due to the

robbing of the ashlar masonry of this facade. Square socket holes high in the tower, each with a small relieving arch above, housed the beams tying the two concentric walls together. The temple stood within a large rectangular colonnaded temenos. A coin sealed in its foundations shows that the complex is no earlier than Trajan, and, like the Roman Pantheon, it may be of the time of Hadrian. Next to the temple, an early Roman house has been excavated and partially restored.

Virtually nothing now remains of the amphitheatre, though in the eighteenth century substantial ruins survived within the gardens of a convent. Its outline is preserved in the oval Boulevard des Arènes, around the Jardins des Arènes. Grenier thought it mid-first-century in date, contemporary with that at Saintes. In the fourth century, it was incorporated as a projecting strongpoint or bastion in the town walls, as at Tours or Amiens. The town walls enclosed an area of some 5.5ha. There is some evidence of buildings in the area being levelled around 300-50, which may give a broad indication of date. The Gallo-Roman collections of the Musée de Périgord (Cours Tourny) are particularly rich.

Grenier III, 440-7, 670-74. Town walls — Garmy and Maurin (1996), 127-54; J. Lauffray et al, *La Tour de Vésone à Périgueux, temple de Vesunna Petrucorium* (49th supplement to *Gallia* 1990).

# GERS

Gers was the ancient County of Armagnac, a name perhaps more familiar in Britain as that of a brandy. It contains several Roman hill towns and a series of spectacular late Roman villas which were being enlarged and equipped with luxurious mosaics and items of St Béat marble to the very end

of the fourth century, and probably well into the fifth. In some cases, as at Séviac, there seems to be continuity between late Roman Lullingstone style Christian villa-chapels and a Christian church lasting into medieval times (Balmelle 1987). Gers contains three of the twelve 'cities' of Novempopulanae, at Eauze (the capital), Auch and Lectoure.

## Auch (Augusta Auscorum)
M82 5 IGN63 B8
The tribal capital of the Ausci stands on a prominent hill, and a late eighteenth-century sketch shows an oval late Roman *enceinte* with mural towers, of which some traces still remain.
Johnson (1983), 108; *Gallia* 20 (1962), 578.

## Beaucaire Villa
M82 4 IGN63 B7
A huge luxury villa, with impressive spreads of fourth-century polychrome mosaic. Like many others in the area it was later reused as a cemetery, which remained in use for a long time. Over 120 sarcophagus burials are known, as well as many simple earth graves. The nearby Romanesque church has three columns with reused early capitals.
Balmelle 1987, 202-5.

## Lectoure (Lactora)
M82 5 IGN63 A8
Capital of the Lactorates, one of the 'nine peoples'. The old hill town has an oval of medieval walls which still show Roman work in places, in the form of *petit appareil* and tile courses. Some reused material is known from their foundations.

The museum, in the old bishop's palace next to the cathedral of SS Gervaise and Protasius, has an important Gallo-Roman collection, including 20 second-century altars found when the chancel of the cathedral was rebuilt in 1540. They record taurobolium ceremonies (*'Taurobolium Fecit'*)

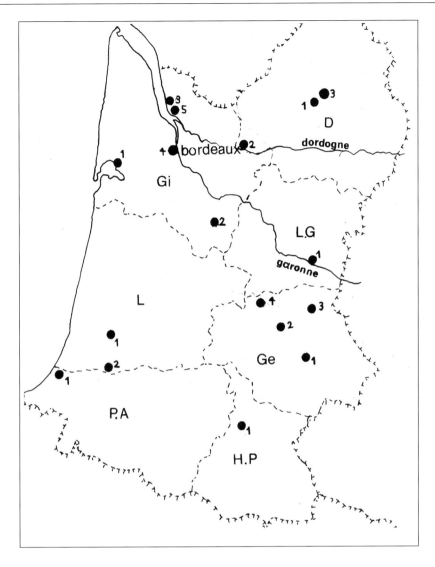

31 Aquitaine and Gascony (Aquitania Secunda and Novempopulanae)
  **D** Dordogne *1 Coulounieux 2 Montcaret 3 Périgueux*
  **Ge** Gers *1 Auch 2 Beaucaire 3 Lectoure 4 Montréal-Séviac*
  **Gi** Gironde *1 Andernos 2 Bazas 3 Blaye 4 Bordeaux 5 Plassac*
  **HP** Haute-Pyrénées *1 Tarbes*
  **PA** Pyrénées-Atlantique *1 Bayonne*
  **L** Landes *1 Dax 2 Sorde L' Abbaye*
  **LG** Lot et Garonne *1 Agen*

associated with the cult of the Great Mother M(agna) M(ater), involving the sacrifice of a bull and washing in his blood. The display of Roman burials, ranging from Gaulish cremations to Christian sarcophagi, is particularly interesting. The latter include a number of the fifth to sixth century: 'SW Gallic' or 'Aquitanian' sculptured sarcophagi of St Béat marble from the Roman cemeteries of the town.

*C.I.L.* XIII, 504-525; Johnson 1983, 109.

## Montréal-Séviac Villa

M79 13 IGN63 A5

2km SW of Montréal is the luxury villa of Séviac, with ranges of rooms set around a large courtyard, an elaborate apsed bath suite and some 25 carpet-like spreads of polychrome mosaic. Excavated by Mme Paulette Aragon-Launet, many of the mosaics have now been conserved and are on display on site or in the museum at Montréal. That in the *frigidarium* sealed a coin of Decentius (350-3) and Catherine Balmelle has argued that some were laid in the fifth century. The mosaics show a fluent range of abstract or vegetal patterns in subtle and harmonious colours, using a range of natural limestone and sandstone, blue-grey St Béat marble and green ophite from the Pyrenees. The Byzantine-looking mosaic now in the museum, with wind blown fruiting trees and baskets of flowers, is particularly impressive.

Séviac is also an example of the way in which a villa could give rise to a Christian church, by way of a villa-chapel. An oval room with a large circular *labrum* (water tank) has been identified as a baptistery. Later, a structure with a square 'nave' and eastern apse was built projecting out from the baptistery, perhaps after the villa had gone out of use. This was followed by an unmistakable small church, with burials around it.

P. Aragon-Launet and C. Balmelle, 'Les structures ornementales en acanthe dans les mosaïques de la villa de Séviac près de Montréal' *Gallia* 45 (1987-8), 189-208; Balmelle 1987, 151-94, nos. 285-310; J. Lapart and J.-L. Paillet, 'Ensemble paléochrétien et mérovingien du site de Séviac a Montréal de Gers' in P. Périn (ed), *Gallo-Romains, Wisigoths et Francs en Aquitanie, Septimanie et Espagne* (Rouen 1991), 171-80.

## GIRONDE

Apart from Bordeaux, capital of Aquitania Secunda, the area to its S and W included two 'cities' of Novempopulanae, at Bazas and the vanished Boatium at La Teste de Buch near Arcachon.

## Andernos Christian basilica

M71 19 IGN46 J1

This simple early Christian basilica, with a rectangular nave and E apse, next to the medieval church of St Eloi, was found in 1902 on the site of an ancient cemetery. Sarcophagi and long cist graves can be seen in the added north aisle, which may have been a funerary annexe. On the S was an arcade or courtyard, whose pillars rested on monolithic stone blocks.

M.M. Gauthier, 'Andernos aux premiers temps chrétiens' *Cahiers Archéologiques* 41 (1993), 47-62.

## Bazas (Cossio)

M79 2 IGN56 B4

Bazas appeared in the Notitia Galliarum as the Civitas Vasatica. Its late Roman walls enclosed about 1.8ha, but were incorporated in the medieval ramparts, and little is known of them. They belong with the group of late town walls in Novempopulanae, including St Lizier and St Bertrand, which may date from the later fourth century.

Garmy and Maurin 1996, 156-65.

## Blaye (Blabia)

M71 8 IGN46 G3

Vauban's fort of 1685-9, guarding the

estuary of the Gironde, with his Fort Médoc opposite, may have been on the site of the late Roman fort of *Blabia*, mentioned in the *Notitia Dignitatum* as that of the *Militum Carronensium* (*Garronensium*, 'of the Garonne'). The Merovingian king Charibert died at Blaye in 567 and Charles Martel was here with his army in 733. The Roman fort would have been destroyed when Vauban's fortifications were built, and much Roman material was found at the time.

S. Johnson 1976, 76-7.

# Bordeaux

M75 11 IGN47 D2

Bordeaux, already the *emporion* or trading port of the Bituriges Vivisques under Tiberius (Strabo IV, 2.1) was founded on the left bank of the Garonne at a point where the stream of La Devèze (Ausonius's *Divona*) ran down to the river between low flanking hills, making a convenient river port. Under Claudius, a local magnate, C. Julius Secundus, gave a water supply and fountains to the town (*C.I.L.* XIII, 590, 596-600) and Ausonius speaks of the Fountain of Divona, of 'Parian' marble. There may have been an early forum on the Mont Judaïque, where sculptures and inscriptions, including dedications to Drusus and Claudius, were found in 1594. However, most of the known monuments of Bordeaux — the amphitheatre, the 'Pillars of Tutela' and the city walls — belong to the later Empire. Only the first of these is still visible above ground. The Pillars of Tutela stood on the site of the Grand Theatre until demolished by Louis XIV in 1677. They consisted of a rectangle of tall Corinthian columns set on a high podium, enclosing an open space. Above was an arcade of arches, the pilasters decorated with female caryatid figures and urns. Architectural parallels suggest a Severan date and excavations

have shown that it stood within a colonnaded monumental precinct. It may have been an open air altar, perhaps for the Imperial cult.

The remains of the amphitheatre have been known since the fourteenth century as the 'Palace of Gallienus', said to have been a mythical queen of Charlemagne, not the third-century Emperor. The building is of *opus mixtum* — mixed brick and tile — and the bands of brickwork are a striking feature of the ruins. Its arches are turned with alternate stone and brick voussoirs like those on the late Roman walls of Le Mans. Though the technique can already be found at Pompeii, here it suggests a date in the late second or third century. The square socket holes (putlog holes) for the timber scaffolding are very clear on the upper parts of the walls and show how they were built in 'lifts' of one brick band and one-and-a-half bands of stonework before the scaffolding was raised to the next level.

The late Roman walls enclosed a rectangular area of 31.5ha, but were demolished piecemeal, producing a rich harvest of sculptures and inscriptions in the process. Etienne has a striking photograph of reused architectural pieces in situ at 7, Rue Guillaume-Brochon. There is an old record of a coin of 270 (a posthumous *Consecratio* issue of Claudius Gothicus issued by Aurelian) being found sealed in one of the mortar beds of the wall, and a bath complex outside their SW corner was demolished in about 275-325, perhaps to provide building material, but more evidence of their date is needed. They were protected by about 46 solid half-round towers at intervals of 50m with larger hollow three-quarter round towers at the angles.

Orientalis, present at the Council of Arles in 314, may have been the first bishop of Bordeaux. Later the cult centred around the church of St Seurin, NW of the walled town, where a Christian cemetery was in use from the fourth century onwards. The church of St Etienne, demolished in 1787, was either an early cathedral or a cemetery basilica like that excavated at Colchester. Several late Roman mausolea were nearby and the existing basilica of St Seurin was built over the tomb of St Severinus, said to have been an early fifth-century bishop.

Etienne *Bordeaux Antique* (1962); Barraud, 'Le site de "la France": origines et évolution de Bordeaux antique' *Aquitania* 6 (1988), 3-60; Town walls — Garmy and Maurin (1996), 16-80.

**Plassac** Villa
M71 8 IGN46 F3
North of the village church, a Roman villa (signposted 'Fouilles Archéologique') que'), discovered in 1883, is on display, with an excellent site museum (open June-September). Three successive villas cover the entire Roman period. The first had wall paintings of the third Pompeian style of *c*.AD 40-50 now displayed in the museum. The mosaics on site belong to the third villa, of late Roman date.

## HAUTES-PYRÉNÉES

The medieval lordships of Bigorre and Comminges only became part of the kingdom of France in 1607, having been part of English Gascony until the fifteenth century. The County of Bigorre was the territory of the Gallo-Roman Bigerriones, whilst the Comminges took its name from the Roman town of Lugdunum Convenarum (St Bertrand de Comminges, Haute-Garonne).

**Tarbes** (Turba)
M85 8 IGN70 B5
Tarbes, in the valley of the Adour, was one of the small civitas capitals of Novempopulanae. Early in the fifth century, it acquired relics of the martyr Genesius of Arles. By the following century, Genesius of Tarbes was seen as a local martyr-priest and bishop Avitus of Clermont (571-94) built a church over his remains.

Gregory of Tours, *Gloria Martyrorum* 73.

## PYRÉNÉES ATLANTIQUE (BASSES PYRÉNÉES)

Bayonne does not appear in the Notitia Galliarum, despite its late Roman walls, though Oloron appears as the capital of the Ellorones. The fortified medieval bridges at the bastide of Sauveterre de Béarn and at Orthez, the latter still intact, have British parallels (e.g. Monmouth), but they are very rare. Like the Haute-Pyrénées, this became part of France in 1607 under Henry of Navarre (Henri IV of France).

**Bayonne**
M85 2 IGN69 A3
Sixteenth- and seventeenth-century references show that the late Roman walls were then well preserved, and traces of a polygonal oval with the bases of circular towers still remain behind the walls of Vauban's citadel of 1674-9. In places, the brick courses in the late Roman walls have been replaced by flat stones, perhaps because of a local shortage of brick.

Blanchet 192-4.

## LANDES

**Dax** (Aquae Tarbellicae)
M78 6-7 IGN62 C4
Until they were largely demolished in 1856, despite an international outcry led by Charles Roach Smith and Arcisse de Caumont, the late Roman walls of Dax were among the most complete and best preserved in France. They enclosed a rectangular area of some 12.5ha, with

over 40 circular towers, a few of which had been replaced in medieval times. Today, only parts of the N and W sides, around the Parc Th. Denis, and two stretches in the Cours Pasteur remain.

The walls were set on a foundation of basalt slabs, themselves with a base layer of substantial timbers (which should some day make a dendrochronological date possible). Above were massive stone blocks, below small square coursed blocks of stone from the quarries at Bidache, with triple tile levelling courses. There was little reused material in the walls, perhaps because little was available locally. An old record of a coin of Magnentius of 350-3 from between two tile bonding courses (Blanchet p192) is of interest in view of recent evidence from St Bertrand that the walls of Novempopulana may date from late in the fourth century.

Dax is a spa town, whose hot springs are said to have been visited by the Emperor Augustus and his daughter Julia. Augustus was seeking relief for his rheumatism, a complaint for which the waters of the Fontaine Chaude are still used. The town was part of the English possessions in France until 1451.
Roach Smith, *Collectanea Antiqua* V 1861, 226-40; Blanchet 186-92; Garmy and Maurin (1996), 81-125.

## Sorde-l'Abbaye Villa
M78 7 IGN69 A6
The abbey of Saint-Jean, in the centre of this small town, partly overlies a Roman villa with a series of mosaic decorated rooms and corridors around a central courtyard, with a bathhouse to the S. The mosaics made excavation of the earlier levels difficult, but one sealed a coin of Constantine and Sorde takes its place among the many luxuriously appointed fourth-century villas of Aquitaine. Most of the pavements are now displayed in a museum in the former Abbot's lodgings, and the villa can be seen in the adjacent gardens. One mosaic has octagonal panels with ducks, peacocks, vases and abstract patterns. Others have ivy scroll borders strikingly like those in the fifth-/sixth-century Aquitanian sarcophagi. It may not be coincidence that the choir of the abbey church contains a splendid medieval mosaic pavement with lions, eagles, a greyhound and hare, and much else.
Balmelle 1987, 32-54, 293-9.

## LOT-ET-GARONNE
### Agen (Aginnum)
M79 15 IGN56 D10
Capital of the Nitobriges. A theatre or amphitheatre was found about 1773, but details are sparse. The municipal museum (Place d'Hôtel de Ville) contains a fine display of fifth-/sixth-century sculptured 'Aquitanian' or 'SW Gallic' sarcophagi of Pyrennean marble. Nearly all are from the collegiate church of St Caprais, where other fragments are preserved in the chapel of the Holy Innocents.
Grenier III, 836. Inscriptions — *C.I.L.* XIII, 913-1030.

# 9 The Massif Central
## (Aquitania Prima)

## BERRY

Berry (Allier, Cher and Indre) is a broad plateau set between the Paris basin and the uplands of the Massif Central, with its capital at Bourges. The area was celebrated in Roman and pre-Roman times for its iron industry, and Caesar describes how during the siege of Bourges, the Gauls were able to mine under the Roman siegeworks 'for they have extensive iron mines in their country, and are thoroughly familiar with every kind of underground works'. Large slag heaps are known from a number of sites.

## ALLIER

For the Roman archaeologist, Allier has two particular points of interest — the Roman bathing establishments at the hot springs of Néris-les-Bains and Vichy, and the pottery production sites which produced samian ware, white pipeclay figurines and mortaria. The figurines were made at St-Rémy-en-Rollat, Toulon-sur-Allier, Gannat, Moulins and elsewhere. Coulonges was a major centre for the production of mortaria — internally gritted mixing bowls — which were traded over much of France (P. Galliou, 'Pelves en céramique commune importés en Armorique', *Arch. Bretagne* 15, 1977, 11-18). The Guide-Répetoire lists seven hillforts, including the two below.

*Guide-Répetoire* 25 (1970).

**Hérisson** Iron Age hillfort
M69 12 IGN35 D10
The hillfort of Châteloy is protected on all sides save the S by natural defences, including the gorge of the river

Aumance. On the S is a massive rampart and broad ditch of 'Fécamp type'.
Ralston and Büchsenschütz (1975), 9.

**Moulins** Museum M69 14 IGN42 A4
The Musée Départemental (Place de Colonel-Laussedat) contains an important collection of Roman pottery from local production centres.

**Néris-les-Bains** (Aquae Nerii)
M73 2 IGN42 D2
The main Roman baths were on the site of the present bathing establishment. To their south, a small 2ha hillfort, the Camp de César, with a massive single rampart on a rocky spur, may indicate pre-Roman interest in the hot springs. By the time of Tiberius, there was already substantial occupation, including pottery kilns, and in the late first or early second century, Néris acquired a theatre-amphitheatre with seating for about 2,800 people. There were two bathhouses, the better known being the South Bath, a monumental symmetrically planned building from the end of the first century, a smaller version of the Imperial bath type.

Néris was also a thermal establishment utilizing the natural hot springs. Water was carried from the thermal springs to the S through a vaulted channel 1.7m high. From the normal undressing rooms and latrines, bathers progressed to a courtyard with two large open-air swimming pools, flanked by porticoes and paved in white marble. The large circular bath, further from the source, would have been cooler than the square one to the N , rather like the Great Bath at Bath, and the smaller and cooler 'Lucas Bath' fed from its outflow. Beyond was the roofed bath block, with the main hot rooms. The square tower-like central room had the central planning and corner niches of monumental bath suites, and the early Christian baptisteries and mausolea of the late Empire.

In the fifth century, St Patroclus of Bourges founded a nunnery here (Gregory of Tours, *Vitae Patrum* 9) and there are many sarcophagi, some cut from Roman sculptured stones, whilst parts of the parish church are of *opus mixtum* with brick levelling courses in the masonry, and may be early medieval. The modern baths include the Musée Riekotter, with a good collection of local finds.

Grenier III, 910-12. *Gallia* 25 (1967), 297-8, 31 (1973), 459.

### St-Rémy-en-Rollat

Pottery production centre

M73 5 IGN43 B1

Unlike the reddish ferruginous clays used for the production of *terra sigillata*, St Rémy produced white pipeclay, which was used for its widely exported white wares. Some green-glazed ware and a little samian were also made.

### Vichy (Aquis Calidis)

Baths and thermal establishment

M73 5 IGN43 C1

The spa centre at Vichy owes its origin to the cluster of thermal springs which provide hot medicinal waters at differing temperatures. The Romans also used these springs. The Grand Hall des Sources, one of the main modern thermal establishments, is built over the Roman baths, and Roman masonry is known below it. Finds have included an octagonal collecting tank of oak planks, architectural fragments, statuettes of bronze and limestone, often of high quality and a lead pipe with an inscription of Septimius Severus. Vichy was also a production centre for samian

pottery in the period 125-80, an offshoot of Lezoux, and Lezoux-style moulds are known.

Grenier IV, 435-42. J. Corrocher, *Vichy Antique* (Clermont Ferrand 1981).

## CHER

A number of major *oppida* of the Biturges developed into Roman towns or vici, a testimony to their degree of pre-Roman urbanism. Bourges became their Cantonal capital, Châteaumeillant and Drevant important secondary urban centres. Another hillfort, Alléans, became a vicus or sanctuary site (Grenier III, 937-8) with monumental buildings and a small theatre-amphitheatre.

A. Querrien, O. Buchsenschutz and J. Dorion, *Carte Archéologique du Cher* (1979).

### Bourges (Avaricum)

M69 1 IGN35 A7

To the Biturges, the capital of their king Ambigatus, was 'the fairest city of all Gaul, the defence and pride of their nation'. On a limestone hill rising 25m above the surrounding marshy plain, it had a forum or market place, and, according to Julius Caesar, 40,000 inhabitants. During the bitterly fought siege of 52 BC the population may have swelled to something approaching this number by warriors and refugees. Since Caesar inserts into the narrative his famous description of the '*murus Gallicus*', the defences were probably of this type, with a framework of nailed timber beams holding together a rampart of stone rubble. They seem to have followed the same line as that of the late Roman walls.

From the time of Diocletian, Bourges was capital of the new province of Aquitania Prima. Its walls, enclosing a perimeter of 2,100m, were between 2.5-3m thick, with double or triple brick courses at intervals and reused

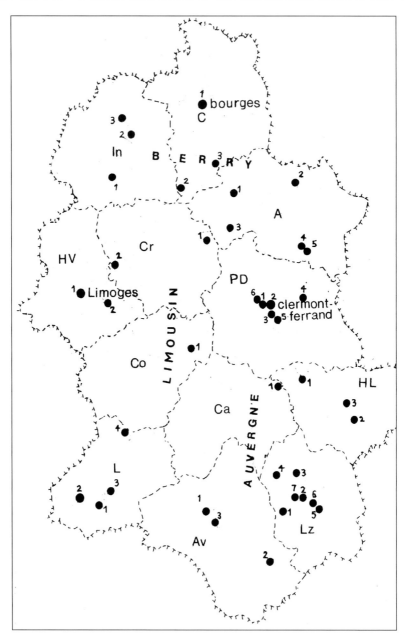

architectural material in their foundations. They were strengthened with 46 projecting D-shaped towers and four gates. The Porte de Lyon in the SE corner was demolished in the nineteenth century, but early drawings survive. A first-century monumental fountain was incorporated in the fabric of the walls, and is preserved in the cellars of the Ducal palace (*Gallia* 35 (1977), 115-40).

In the sixteenth century, Bourges, like many French cities, still had impressive remains of its Roman amphitheatre. In 1536 it was used for a religious pageant in verse 'The Triumphant Mystery of the Acts of the

32 *(opposite)* The Massif Central (Aquitania Prima)
Berry:
**A** Allier *1 Hérisson 2 Moulins 3 Néris-les-Bains 4 St Rémy-en-Rollat 5 Vichy*
**C** Cher *1 Bourges 2 Châteaumeillant 3 Dreux*
**In** Indre *1 Argenton-sur-Creuse 2 Deols 3 Levroux*
Limousin*:*
**Co** Correze *1 Charlat*
**Cr** Creuse *1 Evaux 2 Mont Jouer*
**HV** Haute-Vienne *1 Limoges 2 Villejoubert*
Auvergne:
**Av** Aveyron *1 Caydayrac 2 La Graufesenque 3 Rodez*
**Ca** Cantal *1 Massiac*
**HL** Haute-Loire *1 Brioude 2 Le Puy 3 St Paulien*
**L** Lot *1 Cahors 2 Luzerch, L'Impernal 3 Murcens 4 Puy d'Issolud*
**Lz** Lozère *1 Banassac 2 Clapas Castel 3 Javols 4 Lac de St-Andreol 5 Lanuejols 6 Mende*
*7 St Bonnet de Chirac*
**PD** Pûy-de-Dome *1 Chamalières 2 Clermont Ferrand 3 Gergovia 4 Lezoux 5 Matres de Veyre*
*6 Puy de Dôme*

Apostles', with a cast of 500 and an audience of 25,000, but it was demolished in 1619 and nothing now remains.

Grenier III, 680-81. F. Prevot, *T.C.C.G. VI (Aquitania Prima)* 15-26.

## Châteaumeillant
(Mediolanum Biturgum)
M68 20 IGN35 C6

The Biturgian oppidum of Mediolanum occupied a long oval area of 27ha defended by a timber laced rampart of 'Ehrang' type, like a *murus gallicus*, but without nails — perhaps an indication of an early date. About the time of Caesar's campaign of 52 BC this was strengthened by an earth rampart. It was already a prosperous trading town. Many Graeco-Roman amphorae of about 100 BC are known, and some 300 Italian Republican Dressel 1 wine amphorae, 37 of them found stored in the cellar of a wooden house which had been destroyed by fire, perhaps in 52 BC, when the Biturges under Vercingetorix fired 20 of their *oppida* to deny their use to the Romans. After the Roman conquest, the town failed to develop in line with its early promise.

The medieval walled town and castle occupy a much smaller area at its W end. The *castrum Mediolanense* was still a strong place in the sixth century, fought over by the Merovingian kings Chiperic and Guntrum (Gregory of Tours H. F. X, 19).

Nash 1978, 182-4. *Gallia* 19 (1961), 327-31.

## Drevant (Derventum)
M69 11 IGN35 C8

Derventum means 'the meeting place (or market) by the oak tree' and the way in which the Romano-Celtic temple stands off centre within its otherwise symmetrical temenos suggests where the sacred tree may have stood. A miracle of Martin of Tours depicts him felling a sacred pine tree at a temple somewhere in this region. Drevant was a rural cult centre where the Neris-Bourges road crossed the Cher valley. Across the river is a promontory fort, the 'Camp de César', with 'Fécamp' style rampart. The monumental complex (now a National

Monument) comprises the temple, baths (not visible), and a theatre-amphitheatre with seats for 1,500 people. Three beast-pens opening on to the arena, and a 3m high wall separating the arena from the spectators show its double function. Recent rescue excavations have recovered the plan of a large area of houses north of these, and shown that the site was, like many rural cult centres, abandoned at the end of the third century and totally in ruins by the mid fourth.

The N144 road south from Bourges to Néris follows the line of its Roman predecessor, but between Lissay-Lochy and Levet (IGN35 A7), takes a more direct line and a length of Roman road ('Chaussée de César' on the maps) is visible. Further S at Bruère-Allichamps (IGN35 B8) a Roman milestone stands near the modern road.

Cribellier, 'Un quartier d'habitation de l'agglomération antique de Drevant, Cher', *Revue Archéol du Centre de la France* 35 (1996), 113-52.

# INDRE
## Aregenton-sur-Creuse

(Argentomagus) M68 17/18 IGN 35 C1
2km N of the modern town is the Roman Argentomagus at St Marcel, on the site of the hillfort of Mersans. Enclosing 27ha, it began in the second century BC. The earliest, pre-Augustan levels of the Roman town show a prosperous settlement with evidence for the presence of foreign traders. The first stone theatre and temple were Augustan, and by the time of Tiberius stone-built private houses were appearing. The town, 70ha in overall extent, has been under excavation since 1962. A new museum displays the finds, plus material (including art) from local Palaeolithic sites. On the plateau of Mersans are the 'House of Quintus Sergius Macrinus',

named from an altar dedicated by a local magnate, and a small group of temples. To the E a large monumental stepped fountain (signposted), has recently been re-interpreted as a service gallery for the city's aqueduct channel. The site of the forum is also known. W of the plateau is the outer wall of the theatre of Virou. Excavation showed that an early first-century theatre of classical type had been replaced in the second century by a theatre-amphitheatre characteristic of 'Celtic' Gaul.

*Rev. Archéol Centre* 1975 — special Argentomagus number; Nash 1978, 188-91.

## Déols
Christian mausoleum and sarcophagi
M68 8 IGN35 B3

Two miles from Déols, in a chapel beneath the twelfth-century church of St Etienne, are two fourth-century marble sarcophagi. That of St Ludre has a boar hunt, with wolves and stags. The other is said to be that of his father Leocadius. In the sixth century, Gregory of Tours described how Lusor, son of the senator Leocadius, was buried at Déols, a village in the territory of Bourges. He had died while still dressed in the white robe of baptism, and lay in a crypt in a tomb of 'Parian' marble, with marvellous sculptures. This was a place of pilgrimage, and Gregory describes several miracles here, one involving St Germanus of Paris. Leocadius claimed descent from Vettius Epagathus, one of the Lyon martyrs of 177, and was also a kinsman of Gregory.

Gregory of Tours, *Gloria Confessorum* 90; Viellard-Troiekouroff 1976, 108-9.

## Levroux Hillfort and Roman vicus
M68 8 IGN35 A2

N of the town, on the steep Colline des Tours, is a hillfort with an inner *murus gallicus* rampart, and a secondary outer one of dump construction. The Roman vicus on the site of the present town had a first-century amphitheatre, 'Les Arènes'.

O. Buschenschutz and I. Ralston, 'Découverte d'un *murus gallicus* à Levroux', *Gallia* (1975), 27-48; Ralston and Buschenschutz 1975, 8-18; Nash 1978, 191-4.

## LIMOUSIN

Corrèze, Creuse and Haute-Vienne make up the province of Limousin, with its eponymous capital at Limoges. In ancient times, it belonged to the Lemovices, and was an important mining area. The Creuse contained important gold deposits, used for many Iron Age coins, and in Roman times there was exploitation of gold, tin and argentiferous lead.

## CORRÈZE

The present département contains a number of small hillforts of the Lemovices, studied by Cotton and Frere (1961) and by Desbordes (1985). On present evidence they date from Final La Tène (La Tène III) and Desbordes suggests that they may have been built as a result of the Roman conquest of the area to the S, and the creation of the province of Narbonensis in 127-5 BC. The only larger fort is that at Yssandon (Collis 1975, 190; Desbordes 31).

G. Lintz, *Carte. Archéologique de la Gaule Romaine.* 16 (1981).

**Charlat** Hillfort
M73 11 IGN49 D1
Three miles S of Ussel, a rampart cuts off 1.45ha of an elongated spur. Excavation in 1957-9 showed it was of *murus duplex* technique, with multiple internal stone revetments and timber framing. The rampart overlays sherds of Dressel 1 amphora, and did not long pre-date the Roman conquest. Cotton and Frere suggested that it might be linked with the campaign of Vercingetorix in 52 BC, or later disturbances. They had hoped to excavate the hillfort of Pont-Maure, the scene of unpublished excavations by the British archaeologist Noel Lucas Shadwell, killed in the war, but this proved impossible.

Cotton and Frere 1961, 31-42, with plan.

## CREUSE

The gold deposits of Cruese and Haute-Vienne, used in pre-Roman times, were exploited in Roman times in the vici of *Praetorium* (St Gossuard, Creuse) and *Carovicus* (Château-Chervix), with tin mining centred nearby at *Blotomagus* (Blond). The hilly country N of Limoges has a long history of mining, with many . . .les Mines place names and, today, uranium mines. Desbordes (1985) lists several small hillforts, like those of Corrèze. Those at Puy de Gaudy and Ste Radegonde begin in the Neolithic and continued to late medieval times. The larger Ambusson (15ha) begins in Halstatt times.

D. Dussot, *Carte Archéologique de la Gaule* 23 (1989).

**Evaux** (Ivaunum)
M73 2 IGN43 B5
Roman and modern thermal establishment. Ruins of baths with marble cladding, mosaics and sculpture. Until recently preserved in places to springing of vault. A series of baths used water from different sources and at different temperatures for different treatments. The rooms were set around a rectangular courtyard with a central rectangular water feature. To the N was a large circular hot bath, clad in marble, with other baths grouped in the surrounding rooms.

Grenier IV, 417-23 with plan.

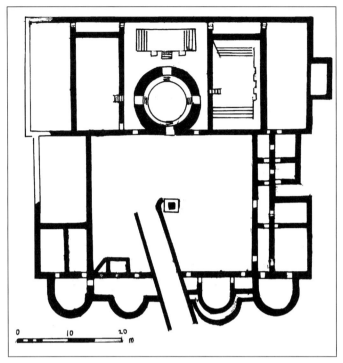

*33 Evaux (Creuse) — plan of bath suite. Grenier IV, 419*

## Mont Jouer

M72 8 IGN41 C7

Near St Gossuard, on the flank of Mont Jouer, is a rectangular temenos containing a Gallo-Roman temple and other buildings, excavated in the nineteenth century. Nearby is a small and simple theatre. The settlement may be associated with the nearby Roman gold mines.

Grenier III, 871.

## HAUTE-VIENNE

J. Perrier, *Carte Archéologique de la Gaule Romaine*, Forma orbis romani XIV (1964).

### Limoges (Augustoritum)

M72 17 IGN41 C5

The new Augustan capital of the Lemovici, at the crossing of the Vienne, acquired all the usual amenities of a Roman city. The Roman bridge, Pont-St-Martial, 'constructed of marvellous work', on which the street grid was aligned, was destroyed in 1182. In the centre of the modern city were the late first-century forum and public baths, matching other Flavian fora e.g. in Paris. The amphitheatre, close to the Roman bridge, Flavian to Hadrianic in date, was known from an account of 1638 before recent excavations. Parts of it are now the only visible portion of the Roman city. The theatre, at the NE end of town, seems to have been mid second century. At its peak, the city covered 100ha. No trace has been found of any late Roman walls, though a sixth-century document refers to a house 'within the walls'.

The first bishop, St Martial, was buried in the Roman N cemetery, and his crypt became a centre of cult. His grave was cut into the cellar of a ruined second-century building, perhaps baths. Fourth-century burials are known near it. By the sixth, Gregory of Tours was describing the crypt and its two sarcophagi (*Gloria Confessorum* 27-8). The Abbey of St Martial was totally demolished at the French Revolution, but the crypt is on display to the public. Grenier III, 2, 834 (theatre); 675-6 (amphitheatre). J. P. Loustaud, *Limoges gallo-romain* (Limoges 1980) and 'Limoges gallo-romain', *Archéologia* 157(1981), 24-9; M.M. Gauthier, 'Le culte funéraire primitif de Saint-Martial de Limoges', *Actes VI Congres Archéol Chrétienne, Ravenna 1962* (Rome 1965), 179-88; F. Prevot, *T.C.C.G.* VI (Aquitania Prima) 67-77; J.-M. Desbordes and J.-P. Loustand, *Limoges Antique* (G.A.F. ); J.-M. Desbordes and J. Perrier, *Limoges, Crypt St Martial* (G.A.F.).

## Villejoubert
'Camp de César', Hillfort
M72 18 IGN41

E of Limoges, at the confluence of the Vienne and Maulde, is one of the largest French hillforts, though this probably reflects its topography rather than its population or importance. The main rampart, said to be of *murus gallicus* construction, crosses the neck of the promontory, cutting off an area of 350ha. An inner cross-rampart, presumably of different date, encloses 120ha. There have been no excavations, but discoveries were made when a road was cut through the main rampart.
Cotton 1957, 189-90; Cotton and Frere 1961, 42-3; J.M. Desbordes 'L'oppidum de Villejoubert', *Travaux d'archéologie Limousine* 4 (1983), 25-28 and 'Les remparts de l'oppidum de Villejoubert' do. 7 (1986), 63-74.

## *AUVERGNE*
The Auvergne, covering the modern départements of Aveyron, Cantal, Haute-Loire, Lot, Lozère and Puy de Dôme, included the territories of the pre-Roman Arverni, the Cadurci of Lot and the Vellavori of Haute-Loire. It contains some important hillforts, including Uxellodunum and Gergovia. In Roman times, it was an important metal mining area, for iron, argentiferous lead and gold, and contained the most important centres for the manufacture of samian ware, both of the south Gaulish industry (Banassac, La Graufesenque) and the later central Gaulish industry (Lezoux, Matres de Veyre). The main Roman centres of the area, Rodez, Clermont Ferrand and Cahors, are all large modern cities with few visible traces of their Roman past.

## AVEYRON
### Caydayrac Mining settlement
M80 2 IGN58 B4
In a remote area of the Causée Comtale, near Salles-la-Source, a group of ruins include a Romano-Celtic temple and a small theatre-amphitheatre, probably belonging to an iron mining settlement. The ac(um) name suggests that this might have been connected with a villa or villa estate.
Grenier III, 927-8.

### La Graufesenque (Condatomagus)
M80 14 IGN58 D8
This site just E of Millau produced much early 'south Gaulish' samian ware. Above the town is its possible predecessor, the hillfort of La Granède, fortified since Hallstatt times. It later held a Romano-Celtic temple and may have been re-fortified under the late Empire. Pottery production began about AD 20, imitating Italian Arretine ware, and it was soon being exported over most of the western world, from Africa to Britain. An unopened crate of samian from La Graufesenque was found at Pompeii, where it had arrived just before the eruption of AD 79, but by the time

of Hadrian its products had been supplanted by those of Lezoux. Among the material from the site are graffiti scratched on wasters and 'seconds' listing potters and the types and numbers of pots produced by them. One set lists a total of 868,000 pots, including 1,295 inkpots — a reminder of how little Roman ink writing survives in Gaul or Britain. The pottery collections of Louis Balsan and F. Hermet are in the museums at Millau and Rodez respectively.

D. Atkinson 1914, 'A hoard of samian ware from Pompeii', *J.R.S.* 4, 27-64; F. Hermet 1934, *La Graufesenque* (Paris, 2 vols); A. Albenque 1951, 'Nouvelles fouilles à la Graufesenque', *Rev. Archéol* 37, 175-91; R. Marichal 1988, *Les graffites de la Graufesenque* (47th supp. to *Gallia*).

**Rodez** (Segodunum)
M80 2 IGN58 C4
The Roman town began as a Gaulish hillfort in a loop of the river Aveyron, on the route between Lyon and Bordeaux. It received early imports, one find being a cache of 25 Dressel 1 amphorae. The exact line of the late Roman defences is uncertain, but they occupied the broad oval hilltop area of the hillfort, as at Bourges. Medieval sources refer to the 'old wall of the city' and its gates, and some traces have been found in excavation. A unit of Sarmatian cavalry was stationed in the area in the fourth century. The early Roman town was, as usual, much larger and lay below the hilltop. The site of an amphitheatre is known on its edge.

There was already a bishop and cathedral in the fifth century, when Sidonius visited to dedicate a new baptistery. Soon after 500, bishop Dalmatius began the predecessor of the present cathedral on the site of a large Roman public building, which had presumably been given to the Church.

The shrine of an early saint or martyr, Amatus, was in the early Roman town to the S, but his church was demolished in 1751.

F. Prevot, *T.C.C.G. VI* (Aquitania Prima), 41-9.

# CANTAL
*Guide-Répetoire* 28 (1972)
**Massiac** Lead mine
M76 5 IGN49 H4
Old workings and an ore roasting furnace, found in 1976 during engineering work on a stream, related to Roman exploitation of argentiferous lead, as radiocarbon dates and pottery showed. However, well-preserved mine timbering proved to belong to an eighteenth-century antimony mine, worked by English miners.

L. Texier, 'Une exploitation minière gallo-romaine à Massiac', *Archéologia* 117 (1978), 30-7.

# HAUTE-LOIRE
Saint-Paulin, chef-lieu of the Vellavori, has been replaced in modern times by Le Puy, which is now capital of the département.

*Guide-Répetoire* 9 (1967).

**Brioude** Martyr shrine
M76 5 IGN50 F1
There are a number of saints with the name Julian, but one was a Gallo-Roman martyr of Brioude. Gregory of Tours and his family had a special devotion to Julian. His uncle Gallus, bishop of Clermont, organized an annual pilgrimage to his tomb, in which, as a boy, Gregory and his entire family took part. Gregory always regarded himself as the 'client' or 'special son' of the martyr. At St Férreol on the N102 outside Brioude, in the private garden of a former convent, is the 'Fountain of St Julian' in which the martyr's head was washed following his execution. In the

twelfth century it was surmounted by what was said to be a Roman aedicula or shrine.

*Guide Repertoire* 31.

## Le Puy Roman sculptures
M76 7 IGN50 H3

Reused in the walls of the cathedral are parts of a sculptured frieze with a lively series of animals — lions, deer, and a chimera. These are said to be Gallo-Roman, though Roman and Romanesque sculpture can be difficult to tell apart at times.

*Guide Repertoire* 34-7.

## St-Paulien (Ruessio)
M76 6 IGN50 G2/3

The cantonal capital may have been the successor of the nearby hillfort of La Roche Lambert. Reused Roman sculptures and inscriptions are built into the walls of various buildings including the parish church and the disused chapel of Notre-Dame-du-Haut-Solier. At the latter is a dedication to the Empress Etruscilla, wife of Decius (249-51) by the Civitas Vellavor(um).

*Guide Repertoire* 41.

# LOT

Until the French Revolution, Lot was Haute-Quercy, Bas-Quercy being the present Tarn et Garonne. The area lay in the territory of the Cadurci, whose capital in Roman times was at Cahors.

M. Labrousse and G. Mercadier, *Carte Archéologique de la Gaule* 46 (1994).

## Cahors (Divona Cadurcorum)
M79 8 IGN57 B5

Occupation of the capital of the Cadurci, in a loop of the River Lot, began under Augustus. To the W are an Iron Age hillfort and the sacred spring of the goddess Divona, now the Fontaine des Chalreux. Baths (the 'Baths of Diana') are known, and a Roman theatre was demolished about 1865. Nothing of either is now visible, and the late Roman

walls are only known from the Life of bishop Desiderius (630-55), which refers to gates, walls and towers of squared stone. Desiderius also repaired the city aqueduct, and wrote to the bishop of Clermont for craftsmen who could make wooden water pipes. A fifth-/sixth-century 'Aquitainian' sarcophagus of St Béat marble with a crowd scene was displayed in the cathedral until the French Revolution as that of Desiderius, but is now in St Petersburg. The fourteenth-century fortified bridge, the Port Valentré, deserves mention.

Calvert, *Congres Archéol de France* 1865, 381; Ward-Perkins 1938 no. 35.

M. Labrousse, 'Les thermes romains de Cahors', *Gallia* 21 (1963), 191-225.

## Luzech, L'Impernal Hillfort
M79 7 IGN57 B4

This 16ha promontory fort in a loop of the River Lot began with a timbered rampart of Hallstatt date, destroyed by fire. A *murus gallicus* followed in the first century BC (there were amphora sherds in its make-up) and a Romano-Celtic temple in the following century. What is described as a 'barbarian wall' on top of the destroyed rampart may indicate re-fortification in late Roman times.

Cotton 1957, 186-9; Collis 1975, 190; Nash 1978, 267.

## Murcens Hillfort
M79 8 IGN57 B5

On a 300ft high plateau at the confluence of the Rance and Vers is a 73ha hillfort surrounded on all sides save the N by high cliffs. The *murus gallicus* rampart is estimated to have used $13,500m^3$ of wood and 11,200kg of iron nails. The site has produced many Republican amphorae, but was abandoned under Augustus.

Cotton 1957, 183-6; Nash 1978, 266-7.

## Puy d'Issolud (Uxellodunum)
M75 19 IGN48 D7

The identification of the hillfort of Puy

d'Issolud above Vayrac with the *Uxellodunum* besieged by Caesar in 51 BC (*Bello Gallico* VIII, 32-44) is confirmed by the Fontaine de Loulie in its rock cut basin just outside the defences, for Caesar describes how a spring outside the walls was cut off by an adit, denying the defenders water. The adit is still visible. The defences, on a high cliff-girt plateau, enclose 120ha — the area, as Hogg points out, of Roman London. From the car park at the N end of the site, the N gateway (rock cut, but widened in modern times), the Fontaine de Loulie and stretches of the defences can be reached. The earlier inner rampart was of earth, the outer and later one revetted in stone.

Uxellodunum withstood full-scale siege by several legions, commanded by Caesar in person. Three siege camps were built and the site surrounded by a circumvallation or siege line. Archers and artillery denied the garrison access to the river for water and a mound 60ft high was built to dominate the spring, topped by a tower of 10 storeys. Eventually, Roman sappers diverted the spring and the Gauls were forced to surrender by thirst.

Hogg (1969), 262-4, with plan; Nash (1978), 263-6.

# LOZÈRE

This hilly and rocky country contains a number of small Iron Age forts, two of which have been investigated. Saint Bonnet has imported Italian and Spanish pottery, and a bastioned wall recalling those of Provence and Catalonia. Late Roman pottery and coins show that some of these forts were reoccupied in late Roman times. Gregory of Tours refers to the people of the area shutting themselves up in a fortified castle at Grèzes, west of Mende, during the third-century invasions (H.F.I, 34). Saint-Bonnet is only 3km from Grèzes, and could well be Gregory's 'castle'.

**Banassac** Pottery production centre
M80 4 IGN58 B9

Between AD 40 and 110, Banassac was one of the main production centres for south Gaulish samian pottery. It also produced drinking bowls with such convivial mottoes as 'Drink friend from my cup' and 'Happy Rheims' — the predecessors of 'A Present from Blackpool'. Examples have been found at Pompeii.

**Clapas-Castel** Hillfort
M80 6 IGN59 C2

Occupation of this tiny hillfort on a rocky spur near Grizac runs intermittently through from late Bronze Age to medieval times. The multiple drystone defences are Iron Age, but could have been modified later. On the N, the neck of the spur is protected by two widely spaced ramparts, the outer with out-turned entrance. A short triple rampart protects a possible approach from the S. The site was abandoned about the time of the Roman conquest, but reoccupied in the fourth century. Rectangular drystone buildings in the interior are probably medieval. Nash has suggested that the site could have been associated with transhumance between winter uplands and summer pastures.

A. Soutou, 'L'éperon barré de Clapas Castel', *Gallia* 22 (1964), 189-208; Nash 1978, 136-7.

**Javols** (Anderitum)
M76 15 M58 A10

The ruins of Javols, the Roman capital of this area, are in a remote and landlocked site, replaced in early medieval times by Mende in the valley of the Lot, which is now the départemental capital. Javols however remained as an abbey of St Privatus, for Gregory of Tours records the murder of its abbot, Lupentius, in 584 (G.T. VI. 37).

## Lac de Saint-Andréol
Pagan water cult and Christian chapel
M76 14 IGN58 A8

Despite its alleged third-century bishop, Christianity may well have come late to this area. In the early sixth century, crowds of country people still came in wagons to a lake in the territory of Javols (almost certainly this one) and spent three days feasting, sacrificing animals, and making offerings of rolls of linen, sheepskins, cheeses, and wax and bread models to the lake. The bishop of Javols built a church dedicated to Hilary of Poitiers near the lake, and diverted the celebrations, and the offerings, to the Church.

Gregory of Tours, *Gloria Confessorum* 2. Viellard-Troiekouroff 1976, 246.

## Lanuéjols
M80 6 IGN59 B1

Mausoleum on D41, SE of Mende. Should not be confused with Lanuéjouls, W of Rodez.

## Mende (Minate)
M80 5-6 IGN58 B11

Mende is an interesting example of a Merovingian martyr cult. The Roman vicus, 28km SE of the Cantonal capital of Anderitum (Javols), is said to have been the scene of the martyrdom of St Privatus, bishop of Javols, allegedly killed by Alemanni during the third-century invasions. A late Roman cemetery is known around the cathedral, and bishop Hilary of Javols moved the see here sometime between 475 and 535. The written *passio* of the saint dates from the eighth century, and in the twelfth, a crypt with a lead coffin (presumably late Roman) was found, and identified as the 'crypta in sutteraneo' in which he was buried. Despite this, there are problems with the tradition, and it could have originated in the fifth/sixth century,

from the presence of the late Roman cemetery and crypt, and a desire to establish the see in its new home.

F. Prevot, T.C.C.G. VI (*Aquitania Prima*), 79-85.

## Saint-Bonnet-de-Chirac
Hillfort M80 5 IGN58 B9

Promontory fort with distinct resemblance to Clapas-Castel, though a larger settlement. A drystone wall defends an oval area of about 1ha at the tip of a rocky spur. This, dated La Tène I by excavation, is similar to Clapas-Castel. About 120 BC a much larger outer enclosure was added, occupation continuing until Augustan times. The most unusual feature of this phase is a half-round bastion on its south wall, recalling Nages or Lussas. Pottery includes Dressel 1 amphorae and Campanian wares from Italy and pottery from Ampurias in Catalonia. Coins of Arcadius and Early Christian grey stamped wares (*sigillée paléochetienne grisé*) show that, like Clapas-Castel, the site was reoccupied as a late Roman refuge.
*Gallia* 27 (1969), 416; 29 (1971), 405.

## PUY-DE-DÔME
Unlike most départements, the Puy-de-Dôme is named not after a river, but after a volcanic peak west of Clermont Ferrand, crowned in ancient times by a temple of Mercury. This is an area of volcanic peaks, the local name for which, Puy, is very common. The area around Clermont Ferrand is rich archaeologically, with the major Iron Age centre of Gergovia, the wooden ex-votos from Chamalières and the pottery production centres of the Allier valley.
*Guide-Répetoire* 28 (1972).

## Chamalières
Water cult and ex-votos
M73 14 IGN42 I4

At the natural spring of the 'Source des Roches' in a suburb of Clermont-

Ferrand, 5,000 wooden ex-votos were found in rescue excavations in 1968-71 around the rock basin where the spring emerges. There are no traces of a temple or of associated structures, save for a rough stone kerb, and this was evidently an open air shrine. The figures include legs and arms, heads, and a series of pilgrim figures in hooded cloaks. Associated coins and pottery suggest a date range from Augustus to Nero.

C. Vatin, 'Wooden sculpture from the Gallo-Roman Auvergne', *Antiquity* 46 (1972), 39-42; A.M. Romeuf, 'Ex-votos en bois de Chamalières et des sources de la Seine: essai de comparaison', *Gallia* 44 (1986), 65-89.

## Clermont-Ferrand

(Augustonemetum)
M73 14 IGN42 I3

The name means something like 'The sacred place of Augustus', *nemet* usually referring to a native shrine or holy place rather than a Roman temple. The reference is to the temple on the summit of the Puy-de-Dôme. There is scattered pre-Roman material, including pottery kilns, under the town, but no real pre-Augustan occupation. The street grid was late Augustan, and the city seems to have reached its maximum extent by the end of the first century. The sites of several large buildings are known, including a possible theatre and baths, but the Roman city is buried beneath its modern predecessor. No traces of late Roman walls remain, but they are thought to have occupied a small rectangular area around the cathedral and there was a garrison of laeti (Germanic soldier-settlers) and Suevian *gentiles* (recruited from prisoners of war). In the late fifth century the writer Sidonius Apollinaris was bishop here and defended the city against a prolonged Gothic blockade.

F. Prevot, *T.C.C.G.* VI (Aquitania Prima), 27-40.

## Gergovia Hillfort

M73 14 IGN42 I3

The rocky plateau of Merdogne, SE of Clermont-Ferrand, is a plug of volcanic basalt rising 369m above the surrounding plain. It was renamed Gergovia in 1862, when it was identified as the site of Caesar's defeat by Vercingetorix in 52 BC after excavations by Colonel Stoffel for Napoleon III. The name had survived locally in medieval documents. The oppidum of the Arverni had stone faced ramparts utilising the natural terracing of the basalt and enclosing an oval area, and a permanent water supply. There was Bronze Age occupation, but then very little until the time of Vercingetorix, who may have re-fortified the site. Most of the excavated material post-dates this. The site was abandoned under Tiberius, but Roman buildings are known, including two small Romano-Celtic temples in a rectangular temenos.

O. Brogan and E. Desforges, 'Gergovia', *Archaeological Journal* 97 (1940), 3-36.

## Lezoux (Ledosus)

Pottery production centre
M73 15 IGN43 D1

Lezoux and Martres de Veyre were two major pottery production centres in the Allier Valley E of Clermont Ferrand. Though they produced a wide range of wares, their best-known product was the familiar red-gloss 'samian' ware. In the second century, Lezoux produced this on a prodigious scale, supplying Britain and the Rhineland. Production started about AD 40 in the reign of Tiberius, and by the end of the century Lezoux had supplanted its south Gaulish rivals. The products were shipped down the Allier to the Loire, from which the Gaulish river network distributed them. Production continued until about 260, but Lezoux was still producing other types of pottery in the fourth century.

## Martres-de-Veyre

Pottery production centre
M73 14 IGN42 J4

Lezoux's neighbour, Martres de Veyre, produced both red-gloss samian ware and black-gloss pottery like the later Rhineland or British 'colour coated' wares. Production reached a peak around 100-120, after which there was a mass migration of potters to Lezoux, though pottery making continued on a reduced scale. 'Martres' is from the early Christian word 'Martyrium', meaning a place with important graves. The Welsh or Cornish place name element 'Merthyr' is directly comparable. It occurs in France in the names of various archaeological sites, often where a large early medieval cemetery is present. In the present case, finds of pots may have led medieval people to assume that the site was that of a cemetery.

J.R. Terrisse 1968, *Les céramiques sigillées gallo-romaines des Matres-de-Veyre* (supplement to *Gallia*); Symonds (1992), 6-17.

## Puy-de-Dôme Temple of Mercury
M73 14 IGN42 I3

The département of Puy de Dôme is named after a volcanic mountain ('Puy') W of Clermont Ferrand. Just below its summit, at an elevation of 1,465m, an elaborate group of terraces and rectangular enclosures mark the site of a temple of Mercurius Dumias, known as the Vasso Galatae, excavated in 1872-8. Pliny the Elder records that in the time of Nero the Arverni commissioned a Greek sculptor Zenodorus to produce a colossal bronze statue of Mercury (*Natural History*, 34. 45), probably for this shrine.

In the sixth century, Gregory of Tours described its ruins, claiming that the temple had been destroyed by the Alemannic king Chrocus during the third-century invasions. 'It had been constructed with great skill, and was solidly built, for it had a double wall, the inner one made of small stones, the outer one of great squared masonry. Altogether the wall was 30 foot thick. It was decorated inside with marble and mosaics, its floor was paved with marble, and the roof covered with lead' (H.F. 1, 32).

Grenier III, 424-33.

# 10  Burgundy and the Upper Rhône
## (Lugdunensis Prima and Maxima Sequanorum)

## AIN

Ain is the SE corner of Burgundy, E of the Sâone. It includes the rich agricultural area of Bresse, celebrated in France for its poultry.

A. Busson, *Carte Archéologique de la Gaule* 19 (1990).

**Briord** Roman cemetery and church
M74 12 IGN44 D4

Excavated since 1956, Briord, in the Upper Rhône valley east of Lyon, shows a remarkable development from an early Roman cremation cemetery to a Christian church and graveyard. Though the site is not without its problems, it is rare for such a sequence to be firmly dated by an assemblage of grave goods and inscriptions.

The early Roman graves have pottery, coins and glassware. This is followed by a late Roman cemetery of E-W tile tombs without grave goods. These were probably Christian, for the sequence continues with a Christian church, with nave, square chancel and flanking square transeptal vestries (*prothesis* and *diaconicon*). A puzzling feature of the site is that the latest series of graves, with long cists and wooden coffins, are said to post date the destruction of the church, though the site has produced an impressive range of dated Christian tombstones of the later fifth to seventh centuries. One possible scenario is that the church fell into disuse, perhaps under the Arian Visigoths, and a later church awaits discovery elsewhere on site. The material from the excavation is in a museum run by a local archaeological society in Serrières de Briord.

## Izenore (Isarnodurum)
M74 3 IGN44 B5

Capital of the small tribe of the Ambarres, Isarnodurum means something like 'City of Iron', presumably referring to local iron mining. It probably succeeded an Iron Age oppidum. The baths and temple were excavated in 1863 and 1913, and there are also traces of a theatre. The temple is a Celtic/Roman hybrid, combining the rectangular form and proportions of a classical temple with the surrounding gallery of a Romano-Celtic temple. Coins from the excavations ran from Tiberius to Commodus, suggesting that the site declined in the late Empire. The remains are on display and the finds are in the Municipal Museum in the Mairie.

Grenier III, I, 403-6 (temple); IV 298-300 (baths).

## CÔTE D'OR

Côte d'Or is the heartland of Burgundy, around the historic capital of the Duchy at Dijon. South of Dijon are the places that have made the name of Burgundy world famous — Beaune and Beaujolais, Nuits St George and Meursault. The archaeology is equally rich, particularly for the Iron Age and early Roman period, with *oppida* like Vix and Alesia, the legionary fortress of Mirebeau and the finds from the Source of the Seine.

**Alise Sainte Reine** (Alesia)
M65 18 IGN28 C6

The Roman siegeworks at the site of Vercingetorix's last stand in AD 52 were excavated by Perret for Napoleon III in 1861-6. An impressive

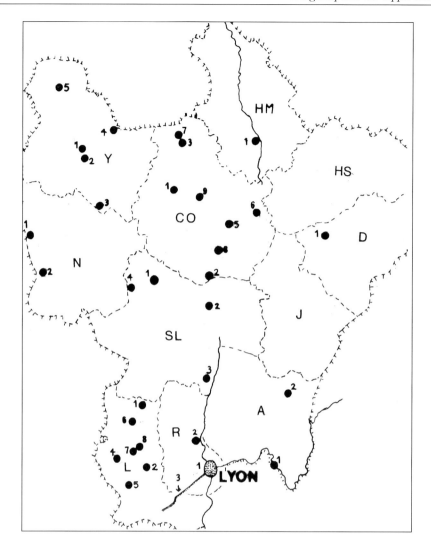

34 Burgundy and the Upper Rhône (Lugdunensis Prima, Maxima Sequanorum)

**A** Ain *1 Briorde 2 Izenore*

**CO** Côte d'Or *1 Alesia 2 Beaune-Archéodrome 3 Châtillon-sur-Seine 4 Cussy la Colonne 5 Dijon 6 Mirabeau 7 Mont Lassois and Vix 8 Nuits St Georges 9 Sources of the Seine*

**D** Doubs *1 Besançon*

**HM** Haute-Marne *1 Langres*

**HS** Haute-Sâone

**J** Jura

**L** Loire *1 Charlieu 2 Feurs 3 Gier aqueduct 4 Höpital-sous-Rochefort 5 Moingt 6 Roanne 7 St Georges de Baroilles 8 St Marcel des Felines 9 St Maurice sur Loire-Joeuvre*

**N** Nievre *1 Bulcy 2 Nevers*

**R** Rhône *1 Lyon 2 Anse 3 Courzieu*

**SL** Saône et Loire *1 Autun 2 Châlons-sur-Saône 3 Mâcon 4 Mont Beuvray*

**Y** Yonne *1 Auxerre 2 Escolives St Camille 3 Fontaines- Salées 4 Jaulges Villiers-Vineux 5 Sens*

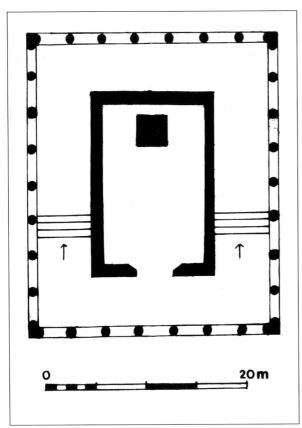

35 *Izenore (Ain) — plan of temple.*
*After De Caumont and Grenier*

0                                    20 m

reconstruction can be seen in the Archéodrome at Beaune (see below). Alesia continued to be occupied in Roman times as a vicus, with the shrine of Apollo Moritasgus 800m to the E. The local tribe, the Mandubii were integrated into the civitas of the Aeduii however, and the site never developed as a Roman capital. Traces of pre-conquest rock-cut structures are known, and a wooden temple existed by *c*.50-30 BC, associated with rectangular wooden houses. The first forum complex dates from AD 20-30, and by the late first century, stone houses were appearing. The vicus was known for its metalworking industries, mentioned by Pliny. Its houses were in streets and blocks, but their plan was determined not by a formal grid but by the relief of the site.

The second century saw the addition of impressive public buildings — a theatre-amphitheatre and a forum apparently modelled on Trajan's forum in Rome as completed by Hadrian. A number of large houses are known, including the Ucuetis monument, which may have been the headquarters of a guild of metalworkers, and the House of Silenus. The shrine of Apollo Moritasgus included an octagonal temple and a large bath building.

Le Gall, *Alésia: archéologie et histoire* (Paris 1980) and *Alésia* (G.A.F.); Cotton 1957, 195-8; R. Martin and P. Varène, *Le Monument d'Ucuetis a Alésia* (26th supplement to *Gallia*, 1973).

## Beaune-Archéodrome
M69 1 IGN37 B3

This splendid open air museum is attached to the Beaune-Merceuil service station on the Paris-Lyon A6 motorway, 7km south of Beaune. The museum presents the archaeology of the area from the Palaeolithic onwards, whilst outdoor exhibits include prehistoric huts, a tumulus grave, early bronze and iron working furnaces, a Gaulish house and farm, a remarkable reconstruction of part of Caesar's siegeworks around Alesia, a Romano-Celtic temple, a Roman cemetery with carved and inscribed tombstones, a potter's workshop and a Roman villa.

## Châtillon-sur-Seine
M65 8 IGN28 A7

The Roman town at Vertault is situated on a spur defended by a cross-bank built in a variant of the *murus gallicus* technique, with squared stone blocks and timber planking. Joffroy thought it to be of Roman date, and non-military.
Cotton 1957, 198; Collis 1975, 174.

## Cussy la Colonne Votive column
M69 9 IGN37 B1

Cussy, between Beaune and Autun, takes its name from a Roman votive column which stands N of the village.

## Dijon (Dibio)
M65 20 IGN37 A4

The description of Dijon as it was in the sixth century, by Gregory of Tours, is well known, but deserves repetition: 'It is a fortress girded around with mighty walls, and set in the middle of a pleasant plain. Its lands are fertile and . . . after a single ploughing, when the fields are sown, a rich harvest soon follows. On the south is the River Ouche, which teems with fish. A smaller river runs down from the north, entering through one gateway, running under a bridge and then out through another gate. This stream washes all the fortifications . . .

and turns the mill-wheels round at wondrous speed outside the gate. The four entrances . . . are placed at the four points of the compass, and twenty three towers adorn the circuit of the walls, which are of squared stones rising to a height of twenty feet, with smaller stones above to reach in all some thirty feet, the whole being fifteen feet thick. Why Dijon has not been raised to the dignity of a bishopric I cannot imagine. Round it are excellent springs of water, to the west the hills are covered with fruitful vines which yield a noble Falernian vintage, that the inhabitants have sometimes preferred to a good Mâcon. The ancients say Dijon was built by the Emperor Aurelian.'

The late Roman walls praised by Gregory enclosed an oval area of 11ha in the centre of the modern city, around the old Ducal Palace and the Palais de Justice. The Archaeological Museum, in the cloisters of the cathedral of St Benigne, has an important collection of Celtic Iron Age religious material, including the statue of Sequana and the wooden *ex voto* figures from the Source of the Seine, a native Mars with his consort Rosmerta from Mavilly, and material from Alésia. Gallo Roman sculptures include (appropriately for Dijon) the tombstones of a butcher and a wine merchant. In the crypt of the Gothic cathedral next door is the sarcophagus of the Gallo-Roman martyr Benignus, enclosed in a rotunda built by William of Volpiano in 1101, with pre-Romanesque sculpture still echoing early Christian models (and echoed in its turn at St Augustine's Abbey, Canterbury).
Gregory of Tours, *History of the Franks* III, 19; Blanchet 27-32.

## Mirabeau Legionary fortress
M66 13 IGN29 H3

A stone-built legionary fortress in the

middle of Burgundy, 25km from Dijon, is an unexpected discovery in Roman France. Stamped tiles of the Eighth Augustan Legion, *Legio VIII Augusta*, the tombstone of a soldier of the legion, and, more mysteriously, stamped tiles attesting the presence of detachments of four other Rhineland legions, were already known when in 1964 a Roman fortress of 22ha was identified from the air by a pilot of the French Air Force. Excavation produced the classic plan of a legionary fortress, with a Principia (Headquarters Building) at the centre, ranges of barracks, a tribune's house and other buildings. The defences, originally timber, had internal stone turrets and gateways with twin semicircular projecting towers.

Outside the fortress, air photography and selective excavation have revealed a civil settlement with houses, a forum, and large bathhouse. To the E is a temporary camp, perhaps preceding the fortress, and outside the W gate were, as at Caerleon, a legionary parade ground and adjacent amphitheatre.

The legion was moved to Gaul from *Novae* in Bulgaria by Vespasian in AD 70, and Mirabeau is contemporary with the British fortresses at Caerleon, York and Chester. About AD 90 however, Domitian moved the legion to Strasbourg, which became its permanent home. The stamped tiles of the other legions have been much debated by Roman historians and associated with preparations for Domitian's war with the Chatti in AD 83. However, as Reddé points out, they suggest building operations rather than a temporary transit camp. Squads of craftsmen ('Arbeitsvexillationen' — work squads) may have been drafted in for the initial building work and the different legions are bracketed together on a single stamp (*Vexil. Legionum I. VIII. XI. XIII XXI*) rather than each having its own, which might be expected if they were present in force.

René Goguey and Michel Reddé, *Le Camp Légionnaire de Mirabeau* (Römisch-Germanisches Zentralmuseum, Mainz, 1995); Reddé 1996, 191-203.

## Mont-Lassois and Vix
M65 8 IGN28 A6

Mont Lassois dominates the Seine valley N of Châtillon-sur-Seine, close to its upper navigable limit. Its summit, crowned by the Romanesque church of St Marcel, was the site of a Hallstatt oppidum which has produced Hallstatt D2 pottery associated with Massiliot wine amphorae and Attic black figure pottery. In the valley below, Rene Joffroy found in 1953 the remarkable grave known as the 'Vix Treasure', now in the museum at Châtillon (Rue du Bourg).

About 525 BC, a woman aged about 35 (the 'Vix princess') was buried in a wooden mortuary chamber under a barrow. The grave goods included a dismantled four wheeled cart; an enormous Greek bronze *krater* or wine-mixing bowl, probably made in Corinth around 575 BC, with decoration of horsemen, warriors and chariots; an Attic black-figure cup of *c.*525 BC; a heavy gold diadem or torque, possibly Spanish in origin; an Etruscan bronze flagon and three basins; the lady's personal jewellery (brooches, bracelets and anklets); and rich textiles. Though earlier than most of the sites included here, Vix is crucial for early contacts between the Classical and Celtic worlds. Already, the Greek and Etruscan wine-drinking kit demonstrates the role of feasting and imported wine in the Celtic world, whilst the grave itself shows the high status that women could attain in that world.

R. Joffroy 1954, *Le Trésor de Vix* (Paris); Cotton in Wheeler and Richardson (1957), 198.

# Nuits-St-Georges

Temple of Mithras

M65 20 IGN37 A3

The name of Nuits-St-Georges may be familiar to some readers in quite another context, but its Roman vicus has produced the only Mithraeum, dedicated to the cult of the Persian sun god, fully explored in inland Gaul. It was discovered by local amateurs and badly excavated before professional archaeologists came on the scene. Probably of the mid-second century, it was a classic Mithraic cave — a rectangular partly underground room, with benches along the sides on which worshippers would recline during the cult ceremonies, similar for example to that at Carrawburgh on Hadrian's wall.

The collection of sculptures from the temple includes heads of Mithras and Sol (the sun); figures of Mithras's helpers Cautes and Cautopates (sunrise and sunset); a sculptured lion ('Lions' were one of the Mithraic grades of initiate); a marble column with sculptured oak branches and fragments of two large monumental inscriptions, one with the name MITHR(AS). David Mouraire's recent study suggests that the temple may have been founded by merchants or traders from Italy or the east.

E. Planson and C. Pommeret, *Les Bolards, le site gallo-romaine et le musée de Nuits-Saint-Georges* (G.A.F.); D. Mouraire, 'La statuaire du Mithraeum des Bolards à Nuits-Saint-George', *R. A. E.* 48 (1997), 261-78.

# Sources of the Seine

Water shrine

M65 19 IGN28 C7

The shrine of the goddess Sequana at the spring marking the source of the Seine has been known since 1845, but owes its particular fame to the collection of *ex-votos* now in the Archaeological Museum at Dijon. The bronze of the draped and diademed goddess of the Seine, standing in a boat whose prow and stern are the head and tail of a duck, holding in its beak a ball or fruit, is justly famous. The bird-ship carrying the goddess clearly has a mythological dimension. She was found in 1933. Thirty years later the excavation of a large water tank fed by a leat from the spring produced the remarkable collection of wooden figures of men and animals, including many *ex-votos* of limbs, heads and other parts of the body. Pottery showed that they were deposited around the time of Claudius. The practice may have lasted much longer however, and Gregory of Tours in the sixth century knew of a shrine near Cologne where wooden models of injured human parts were suspended (*Vitae Patrum* VI, 2).

The spring flows into a rectangular tank with steps leading down into it, perhaps for ritual bathing. A Romano-Celtic temple was built to the N in the mid-first century AD (this could have been when the *ex-votos* around the shrine were taken down and deposited) and in the second century an open enclosure with a portico was added. From the spring, a leat led to the large water basin, where the wooden sculptures were found. Coins showed that the site was frequented by worshippers at least until the time of Constantine.

A second Côte d'Or shrine at Montlay-en-Auxois has now produced a few similar wooden *ex-votos* of AD 150-200 associated with timber tanks.

*Gallia* 1964, 302ff; F. Deyts, *Les Bois Sculptés des sources de la Seine* (Paris 1983); Dupont and J. Bénard, 'Le sanctuaire gallo-romain à bois votifs de la Fontaine Segrain à Montlay-en-Auxois', *R.A.E.* 46 (1995), 59-78.

# DOUBS

Doubs, in eastern Burgundy, is part of Franche-Comté, a French speaking part of the Holy Roman Empire that only became part of France in the seventeenth century. Rhineland and Lutheran influence is still strong, not least because of the Belfort Gap, a natural corridor between the Rhine (which once flowed through it) and central France.

## Besançon (Vesontio)
M66 15 IGN38 C1
Besançon is set in a loop of the river Doubs. A ridge of high ground blocks the neck of the loop, providing a natural defence. Excavations have found late La Tène occupation from 120-40 BC, with Campanian ware the only non-local pottery. Julius Caesar wintered his army here in 58-57. Later, after a brief hiatus at the end of the Iron Age occupation, Roman buildings appear, together with *terra sigillata*. By the beginning of the first century AD a street grid had appeared. The main Roman monuments are a second-century arch, the 'Porte Noire', S of the cathedral, and the Roman amphitheatre across the river. The somewhat restored arch, the work of local craftsmen, stood where the main road from Italy and the south entered the city. Probably commemorating the wars of Marcus Aurelius, it has attached columns; battle scenes with Roman soldiers fighting Parthians and Germans; sculptures of Mars; Jupiter battling with Tritons and a pair of Victories. Incorporated in the late Roman and medieval walls of the town, it was celebrated on its thirteenth-century coins as the 'Porta Nigra'. Fragments of late Roman walls were found in the nineteenth century, with reused architectural fragments and both rounded and square towers.

Near the Porte Noire is the Square Archéologique A. Castan, a small park containing the columns of a Nympheum, an architectural water feature set at the end of an aqueduct. Traces of this aqueduct, bringing water from the source of the Arcier can be seen SE of Besançon on the D67, with a rock cutting known as the Porte Taillée. The amphitheatre (Arènes) lies across the Doubs to the NE, between the Quai Veil Picard and the Avenue Siffert.
Blanchet 137-9; H. Walter, *La Porte Noire de Besançon Contribution à l'étude de l'art triumphal des Gaules* (Paris, 2 vols, 1986); L. Lerat and H. Walter, *Besançon Antique* (G.A.F.).

# HAUTE-MARNE

The Langres plateau is a high limestone area of poor and wooded upland soils at the junction of Champagne, Burgundy and Lorraine, the source of a number of major French rivers, including the Sâone, the Meuse and the Marne.

## Langres (Andematunnum)
M66 3 IGN29 D3
The Roman city of Langres spread for 2,000m along a N-S ridge. By the late Empire, it had shrunk to a quarter of its former size, and the late walls enclosed an area only some $500m^2$ at the N end of the ridge. Much of the walls still survived in the early nineteenth century. A gate known as the Longe-Porte, demolished in 1838, had a sculptured frieze with trophies of arms, and may have been an earlier triumphal arch (if the pieces were not merely reused). Of the two gates, the Porte au Pan had already been demolished, and the Porte de Moab went in July 1840, together with a fine stretch of wall to the E. The demolitions produced the usual rich harvest of sculptures and inscriptions.
Blanchet 20-24; C.I.L. XIII, 5823; Knight 1999, 80-1.

# JURA

The heavily forested Tertiary rocks of the Jura mountains, which also extend over parts of Doubs and Ain, and the Swiss Jura, gave their name to a period of earth history (and to the film Jurassic Park). In the Iron Age they were part of the territory of the Sequani of Besançon, but did not lend themselves to settlement on a large scale. Much of the area was covered in pine forests (Pliny, *Natural History* XVI, 197), which provided timber, floated down the Rhône to the cities on its banks, and the resin and pitch used to line wine containers, an item of commerce in its own right. There were Roman settlements at the salt springs of Salins-les-Bains and Lons-le-Saunier, and at Dole, but these have left no visible remains. The salt, combined with the forests, made the Sequani famous in ancient times for their hams and salted meats. There are good collections of local archaeological material in the museums at Dole (Rue du Collège) and Lons (Hôtel de Ville), including important prehistoric material from the lake settlements of the area.

# LOIRE

Loire was the tribal territory of the Segusiavi. Inscriptions show that Feurs (Forum Segusiavorum) was at one stage the Cantonal capital, though later it was absorbed by its neighbour, Lyon. The *Guide Répertoire* and other sources list eight hillforts, of which at least three had *murus gallicus* defences. Essolois at Chambles, largely destroyed by quarrying, produced large numbers of early Dressel 1 amphorae. It is on the Loire, at its nearest point to the Rhône, and may have controlled the flow of imported goods between the two river systems. Apart from Feurs and the baths at Moingt (Aquae Segetae), there are remains of the Aqueduct de Gier, which carried water from its source at Izieux to Lyon. The area is rich in Roman inscriptions, and a number of particular interest are listed below.
*Guide Répetoire* 14 (1967).

## Charlieu
Sarcophagus of Maria Severiola
M73 8 IGN43 B6
In the narthex of the Abbey is the sarcophagus of Maria Severiola, wife of Titus Magneius Severianus, who died at the age of 24. Her burial crypt is thought to lie below the church.
C.I.L. XIII, 1650; *Guide Répertoire* 12.

## Feurs (Forum Segusiavorum)
M88 5 IGN43 D7
The capital of the Segusiavi had the usual civic amenities, including baths, a theatre and a forum. The latter is the earliest known example in Gaul of the three part forum-basilica complex, with a temple in a monumental precinct, a large central forum and a basilica. Excavation has shown that it dates from *c.*AD 10-30, in the time of Augustus or Tiberius. An inscription in the museum, of the time of Claudius (AD 41-54) records that Tiberius Claudius Capito, Priest of Rome and Augustus, rebuilt the theatre, previously of timber, in stone (C.I.L. XIII, 1642). His names show that he had only recently acquired Roman citizenship. Saintes and Evreux also had Claudian theatres, but the reference to a timber predecessor is unique. There is also an honorific inscription by the Civitas Segusiavorum to a local dignitary, showing that first-century Feurs was a Cantonal capital, though it was later absorbed by Lyon (C.I.L. XIII, 1645). A third inscription confirms the Roman name of the town, otherwise known from literary sources.
P. Valette and V. Guichard, 'Le forum Gallo-Romain de Feurs, Loire', *Gallia* 48 (1990), 109-64.

# Gier Aqueduct

M73 19 IGN51 C2-B2

Hadrian's Aqueduct de Gier was one of four supplying water to Lyon. It begins at a height of 405m on the headwaters of the Gier, at Izieux, 50km SW of Lyon, and follows the line of its valley (and now the A47 motorway), to arrive at the monumental buildings on the hill of Fouvière at a height of 285m. Wherever the Roman engineers could, they conveyed the waters in an underground channel, but where the line of the aqueduct crossed one of the tributary streams running down to the Gier, it was necessary to carry the leat on a series of above ground masonry arches. It is these, often on a monumental scale, as at the Pont du Gard outside Nîmes, or at Segovia in Spain, that the phrase 'Roman aqueduct' brings to mind. However, they were only a small part of the overall engineering complex. Here, for brevity, 'aqueduct' is used in both senses. Nos 1-2 below are south of St Chamond and the A47. Sorbiers (3) is to the NW and the remainder N of Rive-de-Gier, between Chagnon and the départemental boundary. The E half of the aqueduct, nearer Lyon, is in the département of Rhône.

1 *Izieux* The aqueduct starts at a collecting basin at La Martinière, on the southern outskirts of Izieux beside the D2, 400m downstream from the initial damming of the Gier. Its underground channel passes below the village and cemetery and 1,200m W of the church, at Pont-Nantin, crosses a stream on an aqueduct in reticulated masonry, traces of whose five piers can be seen.

2 *Saint-Julien-en-Jarez* 1km W of St Chamond on the N498 is the Café des Aqueducs. There were two masonry aqueducts here, one, originally of nine arches, near the café, carrying the leat over the river Lagonand. 300m E is the remaining part of the other, a five-arched aqueduct over a stream.

3 *Saint-Chamond* Traces of the underground channel have been found at several points.

4 *Sorbiers* E of the village, at la Sarrasinière, is a rock cut channel which carried the waters of a tributary stream down to the aqueduct.

5 *Chagnon* Preserved at the village school is an inscription of Hadrian delimiting the catchment area of the aqueduct, within which water supplies were protected. C.I.L XIII, 1623.

6 *Saint-Genis Terrenoir* La Plombière. Remains of 15 arch bridge 20m high carrying the leat over the valley of the Durèze. Three piers survive.

7 *La Cula* Les Arcs, south of La Cula near the D37. A siphon-reservoir with ten openings, through which lead pipes carried the water into the tank.

8 *Saint-Martin-la-Plaine* 600m SE of the village, at the stream of Fontaines, a section of underground channel emerges near the S angle of the boundary wall of the Château de la Ronze. Cut on the rock face are a trident, a cross and a circle. Their significance is uncertain.

9 *Saint-Joseph* Upstream from the village on the D30 is the pier of a short section of aqueduct over the Vaille stream. The line continues underground through the village to Bissieux, where a bridge of four arches in reticulated masonry carried the aqueduct over the stream which is now the départemental boundary.

C. de Montauzan. *Les Aqueducs de Lyon* (Paris 1909); *Guide-Répertoire* passim.

# Hôpital-sous-Rochefort

Cremation chests M73 7 IGN43 D5

In a variation on the theme of reused Roman building material in churches, the parish church off the N89 NW of Boen has a number of stone cremation chests, presumably from a nearby cemetery, built into its exterior walls.

## Milestones

An interesting group of milestones from the Feurs-Moingt Roman road can be grouped together here. They measure the distance from the Cantonal capital (Feurs), as was normal practice, but unlike milestones in (say) Britain, the distances are in Gaulish leagues (1.5 Roman miles). This practice began in Aquitania under Trajan and Hadrian, and spread to Gallia Lugdunensis and Belgica under Septimius Severus.

1 *Feurs* Four milestones of the Emperor Maximian (235-8) now in the municipal museum, marked in Gaulish leagues (LI, II, III, IV) from Feurs. They were probably never erected, perhaps because of the overthrow of Maximian, who was murdered by his own troops. C.I.L. XIII, 8861-4.

2 *Saint-Cyr-les-Vignes* At the castle is a milestone of Trajan (98-117) from Poncins, marking two leagues (L II) from Feurs. C.I.L. XIII, 8865.

3 *Moingt* A milestone of Maximian records that Moingt was 9 leagues from Feurs. C.I.L. XIII, 8866.

## Moingt (Aquae Segetae)

M73 17 IGN50 B6

The waters of the natural source were collected in a rectangular pool and served large, well-appointed baths. Nearby was a theatre-amphitheatre of the late first century holding 8,000 spectators. The hot radioactive springs at Sail-les-Bains and the mineral springs at Sail-sous-Couzan may also have been utilised in Roman times.

## Roanne (Roidomna)

M73 7 IGN43 C6

Roanne, already a large open settlement in pre-Roman times, became a production centre for high quality pottery, including fine painted wares, some of the kilns for which have been excavated. Occupation continued throughout the Roman period, and Merovingian burials are known. The Musée Joseph Déchelette (22, Rue Anatole France), named after the distinguished archaeologist who was a native of the town and was killed in the First World War, has important collections from Roanne and from other local sites.

M. Bessou, 'La poterie peinte gauloise à Roanne', *Ogam* 19 (1967) 1-2, 109-27.

## St Georges-de-Baroilles, Châtelard de Chazi

Hillfort M73 18 IGN43 D6

Promontory fort, 7-8ha with massive cross ditch and second rampart with *murus gallicus*, on spur 1,300m S of the church, at the junction of the Loire and Aix.

Cotton 1957, 181-2; Collis 1975, 181.

## Saint-Marcel-de-Felines, Le Crêt Châtelard Hillfort

M73 18 IGN43 D6

A high promontory above the Loire, protected on its vulnerable E side by a large rampart (Crêt), enclosing 25ha, and by a weaker rampart on the other sides. The latter proved to be of *murus gallicus* construction, but the Crêt itself was not available for excavation, and could be of a different phase. Gallo-Roman occupation inside the ramparts included buildings with *opus signinum* floors and over 200 pits or shafts containing pottery and organic remains. Châtelard is the universal place name hereabouts for a hillfort.

Cotton 1957, 178-80.

## Saint-Maurice-sur-Loire, Joeuvre Hillfort

M73 7 IGN43 C5

A 75ha promontory on a spur above the Loire, occupied from the sixth century BC to late Roman times. The finds, including Dressel 1 amphorae and Campanian ware, are in the Musée

Déchelette in Roanne.
Collis 1975, 181, *Guide-Répertoire* 20.

# NIÈVRE

The Nièvre was the western part of the territory of the Aedui, between the Rhône and the Loire. They also occupied Saône-et-Loire and southern Côte d'Or.

**Bulcy** Stone quarries
M65 13 IGN27 D9

These quarries, near Mesves sur Loire, produced a high quality building stone which was shipped down the Loire as far as Orleans.

**Nevers** (Noviodunum)
M69 3 IGN36 B2

Noviodunum was an oppidum of the Aedui, used by Caesar as a supply base and holding camp for hostages. It was stormed by the Gauls under Eporedorix and Viridomarus, who massacred the garrison and rescued the hostages (B.G. VII, 55). The late Roman walls enclosed an elongated area of 11ha, possibly following the line of the pre-Roman defences. Sixteenth- and seventeenth-century descriptions and drawings show them 'very high, of good strong masonry' and with a series of half-round towers, surrounding the cathedral and other main buildings. An early Christian baptistery is known from the cathedral.
*Gallia* 8 (1950), 175-6; Blanchet 85-7.

# RHÔNE

The département is basically the hinterland of Lyon, in the hilly country to its W and N. Though not fertile, this was exploited for its natural resources. The Lyon aqueducts drew their water from here, and the area between Lyon and Feurs contained metal mines. Argentiferous lead was mined at St Colombe, Chambost-Longesaigne and Ancy, and copper at Chessy-les Mines.
*Guide-Répertoire* 29 (1973).

**Lyon** (Colonia Copia Felix Munatia Lugdunum)
M73 20 IGN43 D11

The colony of Lyon was founded in 43 BC by the Roman Governor of Gaul, Lucius Munatius Plancus, though the name Lugdunum 'Fortress of the God Lug' might suggest a pre-existing Gaulish oppidum. Augustus was here from 16-14 BC and built the first theatre, with seating for 5,000 spectators. In 12 BC Drusus inaugurated the great altar and temple of the Three Gauls at Condate, and two years later Lyon became one of the main Roman mints, often displaying on the reverse a representation of the Condate altar. At about the same time the future Emperor Claudius was born here. Claudius, on his return from the conquest of Britain in AD 43-4, gave his native city the aqueduct of La Brévenne. Even a serious fire in 65 did not halt progress. Hadrian rebuilt and enlarged the theatre and amphitheatre and gave the city an impressive aqueduct bringing water from the headwaters of the Gier, 50km to the SW. About 160 a well-appointed Odeon, or covered theatre for recitals and concerts, was added next to the theatre.

Later in the century, two tragic episodes prefigured the changes of the later Empire. In the summer of 177, a group of men and women, many of them immigrants from Asia Minor, were arrested as Christians and tortured and executed in the amphitheatre at Condate during the games associated with the annual Council of the Gauls. This is the earliest evidence for a community of Christians anywhere in western Europe outside Italy. Twenty years later, on 17 February 197, Septimius Severus defeated his rival Clodius Albinus in a bloody battle at Lyon, following which the city was sacked and burnt by the victorious army. In place of the Urban Cohort previously at Lyon, it was now garrisoned, like an occupied city, by detachments of the Rhine legions (I.L.T.G. 234). Severus's vindictiveness towards those who had supported his rivals, and his lucrative confiscations of their property, is well known. Lyon had been Albinus's headquarters, but Severus, having been governor of Gallia Lugdunensis under Commodus, may well have felt that he had a claim on the city's loyalty. What long-term effect these events had is uncertain, but the great complex of monumental buildings on the hill of Fouvière was largely abandoned under the late Empire. Various explanations have been offered for this, but the complex must have needed extensive endowments to meet operating costs, and these would have been an obvious target for Severus's confiscations. The lower lying commercial quarters along the Rhône seem to have continued to flourish.

The 177 persecutions did not succeed in destroying the Christian community at Lyon, and when Fouvière was reoccupied it was by the churches and cemeteries of the Christian church.

## Fourvière — The Monumental Complex

The main city-centre complex was on the hill of Fourvière, rising high above the river loop that marked the confluence of the Rhône and Saône. It was here that Augustus built his theatre, and here no doubt was his palace, and that of the members of the Imperial family who governed Gaul on his behalf. Behind the theatre are the ruins of a complex excavated in 1943 and identified until recently as a Temple of Cybele, on the basis of an altar recording a Taurobolium or bull sacrifice. Recent re-examination has suggested a different story however.

### The Theatre and Odeon

The theatre, discovered in 1887, was excavated and laid out for display between the wars. Originally built by Augustus in 16-14 BC, its two banks of seating could hold 5,000 spectators. Rebuilt and doubled in size by Hadrian about 130, with sculptured decoration in white marble and an elaborate facade and *frons scaena*, it could now accommodate an audience of 10,500, about the same size as the theatres at Arles and Orange. The sockets for the wooden stage machinery can be seen, and a model in the museum shows how this worked. The adjacent Odeon was a covered theatre for lectures and recitals, built about 160. 16 rows of seats remain of an original 23. The orchestras of both theatre and odeon retain their polychrome floors of red stone, grey granite and green *cipollino* marble. This flat semicircular area in front of the stage, used for the chorus in Greek plays, was used in Roman times for the reserved seats of distinguished visitors, and in the Odeon the three lowest rows of seats are separated off as reserved seats for dignitaries. Access to the Odeon was by way of monumental flanking stairs on each side, leading to a roadway around its upper perimeter. The massive external wall on this side was needed to carry the roofing.

### 'Temple of Cybele'

Behind the theatre is a large complex identified early last century as a temple of the eastern Goddess Cybele. This was on the basis of an inscribed altar of AD 160 dedicated to Antoninus Pius found here in the eighteenth century (C.I.L. XIII, 1751, also 1752-6). Recently, fresh excavation has shown that the building was a Palace or Governor's Residence dating from about 20 BC and built over structures of the earliest colonial period. The suggested date would correspond

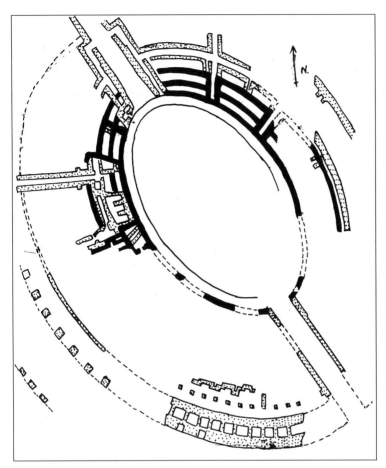

*36 Lyon (Rhône). Amphitheatre of the Three Gauls — Tiberian (black) and Hadrianic (stippled)*

with the residence of Augustus in Lyon, and that of subsequent members of the Imperial House. About AD 10 it became a public building of uncertain function, and it was this which was taken for the 'Temple of Cybele'. Nearby a row of shops ('Boutiques') have been excavated, and the whole complex is now laid out as an archaeological park.

A. Desbat, 'Nouvelles recherches à l'emplacement du Prétendu sanctuaire Lyonnais de Cybele', *Gallia* 55 (1998), 237-77.

## Mur Clebérg

To the N of the theatre (at 1-3 Montée de Fouvière) is a massive retaining wall known as the 'Wall of Cléberg', from the adjacent and parallel Rue Cléberg. 50m long and 14m high it formed a terrace along the S side of the Hill of Fouvière, supporting an unknown monumental structure at the junction of two of the principal roads — the Cardo and Decumanus. The brick courses might suggest a second-century date, but recent work has shown that this technique was already in use in Lyon quite early in the first century.

## Reservoir of the Grotte Bérelle

The monumental buildings on the hill would have needed a good water supply, and several sizeable underground reservoirs are known. One of the largest was under the grounds of the Lycée next to the church of St Just. Water was brought to the trapezoid structure through lead pipes. It consisted of three concentric galleries, roofed with vaults 3.5m high to the crown.

## The Old Forum

To the north was a colossal temple, possibly dedicated to the Capitoline gods Jupiter, Juno and Minerva. This, now under the modern church, was set in a rectangular temenos with a large and much broader piazza in front of it, giving the whole complex a broad T shape. Excavation suggests that it was Augustan in origin, rebuilt and restored in the second century.

## The New Forum

The complex known as the New Forum was excavated in 1957-9. A spacious piazza measuring 118 x 90m, it contained a large temple. Column fragments suggest that this attained a height of 17m.

## Circus

The circus is thought to have lain outside the Roman walls, SW of the Fouvière complex. There was certainly a circus at Lyon, for an inscription recording the honours and benefactions of a local first-century magnate tells how he gave circus games. Two other inscriptions, in an oddly modern touch, tell how Sextus Julius Januarius sponsored a block of ten seats, apparently for free distribution (C.I.L. XIII, 1805, 1919, 1921). A mosaic found in 1806 and now in the Museum of Gallo-Roman Civilisation has a detailed and spirited picture of a chariot race, perhaps in the local arena (Grenier III, fig 322, p981).

## Musée de la Civilisation Gallo Romaine

On Rue Cléberg, this museum is also on Fouvière, near the theatre, odeon and the rest of the monumental complex. It contains major collections covering all aspects of Roman life and Roman Lyon.

The 600+ inscriptions include the dedication slab of the Amphitheatre of the Three Gauls, the famous Celtic calendar from Coligny, and the 'Claudian Tables', two bronze tablets found in 1524 containing part of the text of a speech delivered by the Emperor Claudius in the Roman senate in AD 48, calling for the admission of suitably qualified citizens of the Three Gauls, including citizens of Lyon, to the Senate. A. Audin 1979, *Lyon, Miroir de Rome dans les Gaules* (Paris).

## Lyon-Condate

The altar of Rome and Augustus at the confluence of the Rhône and Saône was dedicated by Drusus in 12 BC as an annual meeting place for the *Concilium Galliarum*, a council of delegates from the tribes of the Three Gauls, who met annually in August, on the anniversary of the Battle of Actium, to elect a chief priest, and to conduct other business. The first priest of Rome and Augustus was an Aeduan, C. Julius Vercondaridubnus. The great altar, of imported marble, with an inscription in letters of gold, stood in front of the temple, flanked by columns with figures of Victory and statues representing each of the 64 tribes. Under Tiberius, an amphitheatre was added and annual games instituted. Hadrian built or rebuilt the temple, and changed the dedication from Rome and Augustus to Rome and all Emperors of good repute. Severus added 'and our Caesars' (Caracalla and Geta) thus associating it directly with the ruling dynasty. Thereafter the cult seems to have declined.

Nothing is now visible, but the Rue Burdeau is thought to preserve the line of its access ramp and the site of the altar, at the upper end of the road, has produced what may be fragments of its structure. The four columns of Egyptian porphyry now supporting the cupola of the eleventh-century church of St Martin d'Ainay are thought to be halves of the two given by Hadrian to replace the original columns supporting the bronze figures of Victory each side of the altar.

The Condate amphitheatre, in which the Lyon martyrs of 177 suffered, was excavated in the 1950s and '60s and is now conserved and on display. One of the three slabs of its monumental dedication slab was found in 1958 (I.L.T.G. 217). Dating from AD 19, it records the building of the amphitheatre under the Emperor Tiberius at the cost of Caius Julius Rufus, Priest of Rome and Augustus, and a native, as he records on the inscription, of Saintes (*'ex Civitat(e) Santon(ensis)'*), where he also built the still surviving triumphal arch dedicated to Tiberius and other members of the Imperial family. The amphitheatre, originally measuring 78 x 54m, was enlarged under Hadrian to a size of 124 x 104m.

Fishwick, 'The temple of the Three Gauls', *J.R.S* 62 (1972), 46-52; Do., 'The development of provincial ruler worship in the western Roman Empire', *A.N.R.W.* II, 16. 2, 120-53; Audin and P. Quoinian, 'Victories et colonnes de l'autel fédéral des Trois Gaules', *Gallia* 20 (1962), 103-16.

## Potters Quarters

West of Condate at La Muette (angle of Quai de Serin and Rue de la Muette), excavation in 1965-6 revealed a potters' and glass makers' quarter, with 5 kilns producing Arretine ware, previously thought to be a wholly Italian product. There is nothing to see on site, but one of the kilns has been reconstructed in the Museum of Gallo-Roman Civilisation.

## The Lyon Aqueducts

The city was served by four aqueducts, with a total length of about 200km, bringing water from the hills W and N of the city. Their estimated capacity was 75,000m$^3$ of water a day. Because of the gradient, most of this was gravity fed, using underground channels only visible where cut by quarries or building works. In some places however, where the line crosses a valley, there are the masonry piers, and sometimes the arches, which carried the water channel — an aqueduct in the narrower sense of an above ground masonry structure. Sometimes, particularly on the Gier aqueduct, a syphon-bridge is used instead of an arched masonry structure. This consists of a collecting reservoir from which the flow is carried in multiple lead pipes through a syphon to a second reservoir. Details of the main visible features are given below. Fuller topographical details will be found in the *Guide Répertoire* (pp30-5) and in de Montauzan. For the W half of the Gier aqueduct see the département of Loire above. A full survey however would need a major field project.

1 *Mont D'Or Aqueduct* Rises at Poleymieux, 11km N of Fouvière, and loops around the Mont D'Or ridge before running south. Few visible remains.

2 *Craponne Aqueduct* From a source at Yzeron, in the hills 15km W of Lyon, follows the slopes of the Yzeron valley. NE of the village of Craponne are two piers ('Les Tourillons de Craponne') of an aqueduct-bridge.

3 *La Brévenne Aqueduct* The gift of the Emperor Claudius to his native city. Its source lies in an area near Aveize, 25km SW of Lyon, though its sinuous course means that its overall length is at least double that. At its source, some ponds and leats are visible and the earthworks can be traced along the contours NE towards Petit-St-Bonnet near St-Pierre-

la-Palud, where a masonry channel, the 'Canal des Sarrazins' is visible. From here, it curves round in a broad sweep to Ecully on the outskirts of Lyon where there are traces of an aqueduct bridge over the stream of des Planches (on private property). The aqueduct arrives in Lyon at les Massues (80, Rue des Aqueducts) where there are remains of a reservoir and a series of arches.

4 *Aqueduct of Gier* Hadrian's Gier aqueduct, 75km in length, begins at Izieux (Loire); for its course until the départemental boundary see above. It was the last of the four Lyon aqueducts, and the most ambitious, both in architectural and engineering terms, and makes an interesting comparison with Hadrian's equally ambitious project on Hadrian's Wall. It enters Rhône over a bridge of 4 arches across the Grand Bosançon river near Bissieux. From here, the line of its rock-cut underground channel can be traced running northwards along the sides of a valley towards *Didier-sous-Rivière*, where it crossed the petit Bosançon on a masonry aqueduct of reticulated masonry like that at Bissieux. One pier survives.

*Saint-Maurice-sur-Dargoire*

The aqueduct now runs NE towards Mornant, carried over a series of stream valleys by a sequence of 7 aqueduct bridges, increasing in size and complexity:

1 *la Billanière* Single arch bridge over stream, 4m high, 12m long.

2 *la Combe Jurieux* Well preserved three arch bridge, 4.5m high, 20m long.

3 *Grange* Five arches in reticulated masonry, 8m high, of which 3 remain intact.

4 *Fondagny* Slight traces of aqueduct bridge at hamlet of la Grimodière. The series of aqueduct bridges continues through Mornant towards Saint-Laurent d'Agny.

5 *Pont du Corsennat* Fragments remain of a once spectacular 44m bridge of 8 arches. Two piers survive.

6 *Pont de la Chavanne* at la Condamine. On a similar scale to the last. Four piers and the central arch remain.

7 *Pont de Mornant* Remains of 4 piers and central arch of a 15m high bridge.

*Orliénas*

6km NE of Mornant, the aqueduct was carried over the Merdansant on a 45m bridge, of which 3 piers remain. Further on, at the hamlet of Violon, its channel is revetted by a wall of reticulated masonry.

*Soucieu-en-Jarez*

The final remains of the aqueduct — and something of a grand finale — are to be found at the end of the Rue Roger-Radison in Fouvière, 400m down the street from the Museum of Gallo-Roman Civilization. The impressive remains show well both the reticulated masonry of Hadrian's aqueduct, and the use of alternate voussoirs of brick and stone in its arches.

C. de Montauzan, *Les Aqueducs de Lyon* (Paris 1909).

## Churches and Cemeteries — Christian Lyon

Lyon had the earliest recorded Christian community in the west outside Italy. That distinction is a melancholy one, for it rests on a letter sent by the survivors of that community back home to Asia Minor and Phrygia after a bloody pogrom in which many of its members suffered torture and death in the amphitheatre of the Three Gauls, whose remains can still be seen and visited (see above). The date was probably August AD 177. A group of Christians under their bishop Pothinus were dragged into the forum, and after interrogation were remanded in custody to await the Governor on his assize circuit. Pothinus, an elderly man, and others, died in prison. The subsequent martyrdom of the remainder, during the annual meeting of the *Concilium Galliarum*, still makes ugly reading. The martyrs included at least two immigrants from Asia Minor — Attalus from Pergamum and Alexander, a doctor, from Phrygia. They also included a deacon from Vienne and a slave woman named Blandina and her mistress. Their bodies were burnt and thrown into the Rhône, perhaps to prevent a martyr cult.

## Fouvière — St Irénée and St Just

The priest Irenaeus (St Irénée) became bishop after the death of Pothinus, and ministered in the area for many years. By the sixth century, his body lay in the church of St Jean, later renamed St Irénée, between the martyrs Epipodius and Alexander. This was in the area of the Roman cemetery SW of Fouvière. Another bishop, Justus, retired to live as a hermit in the Egyptian desert about 381. After his death, his body was brought back to Lyon and buried in a small mausoleum 300m E of St Irénée. This developed into the church of St Just. Christian cemeteries grew up around both churches, the earliest datable Christian tombstone from St Irénée (and indeed from Gaul) dating from AD 334, in the lifetime of Constantine the Great.

The two churches were destroyed by the Protestants in 1562. That of St Irénée, in the Rue des Macchabées, was rebuilt in 1824 on the lines of the original foundations. Below is a vaulted crypt with a polygonal apse. This went through a number of phases in Carolingian and later times (the present columns and arches date only from 1863). It originally comprised a semicircular apse, the burial place of St Irénée and the two martyrs, with a rectangular structure to the west, like the fifth-century arrangement at St Pierre in Vienne.

The church of St Just was moved to a fresh site after the destruction, and the original site was excavated by J.-F. Reynaud in 1971-83. Five successive churches were uncovered. Saint-Just I comprised a small square mausoleum with eastern apse, the original burial place of bishop Justus, NE of a large aisled basilica with eastern apse. This was the church where Sidonius Apollinaris described the feast of St Just which he attended on an October night in the 460s. A procession formed up in the evening light and made its way to the church 'a vast crowd which even that great church with all its galleries could not hold'. After the service of Vigils, chanted alternately by monks and priests, the crowd dispersed to await the coming of the bishop and the main Mass. Sidonius and his aristocratic friends sat around the mausoleum of the praetorian prefect Syagrius, set in its own little park near the church, playing board games or ball, until word came that the bishop was on his way to the church.

Little of the plan of this church could be recovered, since it was overlain by its successor, Saint-Just II, of early sixth-century date (the latest sealed coin prior to the rebuilding was of AD 506-10). This had an aisled nave, a long transept-like crossing with crypts or *confessios* in its end compartments and a polygonal eastern apse. Its planning can be matched in fifth-century churches in north Italy and Rome. There was also a W narthex and a series of porticoes around the nave which would have increased the area available for burials. St Just III was Carolingian.

## The Cathedral Complex

Below Fouvière, on the banks of the Saône, was the cathedral complex. There were three churches, the cathedral of St Jean on the S, the baptistery of St

Etienne (Stephen) in the centre and the church of Sainte-Croix (Holy Cross) to the N. This arrangement can be matched in the late Roman cathedral complexes at Trier and Geneva, and at Sulpicius Severus's villa of Primuliacum. The cathedral is still standing, in a later form, and St Etienne and the eastern parts of Sainte-Croix have been excavated and laid out in an attractive 'Jardin archéologique' N of the cathedral. A poem of Sidonius Apollinaris describes the cathedral built by bishop Patiens between 449-69. Above the pillars of its aisled nave was a gilded ceiling of coffered wood, whilst the light from the green glass windows played on the polychrome marble floor. Outside, probably to the W, was a courtyard or cloister, with rows of columns of Aquitanian marble. 'On one side' wrote Sidonius, 'is the noisy road, on the other the river'. Only its E apse can now be seen, below the crossing of the present cathedral begun in 1170-80.

The other two churches were destroyed at the French Revolution. The Baptistery of St Etienne was originally square, with an E apse and a central octagonal baptismal pool. By the ninth century, this had been replaced by a cruciform structure with three eastern apses. Demolished in 1792, its remains are on view with the baptismal pool covered by a glass and steel cover. The apse and two eastern bays of Sainte-Croix are also visible, and one arch of the nave arcade has been reconstructed to give an idea of scale. The existing remains represent the fifteenth-century rebuilding of a Romanesque church, and though remains on its site go back to the fourth century, these probably did not belong to a church.

*St Laurent de Choulans*

At the end of the Quai Fulchiron below Fouvière, the A7 Autoroute crosses the Saône. Next to the bridge, below a flyover, are the excavated remains of a funerary basilica with aisled nave, surrounding porticoes and E apse. The earliest dated tombstone is of AD 599.

J.-F. Reynaud 1986, *Lyon aux premiers temps Chrétiens* (G.A.F.).

**Anse** Castellum

M73 10 ICG43 C10

In the valley of the Saône north of Lyon, a late Roman *castellum* is built into the houses of the village. Of 15 circular towers, 13 survive, enclosing an oval area 100 x 150m in the area of Place des Frères Fournet. There are traces of two gates, but the date and context of the work are unknown.

*Gallia* 40 (1982), 410-11.

**Courzieu —
Camp de Châtelard** Hillfort

M93 11 IGN43 D9

Fort with drystone ramparts, occupied from early La Tène to Gallo-Roman times. There is a similar hillfort at the Crêt des Fayes at Duerne.

*Guide-Répertoire.*

## SAÔNE-ET-LOIRE

The territory of the Aedui extended over Saône et Loire, Nièvre and southern Côte d'Or, as well as into the fringes of Yonne and Allier. Their great oppidum at Mont Beuvray (Bibracte), where Vercingetorix summoned a meeting of the Gaulish tribes to coordinate resistance to Caesar, was replaced as local capital by Augustodunum ('Fort Augustus') at Autun.

**Autun** (Augustodunum)

M69 7 IGN36 B10

The Augustan walls of Autun enclosed 200ha. The wall, 2.5m thick, had 54 semicircular towers and four gates, and impressive remains still exist. The Porte St-Andre on the E and the Porte d'Arroux on the N are monumental gates with two large vehicular arches

37  *Autun (Saône-et-Loire), Porte Saint-André (upper) and Porte d'Arroux in the nineteenth century. Blanchet pl. XX, 1-2*

flanked by two smaller ones for foot traffic. Above is a gallery with arcades of tall slender arches flanked by Ionic pilasters, with a moulded cornice above. Architecturally impressive and elegantly proportioned, they were intended to impress visitors rather than defend against attack. The Porte-St-Andre, restored by Viollet le Duc in 1844-9, is particularly complete, with a pair of flanking D-shaped towers. The Porte du Rome, on the S, was demolished several centuries ago. A later wall containing reused material, cutting off 10ha of a projecting salient of the walls at their SW corner, may be late Roman, but is not closely dated.

As at Arles and elsewhere, the theatre and amphitheatre were within the walls, near their SE angle. The amphitheatre is known only from a drawing of 1610, being demolished soon after, but there are considerable remains of the theatre, the largest in Gaul.

N of the town, alongside the Roman road to Autun, was the early Christian cemetery of St Pierre l'Estrier (*de strata via* — 'on the Roman road'). It has produced Christian inscriptions of the third and fourth centuries (the former in Greek) and excavation around the disused church (now a barn) showed how this developed from two late Roman mausolea into a fifth-century church.

A. Rebourg, 'L'Urbanisme d'Augustodunum (Autun, Saône-et-Loire)', *Gallia* 55 (1998), 141-236; M. Pinette and A. Rebourg, *Autun: Ville gallo-romaine* (G.A.F.).

A. Rebourg and A. Olivier, 'Le théâtre antique d'Autun: Nouvelles observations et restitution', *R.A.E.* 42 (1991), 125-52; C. Sapin, 'L'ancienne église de Saint-Pierre à Estrier à Autun', *Archéologie Médiévale* 12 (1982), 50-105.

## Chalons-sur-Saône (Cabillonum)
M69 9 IGN37 C3

Although the *Notitia Galliarum* lists Chalons as a mere *castrum*, other sources call it a civitas. It was important for pre-Roman trade, and wine amphorae, shipped up river by Roman merchants, were decanted into barrels or other containers here for transmission onwards into 'Celtic' Gaul. The empties were dumped in the river and some 24,000 have been dredged from its bed.

The late Roman walls enclose a semicircular area backing on to the Saône, rather like those of Toulouse. There were 18 circular towers on its landward circuit, none on the river wall, which, as at Toulouse and London, could be secondary. The best preserved section is in the garden of the Hotel Montcoy. A foundation of large blocks of white limestone from the quarries around Givry and Villar W of the city supports a wall of small coursed blocks with tile levelling courses. The main gate, the Porte de Beaune, at the apex of the walls, was directly opposite the bridge, and Chalons could have been a fortified bridgehead protecting the river crossing and the road leading from it. Eighteenth-century references to a *Clos Rond* and a sculpture of a gladiator suggest an amphitheatre.

Grenier III, 647; A. Tchernia, 'Italian wine in Gaul at the end of the Republic' in *Trade in the Ancient Economy* ed. P. Garnsey, K. Hopkins and C.R. Whittaker (London 1983), 87-104; Blanchet 24-7.

## Mâcon (Castrum Matisconense)
M69 19 IGN44 A/B1

Though already famous in the sixth century for its wines (Gregory of Tours could think of no higher praise for those of Dijon than that they bore comparison with a good Mâcon), Mâcon was neither a civitas capital or a bishopric. It is assumed to have been fortified, in view of the name and since it housed a state armaments factory for arrows, but no trace of any late walls has been found.

The Musée municipal des Ursulines (5, Rue des Ursulines), in a former nunnery, has rich Gallo-Roman collections, plus material from the rock of Solutré outside Mâcon, type site of the Palaeolithic Solutrean culture. A huge collection of horse bones found in 1866 at the foot of this spectacular isolated rock marked the place where herds of wild horses were rounded up and slaughtered on their spring migration. The rock (IGN43 B10) is near the D54, SW of Macon, beyond the village of Solutré. There is another museum at its foot.

## Mont Beuvray (Bibracte)
M69 6 IGN36 B8

This great Gaulish oppidum W of Autun, on the border of Saône-et-Loire and Nièvre, is one of the best-known sites of French archaeology. Identified as Caesar's Bibracte by J.G. Bulliot, a wine merchant with a classical education, he dug here with his nephew Joseph Déchelette in 1865-1907. Déchelette was killed in the First World War. New excavations began in 1984, involving a major reassessment of all aspects of the site. Capital of the Aedui, it was founded late in the second century BC and occupied to Augustan times. A massive rampart twists around the contours of the hill, enclosing an irregular area of some 135ha within a *murus gallicus* of drystone construction with an elaborate nailed timber framework. A second line of defences was recognised outside the first in 1986, increasing the size to nearly 200ha. The relationship of the two is unknown, but recent excavation has revealed five successive periods of rampart, starting with Neolithic defences, followed by a rampart from early in the Iron Age, preceding the

*murus gallicus*, which itself is of two phases, and ending with a massive earth 'dump' rampart. The Bibracte *murus gallicus* was, with Murcens (Lot), one of the first to be identified. Déchelette estimated that the 2km of rampart would require 13,500m$^3$ of wood and 11,200kg of iron. With the newly discovered ramparts, these figures have to be upgraded to around 40,000m$^3$ of wood.

Bibracte was 'by far the largest and richest town of the Aedui', and the finds from the site, including a prodigious number of imported Italian wine amphorae (Dressel 1) confirm Caesar's description. In 52 BC Vercingetorix called a general assembly of the Gallic tribes here to coordinate resistance to Caesar and was made commander in chief. In Augustan times, the capital moved to the new city of Augustodunum (Autun), but occupation continued at Bibracte, the site ranking as a vicus. There are Gallo-Roman buildings of first- to third-century date. The Chapel of St Martin within the S defences has a remarkable history. Beginning as a Romano-Celtic temple, the ambulatory was later demolished and a small square annexe added to the east, evidently as the nave and chancel of a seventh- or eighth-century church. An E apse was added in the tenth century, but by the thirteenth it had become a simple rectangular chapel connected with a Franciscan Friary to the north. A seventeenth-century oratory now marks the site. There is an excellent site museum and a partial reconstruction of the *murus gallicus* timber and dry-stone defences on the NE. Outside, a cemetery of graves set in square enclosures has been excavated.

Cotton 1957, 190-5; *Gallia* 55 (1998), 1-140, special 'Dossier' on Bibracte; C. Goudineau and C. Peyre, *Bibracte et les Eduens: A la découverte d'un peuple Gaulois;*

D. Bertin and J.-P. Guillaumet, *Bibracte: une ville Gauloise sur le Mont Beuvray* (G.A.F.).

# YONNE
## Auxerre (Autessiodurum)
M66 5 IGN28 A3

Even in the nineteenth century, there was little to see of the late Roman walls here, which had been rebuilt in medieval times. Like Meaux, they enclosed a long irregular rectangle, its short E face fronting the river, suggesting ribbon development along an E-W road.
Blanchet 68-70.

## Escolives-St-Camille (Scoliva)
M65 5 IGN28 B4

In the Yonne valley S of Auxerre are the covered remains of a large Roman villa and baths, which, like many in the region, has a Merovingian cemetery of over 200 graves cut into its ruins, some with sixth-/seventh-century buckles. The Romanesque church 200m E contained the relics of the fifth-century female saint Camille, a disciple of Germanus of Auxerre. Possibly the cemetery grew up around the grave of the saint, who may have been buried in a late Roman villa chapel. The site is on the N edge of the village, in the Rue Raymond-Kapps.

## Fontaines-Salées Rural sanctuary
M65 16 IGN28 C5

The salt springs here have been used since Hallstatt times, when wooden water pipes of hollowed tree trunks were used to extract brine. The Roman precinct around the sacred spring, excavated from 1934 on, included a first-century bath building and temple and a paved pool around the spring, enclosed within a large circular ambulatory. The bath building was enlarged in the second century, making a double baths, perhaps for segregated bathing (a decree of Hadrian had forbidden mixed bathing).

This partly overlay the demolished circular ambulatory. The site was destroyed in the late third or early fourth century. Though coins continued to be deposited in the sacred pool until the late fourth, these probably represent folk offerings on a deserted, but still 'magic' site. The finds, including the water pipes, are in the Regional Archaeological Museum at St Père, which also includes a collection of other local Roman and Merovingian material.
R. Louis, 'Les thermes gallo-romains des Fontaines-Salées à saint-Pere-sous-Vézelay', R.A. 6th series 11 (1938), 233-318; Do., 'Les fouilles des Fontaines-Salées en 1942: les thermes, le temple de source et les puits à cuvelage de bois', *Gallia* 1, 2 (1944), 27-70; B. Lacroix, 'Un sanctuaire de l'eau de plan circulaire aux Fontaines-Salées', R.A.E. 14 (1963), 81-114.

## Jaulges-Villiers-Vineux
Pottery kilns M65 6 IGN28 A5

In the second and early third century, potters here were producing samian ware, but after the end of samian production, they switched to a distinctive pottery with painted decoration, which in the fourth century was distributed over most of Burgundy W of the Seine. In the thirteenth century, a tile industry was established on the same site, which lasted into modern times.
J.P. Jacob and H. Leredde, 'Les potiers des Jaulges-Villiers-Vineux: Etude d'un centre de production gallo-romain', *Gallia* 43, 1 (1985), 167-92.

## Sens (Agedincum)
M61 14 IGN21 G/H4

Until the 1830s, the late Roman walls of Sens were virtually intact, surrounding the centre of the city in an oval of walls some 600 x 300m in the angle between the Yonne and its tributary the Vanne. They were then largely demolished to make way for the ring of boulevards around the town centre, whose inner sides now mark their line. There are however some worthwhile pieces remaining to show what was lost. The walls were of the usual construction, massive blocks of stone below, with neatly coursed small square blocks above, and brick levelling courses at regular intervals. There were 23 semicircular projecting towers along the perimeter, with a good surviving example at 49-51 Boulevard du Quatorze Juillet (the inverted keyhole opening in the flank is a much later gunport). The amphitheatre lay outside the walls to the E.

One consolation for their loss is the collection of 500 sculptures and inscriptions from the wall foundations. Many are now on display in the museum in the former archbishop's palace (on the site of a set of fourth-century public baths). Grave monuments show the craftsmen of the Roman town at work: an interior decorator painting and plastering a wall; a fuller standing in his tub; a cobbler; a cloth-worker with a large pair of shears knapping cloth set in a movable frame with peg holes; and a smith with an anvil and hammer. The facade of the public baths was also dismantled and reused in the wall foundations. It has now been reconstructed in the museum. The cathedral nearby was the first of the great Gothic cathedrals of France (1130-68), and the model on which the architect William of Sens based his rebuilding of the Choir of Canterbury cathedral in 1175-92.

C. Roach Smith, *Collectanea Antiqua* V, 1857-1861, 172; Blanchet 61-6; L. Saulnier-Pernuit et al, *La Façade des Thermes de Sens* (7th supplement to R.A.E. 1987).

# 11 The Lower Rhône
## (Viennensis, Narbonensis II)

Under Diocletian, Gallia Narbonensis was divided in two. The main part of the old province, with its capital at Narbonne, became Narbonensis Prima, whilst an area E of the Rhône with a capital at Aix-en-Provence became Narbonensis Secunda. The lower Rhône valley itself became a corridor giving the province of Viennensis direct access to the sea around Arles and Marseilles. The seven cities of Narbonensis II are spread over six present day départements, and correspond neither to modern boundaries nor to the likely itinerary of the traveller. Briefly, they comprise the coastal cities of Antibes (Alpes-Maritimae) and Fréjus (Var); Aix-en-Provence (Bouches du Rhône); the inland cities of Apt (Vaucluse) and Riez (Alpes-Maritmae); and Gap (Hautes-Alpes) and Sisteron (Basses-Alpes) in the Durance valley.

## ARDÈCHE

The Ardèche, an area of wooded and hilly country west of the Rhône below Vienne, lay in the territories of three Gallo-Roman tribes within the province of Viennensis — the Allobriges of Vienne in the north, the Segovellauni of Valence in the centre, and the Helvii of Alba in the south. Only Alba is within its present boundaries.

A. Blanc, *Carte Archéologique de la Gaule Romaine* 15 1975.

### Alba-la-Romaine

(Alba Helviorum, once Aps)
M80 9 IGN59 A8
This little town NW of Viviers, once capital of the Helvii, has been the site of extensive excavations. The Roman theatre, consolidated and on display, forms a good central reference point. Augustan in date, it was remodelled in AD 30-45 and again in Antonine times. One unusual feature is a brook, the Ruisseau St Martin, channelled between the orchestra and proscenium. Around the theatre, the grid plan of the town has been recovered. SE were second- and third-century houses with good mosaics. NW of the theatre lies a temple complex known as 'Le Palais', with shops fronting the road. The forum was S of Le Palais, between it and the theatre.

There are two important outlying sites. 800m NE of the theatre is the suburban villa of la Plaine, whilst 450m to its W is the Roman and early Christian site of St Pierre. The fifth-/sixth-century complex, with a small basilica church surrounded by sarcophagi and tile tombs, overlies a large Severan building of official character. Frequently in Gaul, a large building, often the house of a local magnate, was given to the Church as the site for a cathedral, and this may be another. St Pierre may be an early cathedral, before the removal of the see to Viviers in 517-35. Later it was a medieval priory. There is a museum in the village (open 2-6 pm), which is also the excavation centre, with mosaics and a model of the theatre.

Laurexois et al, *Alba* (G.A.F.); Yves Esquieu and Roger Lauxerois, 'La nécropole de St Pierre à Alba (Ardèche)', *Archéologie Médiévale* 5 (1975), 1-44.

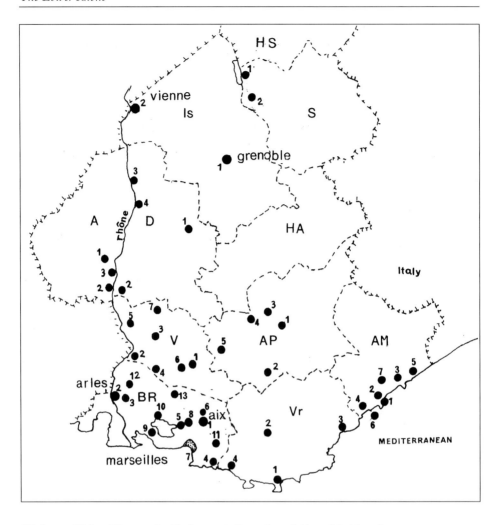

38  Lower Rhône (Viennensis, Narbonensis Secunda and Alpes-Maritimae)

   **A** Ardèche *1 Alba-la-Romaine 2 Bourg St Andreol 3 Viviers*

   **BA** Basses-Alpes*1 Sisteron*

   **BR** Bouches du Rhône *1 Aix-en-Provence 2 Arles 3 Barbegal 4 Ceyreste 5 Constantine*
   *6 Entremont 7 Marseille 8 Roquepertuse 9 St Blaise 10 St Chamas 11 St Jean de Garguier*
   *12 St Rémy-de-Provence. Glanum 13 Vernegues*

   **D** Drôme *1 Die 2 St Paul-Trois-Châteaux 3 Tain l'Hermitage 4 Valence*

   **HA** Haute-Alpes

   **Is** Isère *1 Grenoble 2 Vienne*

   **V** Vaucluse *1 Apt 2 Avignon 3 Carpentras 4 Cavaillon 5 Orange 6 Pont Julien 7 Voison-la-Romaine*
   *(for remaining département see chapter 13)*

## Bourg-St-Andreol

Shrine of Mithras M80 10 IGN59 B8-9

Signposted from the town centre, a relief of Mithras slaying the bull is cut in a niche on the rock face in a small valley. Grooves above suggest a small temple in front of this, but an adjacent cave, perhaps used for rituals, was destroyed by a railway viaduct. A largely illegible inscription may refer to a community of Greek traders.

Bromwich 1993, 21-3.

### Viviers Roman bridge
M80 10 IGN59 B9

The stream valleys running down to the Rhône from the hilly country to the W had to be crossed by Roman road builders with masonry bridges. One over the river Escoutay, with 9 semicircular arches, is on the D107 road N of Viviers. There are remains of single arch bridges at St Fortunat-sur-Eyrieux and Le Pouzin further north.

Bromwich 1993, 43-5.

## ALPES DE HAUTE PROVENCE

Whilst most of the département was in the Roman province of Alpes-Maritimae, Sisteron in the Durance valley was in Narbonensis Secunda, and is therefore included here.

### Sisteron (Segustero)
M81 6 IGN60 B8

Though impressive on its hill above the Durance, little is known of Sisteron's Roman past, though a few buildings and finds are known from excavation. Nothing is visible.

Rivet (1988) 294-5.

## BOUCHES DU RHÔNE

Any départment containing within its boundaries three such unique and diverse cities as Aix, Arles and Marseilles has to be somewhere special. Apart from these, the whole area is archaeologically very rich, with sites like Entremont, Roquepertuse, Glanum, St Blaise, and the Roman water mill complex at Barbegal outside Arles.

*Carte Archéologique de la Gaule Romaine* V (1936).

### Aix-en-Provence (Aquae Sextius)
M84 3 IGN67 G2

The 'Waters of Sextius' owe their name to the general C. Sextius Calvinus. He founded a fort here, near some warm springs, in 122 BC after defeating the Saluvii, whose oppidum, Entremont, is only 2.5km away. This elegant city, whose delights include the broad Cours Mirabeau, with its huge plane trees, and many cafes and bookshops, and Cézanne's studio in the Rue Boulegon (now owned by the University of Aix-en-Provence), has few visible remains of its Roman past. However, excavation early this century under the Palais de Justice found the SE gate, of typical Augustan type, with two round towers flanking a recessed semicircular space, as at Arles or Fréjus. The peristyle of one early Roman house has been laid out as a garden in the Avenue Grassi, and recent excavations elsewhere found a large and well-appointed house of 25-1 BC, which in the second century was equipped with wall paintings and mosaics, with scenes from the Aeniad and roundels with various birds. Coins from the destruction levels suggest that by the end of the century both this and an equally grand house next door had been demolished.

In late Roman times, Aix was the capital of Narbonensis Secunda, and excavation has recovered a remarkable story. Towards the end of the fifth century, the civic basilica was converted into a cathedral, where the bishop and his clergy would have sat enthroned in the apse, just as earlier the city's magistrates would have sat in the basilica. The forum in front of this (the present Place des Martyrs de la Resistance) became a large piazza, with the cathedral at one end, dominated by the new baptistery. Here, crowds from all over the civitas territory would gather on the great feasts of the Church, particularly those at which baptism was administered. The authority of the Church had replaced that of the city magistrates. The baptistery which formed the focus of the piazza can be seen inside the cathedral. A ring of eight tall Corinthian columns of green marble and of granite, reused from some earlier building, surround the central baptismal pool. The stucco decoration above is eighteenth-century, but adds a touch of lightness to an otherwise solemn structure.

The Musée Granet (Place-St-Jean-de-Malte) houses the sculptures of Celtic warriors and horsemen, severed heads and stelae with niches for human skulls from Entremont.

R. Ambard, *Aix Romaine* (Aix 1985); new excavations — *Gallia Informations* 1990, 131-5; inscriptions — *I.L.N.* vol III, ed. J Gascou 1995.

# Arles

(Colonia Julia Paterna Arelate Sextanorum)

M83 10 IGN66 C8

Arles really deserves a chapter to itself. The Greek settlement of Theline, going back to the sixth century BC was possibly a Massiliot trading outpost above the Rhône delta. Initially, the sandy delta made access for large ships difficult, until the Roman general Marius cut his canal, the *Fossa Marianae*, in 102 BC linking it to the sea. A Roman colony was founded here by one of Caesar's generals, Tiberius Claudius Nero, in 46 BC for veterans of the Sixth Legion (hence *Sextanorum* 'of the Sixth'). Thereafter it became an important sea

port, and inscriptions mention carpenters, shipbuilders, a naval architect, sea captains and river boatmen.

The *Augustan City Walls* were rebuilt in late Roman times, in the twelfth century and again in the Hundred Years War, and these later alterations can be confusing. Wheeler showed that the E Gate (La Redoute) and SE tower (Tour des Mourges) were additions, though probably still Augustan. The walls enclosed an irregular area around the low hill on which the city stood. The only visible section is that on the E, between the Tour des Mourges and the church of Notre Dame de la Major, where their line angled sharply W, to pass under the N edge of the later amphitheatre. La Redoute is a typical Augustan gate, with a semicircular court inset into the rampart, flanked by round towers, and with a twin-towered gateway at its centre. The channel by which the aqueduct entered the city can be seen in its threshold. A change in angle under the edge of the amphitheatre suggests another gate here, perhaps lining up on a now vanished triumphal arch which stood near the present Place Voltaire.

The Forum with its cryptoporticus is also Augustan, as is probably the theatre. Outside the limited space afforded by the walls, suburbs rapidly sprang up to the S, as on the Esplanade site off the Boulevard des Lices, where some of the excavated structures are on show; on the riverside area of La Roquette, between the modern Expressway and Trinquetaille bridges and in the cross-river suburb of Trinquetaille, which recalls the similar suburb of St Romain en Gal at Vienne. In the late first century, the city acquired an amphitheatre and circus. Fitting these two massive structures into the existing townscape caused problems. The amphitheatre was squeezed in next to the existing theatre, the two forming an impressive pair. On its N it was necessary to breach the Augustan walls and probably demolish a gateway. On the S, the aqueduct channel can be seen curving around the outside of the amphitheatre on its way from La Redoute to a *castellum* or distribution point, like that at Nîmes, W of the amphitheatre, which was visible in the seventeenth century. The channel in its existing form must be post-Flavian, since it is later than the amphitheatre, but an earlier straight alignment might have been altered when the amphitheatre was built. The circus took up much more room, and needed a clear flat area. It was therefore built parallel to the river W of the city, beyond the La Roquette suburbs. The marshy ground required solid foundations of masonry and oak logs, which should offer the chance of a dendrochronological date for the structure.

Under the late Empire, Arles became an Imperial capital. Constantine held a Church council here in 314, attended by bishops from Gaul, Spain, Italy and Britain and the city acquired a mint, an arms factory, and military workshops. There was presumably an Imperial palace around the area of the Constantinian baths and Place de Forum. At some date, the Augustan city walls were rebuilt on a differing alignment. Part of these late walls can be seen between the S end of the theatre and the Tour des Mourges. The wealth of the late city is shown by its collection of sculptured marble sarcophagi of high quality — the largest such collection outside Rome.

## The Forum Complex and Cryptoporticus

Much of the central area of the Roman city, between the Place du Forum and the Place de la République, was occupied by the Augustan forum complex, presumably comprising a civic basilica, the forum itself and a large temple, probably for the Imperial cult. The huge three-sided underground cryptoporticus is its most impressive surviving feature. Above ground, the Place du Forum takes its name from part of a later monumental entry to the N range of the forum, which survives built into the buildings of a hotel.

The cryptoporticus consists of three ranges, a fraction under 90 x 60m overall. Rows of solid piers down the centre support the vault. There has been much discussion about the purpose of such cryptoportici, but the present one was originally an architectural feature, to level up the sloping ground for the forum and temple precinct. Once the space was created, it could no doubt be put to various uses. In Rome, the cellarage of Aurelian's Temple of the Sun was large enough to store the supplies of free wine for the populace of the city. In the N range, the foundations of the monumental entry seen in the Place du Forum can be seen. This, probably of the time of Constantine II in the fourth century, consisted of a portico and range of shops, rather like a section of a Spanish *Plaza Mayor*, with a monumental central entry and stair. In the surviving part, two columns support part of a richly decorated architrave and pediment. The Egyptian granite obelisk in the Place de la République to the S is not part of the forum complex. Originally on the site of the Circus at La Roquette, it was moved here in 1675 in honour of Louis XIV.

Flanking the W side of the Forum was a long rectangular paved courtyard with an exedra (apse) on its S. This can be seen in the gardens of the Museon Arleten. There was probably a matching apse on the N, and the whole may be the entrance of an early second-century temple enclosure. The public baths lay S

*39  Arles (Bouches-du-Rhône) — Roman theatre. Copyright Chris Dunn*

of the Forum. Whether they were replaced by the Constantinian baths, or whether the latter served only the Imperial palace, is uncertain.

## The Theatre and Amphitheatre

In the sixteenth century, many French cities had ruins of their theatre and amphitheatre. Most were demolished in post-medieval times. Those at Arles owe their survival to their transformation into medieval fortifications. Three of the four medieval towers which rose above the amphitheatre can still be seen, as can the tall rectangular 'Tower of Roland' at one end of the theatre, which preserves the three-storied elevation of the original building. The theatre is the earlier of the two. With room for 10,000 spectators, it occupies an area within the street grid probably reserved for it at the foundation of the colony. A statue of Augustus stood in a central niche, and an altar of Apollo, a favourite god of

Augustus, was wreathed in laurels and oaks, perhaps in celebration of his victory at Actium. Though the theatre was restored by J. Formigé around 1900, and partly reconstructed, some of the seating is original, as is the orchestra floor of pink and green marble. Two columns survive of the many that once adorned the *frons scenae*.

The amphitheatres at Arles and Nîmes are so similar that Grenier thought them the work of the same architect. Externally, they consist of two superimposed ranges of 60 high circular arches, separated by a boldly moulded cornice, with a similar attic cornice (now missing at Arles) above. Between the arches are flat rectangular pilasters at ground level, with attached Corinthian columns above. The ground floor arcade gives entry to a circular access gallery around the perimeter of the arena. Though the exact date is uncertain, the

*40  Arles (Bouches-du-Rhône) — Roman amphitheatre. Copyright Chris Dunn*

building is probably Flavian, when the building of the Roman Colosseum created a fashion for such monumental structures. Inside there is room for 21,000 spectators. A high podium wall separates the arena and the spectators. It still retains parts of its marble veneer, and the inscription of a wealthy local magnate, C. Junius Priscus, records how he paid for the podium, a gilt statue of Neptune, four bronze statues and two days of games and feasting.

## The Circus

The site at la Roquette, was marked until 1675 by the obelisk now in the Place de la République and was identified by J. Formigé in the 1900s. Parts were excavated in the 1970s and can be seen N of the canal basin and at the SW end next to the new *Archaeology Museum* (Musée de l'Arles Antique, Avenue Jean Monnet). It continued in use until the fifth century, Sidonius enjoying circus games here in 461 under Majorian (*Letters* I, 11). The museum has replaced the Musée Lapidaire Païen and the Musée Lapidaire Chrétienne in the centre of the city, of which many visitors will have fond memories. The former contained sculptures and inscriptions from the forum and theatre, and pagan sarcophagi. The latter housed the remarkable collection of sculptured Christian sarcophagi, mostly from Alyscamps. There is an excellent scholarly catalogue of these by F. Benoit.

## The Constantinian Baths

One of the Imperial bath complexes of late antiquity, its walls are of *opus mixtum*, 2-3 courses of masonry alternating with 2 of brickwork, and with large masonry blocks as sills supporting the weight of the window arches. What is visible is less than half of the complex. The great apse with its windows is part of the Caldarium or hot room, probably housing a hot bath. Another hot bath, and a couple of dry sweating rooms are just within the modern entrance. Part of the Tepidarium or warm room is beyond, but the Frigidarium, with its changing rooms and exercise hall, lies outside the excavated area.

## Alyscamps — The Champs Élysées

Alyscamps was a pagan and Christian cemetery on the Via Aurelia SE of the city, a huge field of funerary monuments, marble sarcophagi, many richly sculptured, and around a dozen chapels and funerary churches. Once nearly a mile in length, Alyscamps attracted the usual medieval legends — that it was, for example, the burial place of Charlemagne's soldiers, fallen at Roncevalles. It was known as *Les Champs Élysées* — the Elysian Fields, like the more famous one in Paris — Alyscamps being an Occitan form of this, with the two elements reversed. (Another explanation would derive it from the Alys, an aromatic plant that grew there.) There were once several thousand sarcophagi, but many were given to collectors or to visiting foreign dignitaries before the best of the remainder were removed to the Museum of Christian Art (there are more in the cathedral of St Trophime). The cemetery area has been cut to pieces by a road and canal, and by housing, and the surviving sarcophagi, mostly plain, have been collected together within one of the surviving areas — a unique place full of romantic melancholy, like so much in Arles, but a shadow of its former self.

The flat lands of the *Rhône Delta*, S of Arles, form a natural landscape of considerable interest. W of the Rhône is the Camargue, though anyone wishing to see its famous wildlife should apply in advance for admission to the Réserve Naturelle. Aigues Mortes to the W is one of the most imposing castles and walled towns of medieval Europe, and its setting on the edge of the marshes of the Camargue is particularly memorable. Founded by St Louis, who built the great circular keep, the Tour de Constance, soon after 1240, his son, Philip III, added the rest in 1272-1300. It is thus the exact contemporary of Carcassone, Harlech or Caerphilly. Unlike Carcassone it is intact but fairly unrestored, and has far fewer tourists.

E of the Rhône is the featureless Plaine de la Crau, between Arles and the inland lake of the Etang de Berre. There was extensive Roman occupation here, and air photography has revealed areas of centuriation, the grid-like land allotments for retired veterans of the sixth legion. Fos sur Mer to the S was the outlet of Marius's canal, the *Fossa Marianae* (IGN67 H1). When I first knew Fos, the beaches were littered with Roman pottery of every description — a natural open air teaching collection. Today, the whole area has disappeared under a complex of oil refineries and petrochemical plants, the largest in Europe. There is however an important collection of material from Fos in the museum at Istres, including a bronze ship's figurehead in the shape of a boar and an outstanding collection of amphorae.

L.A. Constans, *Arles Antique* (1921); R.E.M. Wheeler, *J.R.S.* 16 (1926), 174-93; Grenier III, 613-39 (Amphitheatre), 742-53 (Theatre); F. Benoit, *Sarcophages paléochretiens d'Arles et de Marseilles* (Paris 1954); R. Amy, 'Les cryptoportiques d'Arles' in *Les Cryptoportiques dans l'architecture romaine* (Collection de l'école française de Rome 14, 1973), 275-91; C.

41 Barbégal
(Bouches du
Rhône) —
Roman water
mill complex.
Copyright
Chris Dunn

Sintès, 'L'évolution topographique de l'Arles du Haut-Empire à la lumière des fouilles récentes', *J.R.A.* 5 (1992), 130-47; M. Heijmans and C. Sintès, 'L'évolution de la topographie de l'Arles antique', *Gallia* 50 (1993), 135-70 (full catalogue of all discoveries since publication of *Carte Archéologique de la Gaule Romaine* in 1936); M. Heijmans 1999, 'La topographie de la ville d'Arles devant l'Antiquité tardive', *J.R.A.* 12 (1990, 142-67; J.-M. Rouquette and C. Sintès, *Arles Antique* (G.A.F.); Rivet 1988, 190-96; Bromwich 1993, 138-52.

**Barbégal** Water mill complex
M83 10 IGN66 C9
When Arles became an Imperial capital at the end of the third century, the flood of soldiers, civil servants, mint workers and courtiers would have put huge

pressure on available food supplies. On the edge of the Alpilles NE of Arles, where two aqueducts meet, a huge flour mill complex was built, with two parallel rows of eight water mills sloping down the hillside, powered by 16 undershot water wheels, each 2m in diameter. The complex, excavated by Benoit in 1936-8, was, according to the most recent calculations, capable of grinding 2-3 tonnes of wheat a day. The wheels were set in stepped leats outside the mills, which would have been reached via a central staircase. The inspiration may have been the state corn mills on the Janiculum at Rome, also fed by two aqueducts, and used to grind corn for the daily free distribution of bread to the populace of Rome. The site is signposted from the D33b ('Meunerie Romain').

Benoit 1940, 'L'usine de meunerie hydrolique Barbégal', *Rev. Archéol* 15, 42-80; Bromwich 1993, 156-60; M. Bell, 'An Imperial flour mill on the Janiculum', *La ravitaillement en blé de Rome et des centres urbaines* (Actes du Colloque International de Naples 1991, Rome 1994) 73-89.

## Ceyreste (Citharista)
M84 14 IGN67 J3

The Roman small town near la Ciotat, and its neighbour St-Jean-de-Garguier 10km north, possessed Christian churches by AD 417, when they were the subject of a dispute between the bishops of Marseilles and Aix. This obscure quarrel is of wider interest since the dispute concerned the parishes — *parochiae* — of the two churches, the first use of this familiar word in something like its modern sense in Gaul. The two 'parishes' must have covered a substantial area between Marseilles and the present eastern boundary of Bouches-du-Rhône.

Knight 1999, 124, and references.

## Constantine
Iron Age and early medieval fort
M84 2 IGN67 C1

This small fortified site is reminiscent of its better known neighbour Sainte-Blaise. Like Ste-Blaise it stands near the Etang de Berre, in isolated limestone country south of the D10 near Calissane. A squarish area is protected by a dry stone rampart with 11 massive bastions on the N and NW, and by steep natural slopes elsewhere. Inside is a small Gallo-Roman shrine centred around a natural pothole, and 80m WNW an early Christian basilica.

J. Gouvest, *Ogam* 8 (1956), 51ff; Hogg (1969), 267-8 and 272.

## Entremont Oppidum
M84 3 IGN67 F2

The capital of the Ligurian tribe of the Saylii stands on a triangular rocky plateau in the N outskirts of Aix-en-Provence, protected on the SW and SE by cliffs and on the N by a defensive wall of stone rubble, faced with coursed stone blocks and strengthened with rectangular projecting towers with rounded external angles. The first phase of the town was the Ville Haute (Habitat 1), a rectangular area tucked into the S angle of the later town. Dating from about 190-170 BC, it had a defensive wall with towers like those on the outer wall, and a grid plan with rows of back-to-back terraced houses separated by cobbled streets. This might reflect the planning of Greek settlements like Olbia (Var). About 150-140 BC it was expanded to its present size ('Ville Basse' or Habitat 2). This had a less regular layout. Massiliot coins and amphorae, plus a few Italian Dressel 1 amphorae show Entremont's links with the outside world before it was destroyed by the Romans in 125 or 124 BC, though occupation may have lingered until around 90 BC.

Most of the sculptures of Celtic warriors and severed heads now in the Musée Granet at Aix were found smashed near Block XIII, a building with an external portico and carvings of a snake and of severed heads on its sill. Twenty human skulls were scattered in the portico and roadway, some with holes for nails or spikes. This shrine for the severed head cult was probably destroyed by the Romans when they captured the site.

F. Benoit 1968, 'Résultats historiques des fouilles d'Entremont 1946-7', *Gallia* 26, 1-31; Do. 1981, *Entremont: Capitale Celto-ligure des Salyens de Provence* (Gap); New excavations 1984-90 — *Gallia Informations* 1990, 127-31.

## Marseilles (Massilia)
M84 13 IGN67 I2

The centre of animation (as the old Blue Guide used to say) of Marseilles is the Vieux Port, a large natural harbour in the centre of the city, from which the Canebière, the main street of the city, runs up towards a large park. Recent excavations have shown that occupation around the Vieux Port goes back to the Middle Bronze Age, around 3400-3000 BC, long before the foundation of the Greek city of Massalia. This was a colony of Phocea near Smyrna in Asia Minor, and there had been Greek and Phoenician contacts along these coasts even before its foundation around 600 BC. Massalia was sited on a promontory N of the harbour of Lakydon, the present Vieux Port. There may have been a second harbour on the opposite flank of the promontory, at the bay of La Joliette, but the modern docks here have totally changed the topography. The city lay along a chain of three hills, St Laurent on the W, near the tip of the promontory, Les Moulins in the centre and Les Carmes to the east. N and E of Les Carmes, the city walls curved round

across the neck of the promontory from La Joliette to the 'horn' at the inner tip of Lacydon, where there have been extensive excavations at the Bourse (stock exchange) and where remains of the Greek and Roman city are on display next to the Museum of the History of Marseilles.

In the flank of the hill of St Laurent are remains of a Roman theatre, known locally as the 'Théâtre Grec', incorporated in the buildings of a modern school in the Rue des Martégales. A short distance to the E, at the Place Lenche, is the site of the Greek Agora or market. A series of vaulted cisterns or water reservoirs of the second century BC are known here, under the convent of St Sauveur. Below, towards the Vieux Port, is the Musée des Docks Romains. The present Vieux Port does not correspond exactly with the area of the ancient Lacydon. In particular, its all important north shore, where the quays of the ancient city lay, was some 50-100m inshore of its modern counterpart. Excavation in the Place Vivaux and Place Jules Verne has revealed extensive remains of the Roman dockside, and half of a warehouse, which have been incorporated in a museum on the ground floor of an office block in the Place Vivaux. This includes a reconstruction of the Roman quays, a series of 33 massive storage jars (*pithoi* or *dolia*) in situ (more have been found recently under the Place Jules Verne), part of a merchant ship reused in the quay structure, and a display of amphorae and other items of maritime archaeology, including exhibits on several excavated shipwrecks from the bay.

More remains of the Greek and Roman city are to be found on the Bourse site, which lay just outside the SE city gate. This has been laid out as an archaeological park, the 'Jardin des Vestiges' with an adjacent museum, in the Rue Henri Barbusse, on the N side of the Canebière, just before the Vieux Port. The 'horn' of the harbour, which formed the tip of Lacydon, has been grassed over as an expanse of lawn. Its stone revetment wall, with flights of steps originally leading down to the boats, dates from the time of Vespasian. To the E, next to the museum, is a rectangular masonry tank of the early second century AD, filled from a nearby spring, which may have served to supply fresh water to ships in harbour. On the opposite (W) side of the harbour are the remains of the Greek city wall of the second century BC, the so-called 'Wall of Crinas'. Crinas was a wealthy Massiliot doctor of the time of Nero, alleged to have financed the building of the town walls, which are actually 200 years earlier.

The wall, of large rectangular ashlar blocks from the quarries at La Couronne, is impressive, but anyone used to later city walls or castles will be surprised by the way in which it zigzags across the site. The aim was to break up the wall face into short stretches, all flanked at short range by the adjoining length. This technique is found in other ancient Greek cities, but does not seem to have caught on in the west, since it presents a series of vulnerable right angles to any determined attacker with siege engines. Midway along the preserved section is the City Gate. This comprised two square towers flanking an entrance, with a paved roadway of large neatly-fitted stone slabs like crazy paving. The gate, with two archways, is set back, so that the space between the towers forms a recessed rectangular courtyard in which attackers could be trapped. The S tower of the gate, the Tour Penchée, has (a rare survival) two

loops or arrowslits facing outwards. There is another pair in the S Tower a little further on. In front of this southern stretch is a fifth-century AD Roman outer wall ('Avant-Mur'), a crude approximation to 'concentric' defences such as those of the land walls at Constantinople, though here presumably designed simply to deny attackers access to the vulnerable angles of the main wall.

The *Musée d'Histoire de Marseilles*, on the Bourse site, contains the freeze-dried remains of the Lacydon ship, which was probably abandoned in the silted up end of the harbour around AD 200. Nearby is a full-scale model of the ship, loading a cargo of genuine amphorae and ingots by crane. The material from Roquepertuse (q.v.) is found in the *Musée de la Vielle Charité*, housed in a seventeenth-century charity hospital in the Rue de la Charité on the hill above, towards the cathedral.

Recent excavations have found the remains of a large Roman bath building in the port area (Place Villeneuve-Bargemon), built around AD 25-50 and refurbished in late Roman times, and, for good measure, in the Rue J.-F. Leca, a Hellenistic bathhouse of the fourth century BC, with parallels at Gela and Syracuse in Sicily. Perhaps the most important results of the recent programme of rescue excavations however has been the new light thrown on the later history of the Roman city (for details see *Parcours de Villes*). Throughout the city, well established Roman houses were abandoned in the course of the third century, matching the urban recession seen at this time in Aix-en-Provence, Vienne and elsewhere. Large parts of the upper city lay empty in late Roman times, and were not reoccupied until the twelfth or thirteenth century.

In contrast, the lower lying area around the Vieux Port saw a remarkable renaissance in the fifth to seventh centuries. Excavation in a number of areas has revealed a flourishing town of simple houses with beaten earth floors housing a variety of craftsmen — iron workers, glass blowers, salt makers and workers in bone, leather and wood. The area around the Bourse was even compared by its excavator to an eastern Souk or market. This was not wholly unexpected, since written sources, used to great effect by Henri Pirenne in his *Mohammed and Charlemagne*, show Marseilles in this period as a flourishing port, through which eastern luxury goods such as papyrus, fine wines, dyestuffs and oil were redistributed throughout Gaul. Loseby has characterised Marseilles as a 'late antique success story' and these new excavations have shown that this was not simply, as is sometimes claimed, an élite trade in luxury goods.

This late antique prosperity was also apparent in the fifth-century cathedral and baptistery, with their spreads of mosaic. The cathedral was rebuilt in medieval times, but fragments of its mosaics have been found in excavation. The baptistery to its south was still intact in the sixteenth century, known to antiquaries as the Temple of Diana. Its last remnants were removed in the 1850s. The largest in France, its roof was carried on an octagon of reused Corinthian columns, and its floor was carpeted with mosaic. In contrast to Arles however, little is left of Marseille's late antique sarcophagi, which suffered severely in the Revolution. Most of what is left is in the crypt of the *Crypt of St Victor* (Place St Victor). Victor was a third-century martyr, over whose tomb the writer Cassian established his pioneer monastery in the opening years of the fifth century.

Roman Docks — Benoit in *Gallia* 6 (1948), 208; 18 (1960), 286-8; Y. Barral, X. Altet and D. Deocourt, 'Le Baptistère Paléochrétien de Marseilles', *Archéologia* 73 (August 1974), 6-19; S.T. Loseby, 'Marseilles, a late antique success story?', *J.R.S.* 82 (1992), 165-83; *Parcours de Villes. Marseilles: 10 Ans d' Archéologie, 2,600 Ans d'Histoire* (Catalogue of exhibition, Musée d'Histoire de Marseilles, Nov 1999-Jan 2000).

## Roquepertuse Pre-Roman cult site
M84 2 IGN67 G2

The sanctuary site is tucked into a natural hollow on the slope of a wooded ridge just S of the Chemin Roquepertuse (the straight E-W road immediately S of the railway line N of Velaux). It was excavated in 1919-27 and again in the 1960s. A platform, with steps in front, provided the setting for the sculptures now in the Musée de la Vielle Charité at Marseilles. They included the lintel and jambs of a doorway decorated with engraved heads and niches for human skulls; a sinister bird with clawed feet and a seated armoured warrior. They had been smashed, and ballista bolts and catapult balls showed that this was the work of the Roman army.

## St Blaise (Ugium)
M84 11 IGN67 G1

The early fortified site of Ugium, excavated by Henri Rolland, overlooks the Etang de Lavelduc, a marshy inlet of the Gulf of Fos, ideal for fishing and salt making. It originated as a native settlement of the sixth century BC (St Blaise III), receiving much Greek and Etruscan pottery including Attic black figured ware and Ionian amphorae. A stone with a hollow for a skull, like those from Entremont and Roquepertuse, was found reused in the later defences. Its ancient name is unknown, though it may have been Mastrabala.

The site later passed under Massiliot influence. The massive Hellenistic-style rampart with rectangular towers dates about 170-140 BC (St Blaise V) Along the SE side of the high triangular promontory, it is faced with large ashlar blocks with herringbone dressing which can be matched in Greece, in Sicily and in the wall of Crinas at Marseilles. Some blocks have mason's marks in the form of archaic Greek letters. Round-headed merlons or battlements from the wall are displayed on site. Again, there are Sicilian parallels. St Blaise V had mortared stone houses in a grid pattern based on a N-S road. A scatter of Roman catapult balls and ballista bolts suggest that it was captured and destroyed in 124 BC, at the same time as Entremont.

Ugium was reoccupied in late Roman times (St Blaise VI), with a new stone rampart strengthened with a series of towers. It continued as a community of salt workers and fishermen into medieval times. Late Roman and Merovingian coins of the fourth to seventh centuries were accompanied by pottery and lamps, including North African red slip ware and local Terre sigilée grise pottery. Inside the rampart are remains of the early Christian church of St Pierre, with a portico along its north wall, and an eastern apse, partitioned off from the nave by a screen whose sill and socket holes remain. An altar table on four legs projected into the nave. Cubes of blue and white mosaic showed that part at least had a mosaic floor, and roof was of Roman tiles. Around the church was a cemetery of rock cut graves. The present name derives from St Blaise of Sebaste, an eastern saint whose cult was spread by the crusaders.

Rolland, *Fouilles de Saint-Blaise* (2nd supp. to *Gallia*, 1951); Do., *Fouilles de Saint-Blaise, 1951-6* (7th supp. to *Gallia*

1956); B. Bouloumié, *Gallia* 37 (1979), 234-5.

**St Chamas** Roman bridge
M84 2 IGN67 F1

Despite its local name, the 'Pont Flavien' dates from about 20-10 BC, perhaps in the time of Agrippa. Lucius Donnius Flavos, priest of Rome and Augustus, left money for it in his will, as the inscription on the bridge tells us. The monumental arches at each end, with their fluted Corinthian pilasters and elegant proportions, make it particularly memorable. It has needed repair over the centuries, both from wear and tear and from accidental damage (including from a German tank). The roadway, parapets and three of the four lions are restorations.

**St-Jean-de-Garguier** (Gargarius)
M84 14 IGN67 I3

The Roman vicus was a flourishing place, judging by the sculptures, mosaics and inscriptions found there. Under Antoninus Pius the country-folk of the *pagus Lucretius* set up an honorific inscription to their patron, Q. Cornelius Zosimus. By 417, the little town had a Christian church, and the parishes of this and its southern neighbour Ceyreste were involved in a boundary dispute between the bishops of Marseilles and Aix. This was the first recorded use of *parochia*, 'parish' in Gaul and by an odd coincidence, the dispute was settled by Pope Zosimus.

Knight 1999, 124; C.I.L. XII, 594.

**Saint-Rémy-de-Provence-Glanum**
M83 10 IGN66 B9/10

Glanum is one of the most memorable Roman sites in France, a Greek, Ligurian and Roman city set in a narrow rocky valley and prefaced by two impressive first-century memorials, a mausoleum and arch known locally as 'Les Antiques'.

*42  Glanum (Bouches du Rhône) — House of Cybele and Attis. Copyright Chris Dunn*

The arch, Augustan or early Tiberian, has lost its upper part and is now rather oddly crowned with a slanting eighteenth-century roof. The carving shows a variety of fruits and flowers, musical instruments, the thrysus staff of Bacchus, and the usual victories and bound prisoners. The contemporary tomb of the Julii, three stages high, stands next to it. A tall rectangular plinth has sculptured scenes of war and hunting. These are not altogether straightforward, and mythological elements seem to be involved. The arched quadrifons (four-arched) stage above supports a richly carved cornice. Over this, a lantern-like circular colonnade, enclosing statues of two male figures, supports a conical top. The figures may be those of Lucius and Gaius, the intended heirs of Augustus. Only the sculptured pine cone cap is missing. An inscription records that it was set up by 'Sextius, Lucius (and)

Marcus, sons of Caius Julius, to their parents'. The father was presumably a Gaul who acquired Roman citizenship under Caius Julius Caesar. One interpretation of an enigmatic sculpture of a winged figure reading from a scroll to a group of onlookers on the E facade is that it represents the reading out of the grant of citizenship. In another version however, the figure is reading out the news of the death of the two young heirs of Augustus.

Glanum was excavated by Jean Formigé and later by Henri Rolland. Since his death, new excavations and research have continued. By the sixth century BC a small sanctuary occupied the rocky valley, next to a perennial spring. By the second century BC this had developed into a small town (Glanum I), with a Hellenistic enclosure wall around the sanctuary site and Greek style buildings. The masonry of this phase is mostly of large stone blocks without mortar. Destroyed by the Romans around 120 BC and again some 30 years later, Glanum II, from around 100 BC to the time of Caesar, was a small town with buildings of smaller irregular masonry. The Roman remodelling of the site under Augustus (Glanum III) resulted in baths, a forum complex, and temples in regular well-mortared Roman masonry. By the later Empire, the site was largely abandoned.

The visitor enters Glanum at the S end. Each side of the road are shrines which stood outside the town gate. In Hellenistic times (Glanum I) these included a rectangular nympheum or water basin, with flights of steps leading down to the sacred pool. Part of the arch over the pool survives. Opposite, flights of steps climb the hillside to a native hilltop sanctuary of Glanis or the Glanic mothers, which produced a sculpture of a squatting torque-wearing native god. Near the steps were two small square rooms perhaps for ritual bathing. Later (Glanum II) a shrine of Hercules was added next to the Nympheum. A group of Roman altars dedicated to the god, and the base of his statue, stand outside it. Under Agrippa, a temple of the god Valetudo was added on the opposite side of the nympheum. Parts of its fluted columns have been restored.

Beyond is the Hellenistic town gate, flanked by a single rectangular tower, though it is not clear whether this was defensive, or simply defined the sacred temenos of the sanctuary. The rampart wall was of massive blocks of cut stone. Its cornice (now in the museum) was an extraordinary blend of Greek and native, for below an ovulo moulding in impeccable classical style were a series of oval recesses apparently for severed human heads.

Two Roman porticoes define an open space inside the gate. They may have had Hellenistic predecessors and a small Greek exedra stands beside one of them. The open space was defined on the W by a temple, of which foundations remain, whilst to the SW was the Greek Bouleuterion or council chamber, demolished in Roman times to make way for the twin temple complex. Similarly, at the S end of the Roman forum complex, a series of square pier bases define the trapezoid area of a demolished Hellenistic portico, whose columns originally had a series of capitals each with four sculptured heads in a central Italian style.

These Hellenistic structures were replaced in early Roman times by a monumental complex including a forum and basilica, a theatre, part of which can be seen NE of the forum complex, a pair of temples, and a set of public baths to the N. The space at the N end of the Greek agora, in front of the forum facade, was occupied by a group of structures including a fountain, an altar or monument, and a Hellenistic tholos, a domed circular structure which often commemorated some heroic figure — appropriate features for a public open space.

The twin Augustan temples to the W were built around 9-7 BC. Dedicated to the Imperial cult and family, they are among the earliest Roman temples in Gaul. Though largely destroyed, much of their rich Corinthian style decoration was recovered during excavation. They stand within a three-sided peribolos or enclosure. From a well in front of the temples came the sculpted heads of two women, identified as Octavia, sister of Augustus, and Julia, his daughter, wife of Marcus Agrippa. Julia was mother to Caius and Lucius, the adopted heirs of Augustus, commemorated both in the Maison Carrée at Nîmes and possibly in the arch and monument at Glanum.

The Roman forum, also Augustan in date, comprised the forum proper, a large colonnaded piazza, and the basilica at its upper end, marked by the rows of rectangular pier bases which supported the roof of its nave and aisles. At the lower end of the forum, an apse would have held a statue, probably of Augustus, whilst behind the basilica are the massive foundations of a rectangular apsidal structure of uncertain purpose (the small square courtyard behind is part of a Hellenistic house).

The Roman bath building to the N dates from about 40 BC, one of the earliest in Gaul. It is on a different alignment to the earlier buildings flanking it, which lie parallel to the street. There is the usual arrangement of cold, tepid and hot rooms (the latter nearest the road), with a palestra or exercise court to the right and a swimming pool beyond. There are earlier houses, of Glanum II, each side of the baths, with traces of Hellenistic buildings behind. On the opposite side of the road are a row of well-preserved Hellenistic houses, modified in later periods, and a small market. The latter consisted of a colonnaded courtyard with surrounding shops, with an inserted Roman shrine of the Goddess Bona Dea.

In the town of St Rémy, the Musée des Alpilles (aptly in the Place Février) displays the more choice pieces of sculpture. The remainder of the material is in the Hôtel de Sade in the Rue de Parage (guided tours) — the family home of the notorious Marquis, though he never lived here. Behind it are the standing remains of late Roman baths associated with a villa or mansio.

H. Rolland, *Fouilles de Glanum* (Paris 1958); *Le Mausolée de Glanum* (Paris 1969); *L'Arc de Glanum* (Paris 1977); A.R. Congès, 'Nouvelles fouilles à Glanum 1982-1990', *J.R.A.* 5 (1992) 39-55; F. Salviat, *Glanum, St Rémy de Provence* (G.A.F.).

**Verneguès** 'Temple of St Césaire' M84 2 IGN67 E1

The early first-century Graeco-Roman temple whose ruins stand within a buttressed hemicycle cut into the hillside near a spring was originally one of a group of three, possibly dedicated to the Capitoline trio of Jupiter, Juno and Minerva. The central temple is approached by a flight of monumental steps. Its W wall is largely intact, having been incorporated in the medieval chapel of St Caesarius of Arles, whose apse adjoins it (c.f. Langon, Ille et Vilaine). The right-hand temple is known from excavation. Finds include a dedication to *Jovi Tonanti*, an inscription with a possible reference to a Priest of Rome and Augustus, (C.I.L. XII, 513) and the marble head of a young man, now in the Musée Calvert at Avignon. These suggest that this elegant group of buildings was founded by a local magnate, perhaps the owner of a neighbouring villa.

Benoit, *Carte Archéol de la Gaule* 112, no. 270; Formigé, *Congrès Archéol Francais* 1932, 152.

## DAUPHINÉ (Drôme, Hautes-Alpes and Isère)

The rulers of the medieval realm of Dauphiné took the surname and title of Dauphin ('Dolphin'). When the last sold his realm to the king of France in 1349, this became the title of the French heir-apparent. In 1792 Dauphiné was divided into the present three départements.

## DRÔME

Ardeche and Drôme form a compact geographical unit either side of the Rhône between Vienne and Orange. Drome, east of the river, lay in the territories of a number of tribes — the

Allobriges of Vienne, the Segovellauni of Valence and the Vocontes of Die and Voison. There were also the Augustan colonies of Valence and St Paul-Trois-Châteaux. The area thus contained several Roman cities, which have left interesting remains.

*Carte Archéologique de la Gaule Romaine* XI (1957).

## Die (Dea Augusta Vocontium)
M77 13-14 IGN52 C8

Die and Voison were the two cities of the Vocontes. Public baths, an amphitheatre and two aqueducts are known (partly from inscriptions). The main Roman survivals are the Porte Saint Michel, a triumphal arch with floral decoration in its vaults, and carvings of a bull and a triton on the keystone and spandrel; and the late Roman town gate in which it was later incorporated. The impressive gateway, of large dressed blocks, has a central arch flanked by two large circular towers. Above, a moulded string course runs around both the arch and the towers. The walls enclosed an oval area running N from the Porte Saint Michel along the Montée des Usines, the Rue de la Citadelle and the Boulevard de Cagnard. Though rebuilt and repaired in medieval times, stretches of characteristic late Roman work, with large blocks of stone below, *petit appareil* above, and traces of brick levelling courses can be seen, particularly in the Boulevard de Cagnard E of the cathedral and in the Rue de la Citadelle. Both circular and rectangular towers occur.

The reused sculptures and inscriptions from the foundation of the wall are in the museum (Rue Camille Buffardel), and include altars recording the taurobolium bull sacrifice ceremonies of Cybele and the tombstone of a gladiator.

Rivet 1988, 291-3 and fig. 41; Bromwich 1993 23-6.

## St Paul Trois Châteaux
(Augusta Tricastinorum)
M81 1 IGN59 C9-10

Not a great deal is visible of this Augustan colony, save for slight traces of the Augustan town walls, whose line, enclosing a rectangular area, is known from excavations and early plans. The old part of the present village lies within an oval area, perhaps a medieval enclosure, around the cathedral, overlying one angle of the Roman defences.

Rivet 1988, 277-82; *Gallia Informations* 1996, 75.

## Tain L'Hermitage Altar
M77 2 IGN52 B4

In the Place de Taurobole, in the centre of the village, is an altar recording the bull sacrifice and blood-washing ceremony of the Taurobolium, in honour of the Great Mother Cybele.

## Valence (Valentia)
M76 20 IGN52 C4-5

There are no visible remains of the Roman colonia founded by Julius Caesar in 46 BC though the Republican and Augustan town walls have been found in excavation and are thought to enclose a rectangular area of 700 x 350m (*c*.30ha). The site of the theatre has been identified from aerial photographs and foundations in cellars, but again nothing is visible.

A line of three early churches is known from excavation, running E-W under the S side of the cathedral, though nothing is visible. Bishop Apollinaris, a kinsman of Sidonius Apollinaris, built two churches within the Roman walls between 490 and 518. The central one of the three may have been his cathedral of St John the Evangelist. To its W was the square cruciform baptistery of St Stephen, with a mosaic floor. This was very similar to some late fifth-/sixth-century baptisteries and martyr churches in north Italy. The eastern of the three churches was a polygonal rotunda known as Notre-Dame de la Ronde, possibly a converted Roman temple.

The mosaic from the baptistery, now in the museum in the Old Bishop's Palace (4, Place des Ormeaux) has a deer drinking from the water of life, and various animals and birds. It is probably sixth-century, but could be later. The museum also contains mosaics from a villa at St Paul les Romans, one showing the labours of Hercules, another Orpheus charming a circle of beasts. Another, from Luc-en-Diois, carries, most unusually, the signature of its maker, Quintus Amiteius. There is also a collection of Roman inscriptions, including some recording taurobolium ceremonies, and other Roman and early Christian material.

Rivet 1988, 300-4; A. Blanc, 'Le baptistère de Valence (Drôme)', *Gallia* 15 (1957), 87-116; Do., 'Autour de Saint-Jean l'Evangeliste de Valence', *Rivista di Studi Liguri* 37 (1971), 77-82.

## HAUTES-ALPES

What is now the Hautes-Alpes was in Roman times split between the provinces of Narbonensis II on the west and Alpes Maritimae on the east, the boundary running through the mountainous country east of the Durance valley. Gap (Vapincum — M77 16 IGN60 A9) lay in Narbonenesis, Embrun (Ebrodunum) in Alpes Maritimae, but neither of these Roman towns has left any visible remains.

## ISÈRE

The large pre-Roman territory of the Allobriges stretched between the Rhône and Isère as far as the Lake of Geneva. Subdued by Rome in 61 BC, shortly before Julius Caesar, their capital of Vienne became a Colonia under

Augustus, and rapidly developed as one of the major cities of Gaul. In the fourth century, the territory was divided between two civitates, centred on Vienne and Grenoble. The two medieval bishoprics which replaced these were united into the present department at the French Revolution.

### Grenoble (Cularo)
M77 5 IGN52 A10

Cularo, first mentioned in 43 BC, was a vicus of the Allobriges until the late Empire. Two lengthy inscriptions *in situ* in the oval circuit of town walls were destroyed at the Revolution. They recorded how Diocletian and Maximian (284-305) had built 'The walls of Cularo with their interior buildings' as well as the two gates, the Gates of Jove and Hercules (C.I.L. XII, 2229). In 375-83 Cularo was promoted to a civitas, and in 379 was renamed Gratianopolis in honour of the Emperor Gratian. It stands on a strategic river crossing, commanding the main overland route from Italy into Gaul, and the walls of Grenoble may not have been typical of other town defences, which may have functioned in a less strategic role. They enclosed some 9ha, probably slightly less than the extent of the earlier town. Only a few scraps survive above ground. The Vienne gate stood W of the cathedral and part of one of the 30 semicircular towers of the wall circuit is incorporated in a photography shop in the Place Notre Dame. A short stretch of wall survives in the garden of the Hôtel de Ville, and another tower can be seen in the passage de la République opposite the Maison de Tourisme.

Grenoble had a Christian bishop by 381, and a cruciform early Christian baptistery has now been excavated at the cathedral. Across the river from the walled city were the Roman and early Christian cemeteries, two of them marked by the churches of St Laurent and St Ferréol. Excavation of the former, now a museum, by Mme Renée Colardelle has revealed a remarkable story. The visitor enters through the Romanesque west tower to a gallery giving an overall view of the site. The remains are complex and not easy to grasp at first sight.

A stone pavement of early Roman date under the tower perhaps belonged to a funerary structure. In the third or fourth century, this was replaced by two rectangular mausolea along the axis of the later church, one under the tower, the other immediately east of the apse. The W crypt survives under the bell tower, but is not accessible to visitors. The E one is known from excavation. Similar late Roman mausolea occur at Lyon, at Autun, Dorchester in Dorset, and elsewhere. Later, a rectangular annexe was added to the W crypt containing a number of tombs, one with a coin of about 420.

In the sixth or seventh century, a cruciform building of complex plan was built between the two mausolea. From a square central space, four trefoil-shaped arms radiated out, each with three apses, though on the W one apse was replaced by the W door. The E arm was elaborated into a cruciform crypt, with a fourth, western, apse. This crypt of Saint Oyand was remodelled in Carolingian times, with a series of reused Roman columns with carved Corinthian marble capitals. The lateral stairs giving access to the crypt is probably of this phase. The W mausoleum was evidently still frequented by pilgrims, and given a new entry stair of brick, and wall paintings, including an elegant white cantharus (vase). In 1012 the church was granted to a Benedictine monastery, and the existing church, including the vaulting in the crypts, is twelfth-century and

later. The crypt of St Oyand was also heavily restored in the nineteenth century.

Rivet (1988), 320; R. Colardelle, *Grenoble aux premiers temps Chrétiens* (G.A.F. 2nd ed. 1992); *Gallia Informations* 1996, 102-5.

# Vienne (Colonia Julia Viennensium)
M73 20 IGN51 C4

The capital of the Allobriges was already occupied in pre-Roman times, with a hillfort on Monte Ste Blandine and Mont Pipet. An open settlement in the plain below lay on the Rhône valley trade route between the Mediterranean and inland Gaul, at a river crossing where routes led W to the Loire and E to the Alps and Italy via Grenoble. The date of foundation of the Augustan colony is uncertain, but two fragments of a monumental inscription recording the building of its walls and gates — *Muros Portasque* — survive, reused as early medieval sarcophagi. The Augustan city walls climbed between four of the surrounding hills, with an overall length of 7km, enclosing an area of 30ha. They were clearly meant to express the city's statue rather than to defend it from attack.

## Temple of Augustus and Livia

This, very like the Maison Carrée at Nimes, survives in the centre of town after a varied career that saw it converted into the church of Notre-Dame de la Vie, then into a Temple of Reason at the French Revolution, then into a museum, before it was conserved as an historic monument. The dedicatory inscription on its facade has been reconstructed (in more than one version) from the socket holes of its bronze letters. Originally dedicated to Rome and Augustus, the name of Livia Augusta, wife of Augustus, was added later. A recent study by Pelletier suggests that it may originally have been built about 27-25 BC, at the time of Augustus's visit to Gaul, and remodelled about 10-5 BC. The earlier work, including the pilasters and the S column capitals recall contemporary work at Glanum, the later work is similar to that of the Maison Carrée at Nîmes. Now crowded in among the buildings of the town, it would originally have stood in a spacious monumental precinct, traces of which have been found in excavation.

Near the centre of the city, between the Theatre and the Temple of Augustus and Livia, an area excavated between 1945-68 has been put on display. The S part was identified by the excavator as a *metroon* or *Temple of Cybele*. It should be noted however that the alleged 'Temple of Cybele' at Lyon, which influenced this interpretation, is now believed to have been an Augustan palace. A rectangular temple podium on the west was backed by an elaborate group of rooms containing water tanks which could have been used for ritual baths by the priests of the cult. Behind is what has been seen as a small ritual theatre, with a buttressed wall. An alternative view would see the *metroon* as a large domestic house like those in St Romain en Gal, with the buttressed wall supporting a stairway up the hill. The other half of the site contains parts of a monumental portico and a public baths.

A. Pelletier, *Le Sanctuaire Métroaque de Vienne* (Leiden 1980).

## Theatre and Odeon

These are impressive. The theatre, cut into the slopes of the Mont Pipet, is the largest in Gaul after Autun, with room for 13,500 spectators. It is entered via the N lobby, from which staircases would originally have led to the upper parts. Traces of the stage fittings remain, including the foundations of the *pulpitum* or timber stage and the holes for the counterweights which worked

the stage curtains. The areas in front of the stage were richly adorned. The orchestra floor was of patterned pink and yellow marble and the four front rows of seats, for distinguished members of the audience, of white marble, separated from those of lesser folk by a balustrade of green marble. The date of the theatre is uncertain. The early second-century Odeon, with room for 3,000 spectators, was cut into the hillslope SE of the theatre. Excavated more recently than the theatre, it is not yet open to the public.

A. Pelletier, 'Fouilles à l'Odéon de Vienne', *Gallia* 39 (1981), 148-69.

## Circus

The only visible part of the Vienne Circus is the 'Pyramid' or 'Aiguille' (needle). Thought in the Middle Ages to be the tomb of Pontius Pilate, it was one of the markers on the central spine of the racetrack. Unlike its fellow in Arles, it was not an ancient import from Egypt, but of local stone. A square four-way arch supports a tapering masonry obelisk 23m high. The style suggests a late second- or early third-century date. Other parts of the circus have been found in excavation.

Formigé, *Congrès Archéol de France* 1923, 18-23, Grenier III, 989-93.

## Museum collections

Vienne has three important Museum collections (four, counting St Romain en Gal). The *Musée lapidaire païen* in the deconsecrated church of St Pierre contains Roman sculptures and inscriptions from the city, and a number of mosaics. In the Place Miremont is the *Musée des Beaux arts et d'Archéologie*, with some of the major archaeological finds from Vienne, including the life-size bronze statue of C. Julius Pacatianus and a hoard of Roman silver vessels. One often reads in literary sources of someone having his statue erected in a forum or elsewhere. Here we can see what that really meant, for the statue of some forgotten first-century magnate was fitted with a new head — that of Pacatianus — in Severan times, with an accompanying inscription.

The *Musée lapidaire Chrétienne* in the cloisters of St Andre-le-Bas has a unique collection of Christian memorial stones showing the continuing Christian-Latin culture of the fifth to seventh centuries. One commemorates a lady named Foedula, baptized by Martin of Tours, and many are dated by the consul or consuls of the year. They also show the characteristic early Christian art of western Europe, with doves (representing the soul) or peacocks (a symbol of immortality since their flesh was allegedly incorruptible), often drinking from chalices from which spring vinescrolls — a clear eucharistic reference ('I am the True Vine').

Intending visitors should note that in the first two weeks of July, Vienne hosts a renowned Jazz Festival. The city is crowded with fans, with the Roman theatre serving as the focal point for concerts, and a tented village and stage in the archaeological gardens around the Temple of Cybele. A colourful and lively event (the publicity tells visitors to get some sleep in before they arrive), but not the best time for a serious study of the Roman remains, unless of course you enjoy combining archaeology and jazz.

## St Romain en Gal

A cross river suburb of Vienne, something of a French Pompeii, for a whole district of 6ha of the Roman town has been excavated and laid out on display, with rows of shops, workshops, a storehouse or *horreum*, public lavatories, and a series of palatial houses of Pompeian type with mosaics, fountains and ornamental pools. There is an excellent site museum, exhibiting mosaics and other finds from the excavations. The site is actually in the department of Rhône (the river being the boundary), but since it is a suburb of Vienne, it is included here.

Occupation began in Augustan times. The House of the Ocean Gods was one of the first large houses here (in a smaller and simpler form). Other parts were occupied by pottery kilns and other industrial activity. The area was developed under Tiberius, when streets, drainage and piped water were installed. Via II (Rue du Commerce) has an impressive central sewer below it, with manholes for access. The visitor enters at the S end of the site. The *Grand Portico*, along the edge of the site, is a monumental structure enclosing a large area to the S and returning along the Rhône in a riverside terrace. It may have enclosed the still standing baths known as the *Palais de Miroir*, though this is on a quite different alignment.

Because the water table was so high on this alluvial flood plain, lavish use could be made of water for fountains, ornamental pools, industrial activities and flush lavatories. On the right of the entrance is the *House of the Ocean Gods*, named from a late second-century mosaic. The house went through several phases between Augustan times and its mysterious abandonment, with the rest of the quarter, during the third century. In its final form, it was in four parts. The entrance lobby on the S led to a vestibule with a central circular fountain and, in its final phase, the ocean gods mosaic, with fishes and the heads of marine gods. Around were service rooms and a porter's lodge. Beyond, a peristyle courtyard like those at Pompeii, with a central garden surrounded by long elongated ornamental pools, led to the residential rooms of the house. A passageway at the side of these led to a smaller peristyle court with a fountain. Beyond was a later addition to the house, a large porticoed garden again surrounded by long narrow pools — almost moat-like — with two gazebos or garden houses in the centre.

## Shops

Even such a luxurious house however could not expect to take up valuable high street shopping frontage. Along Via II (Rue du Commerce) to the E are a row of shops. The corner shop may have been a dyers, for colouring matter was found here and there are two tanks emptying into the street drain. One room had under-floor drainage consisting of a layer of upturned amphorae. There is also a reconstructed door, with stone jambs and lintels. Buildings further up the street were demolished to make room for a smaller peristyle house, the *House with the Five Mosaics* Here, the central peristyle, with simple geometric mosaics and an ornamental pool flanks the Triclinium or dining room on the S, with an elaborate figured mosaic, and on the N, the domestic apartments.

Beyond is a large rectangular commercial building, a *Horreum* of Flavian date. This may have been a macellum or shopping precinct like that at St Bertrand de Comminges, but was perhaps a wholesale store or warehouse. Like St Bertrand, it has a central entrance on one side, a central court with two rows of identical shops or stores, a portico at each end and a central pool. A series of square piers imply an upper floor. Opposite is a triangular *Industrial Area*, taken up with workshops of various kinds. There are a number of tanks, using the ample water supplies of the site for industrial processes. The central area, with a row of tanks, may be a *fullonica* or fuller's workshop, where raw wool and cloth was cleaned.

J. Laroche and H. Savay-Guerraz 1984,

*Saint-Romain en Gal: un quartier de Vienne antique sur la rive droit du Rhône* (Paris) and *Saint-Romain-en-Gal* (G.A.F.); M. Jannet-Vallat et al, *Vienne aux premiers temps Chrétiens* (G.A.F.); A. Pelletier, *Vienne Antique* (Roanne 1980).

# VAUCLUSE

Unlike most French départments, the Vaucluse takes its name not from a local river, but from a natural feature, the *Vallis Clausa* or Fontaine de Vaucluse, a natural phenomenon famous since the time of Petrach, where an underground river gushes out at the foot of a limestone cliff (IGN67 C1). In pre-Roman times, this was the territory of the Cavares, whose main centres were at Avignon, Cavaillon and Orange.

*Carte Archéologique de la Gaule Romaine* VII (1939).

## Apt (Apta Julia Vulgientes)
M81 14/84 3 IGN67 C2

After Julius Caesar's conquest of the Albici in 49 BC, a Latin *Colonia* on the road from the Alps to the Rhône replaced the hillfort of Perréal, 6km to the NW. Little of the Colonia is visible today, though the sites of the Theatre and Forum are known from excavation and part of the former is visible in the museum cellars.

The most unexpected discovery however was part of a metrical inscription found in 1604 or 1623 (C.I.L. XII, 1122, ILN33) recording that Hadrian buried his favourite horse Borysthenes here. Cassius Dio tells how Hadrian, who is known to have written verse, 'prepared a tomb for him, set up a slab, and placed an inscription on it'. The full text is known from a book of epigrams published in Paris in 1590 which attributes the poem to Hadrian and claims to derive it from 'an old manuscript'. It may have been copied from the stone when the latter was complete. The inscription (which no longer exists) aroused great interest. In Norfolk, Sir Thomas Browne remarked how 'Time hath spared the Epitaph of Adrian's horse, confounded that of himself' (*Hydriotaphia, Urne Buriall* 1658), but it fits so remarkably with Dio that some scholars have been sceptical of the discovery, particularly as a seventeenth-century local clergyman claimed to possess a second-century manuscript by a certain Marcus Uxellicus Bassus, full of druids and Celtic kings, giving a remarkable early history of Apt.

G. Barroul and A. Dumoulin 1968, 'Le théâtre romain d'Apt', *R.A.N* 1, 159-200; Inscriptions — *I.L.N.* vol IV, ed. J Gascou, P. Leveau and J. Rimbert (1997); Clébert 1970, 194-5; Rivet 256-61.

## Avignon

(Colonia Julia Hadriana Avenio)
M81 20/83 10 IGN66 A9

Like most Roman towns of this area, Avignon originated as a pre-Roman hillfort of the Cavares, situated on the Rocher des Doms, above a crossing of the Rhône. It became a Latin colony under Claudius, and its first-century walls enclosed an area of 46ha, though they have been obscured by the medieval circuit, which follows much the same line. Later, the town evidently received some favour from Hadrian, whose name it added to its own. The only *in situ* relics of the Roman town are the Arcades des Fusteries, now largely built into modern buildings in the area of the Place de l'Horloge. They supported a series of flat terraces built into the sloping ground under the structures of the Roman forum, rather in the manner of the cryptoporticus at Arles.

The most impressive buildings of Avignon are of course medieval — the Papal Palace, the impressive city walls (restored by Viollet le Duc), and of course the celebrated medieval bridge

(Sous le Pont, d'Avignon). It was of course on the grassy meadows under (*Sous*) the bridge that the dancing took place, not on (*Sur*) the bridge itself.

There are some good things in the Musée Lapidaire (27, Rue de la République). The 'Tarasque' came from the Iron Age oppidum of Noves, 10km S of Avignon. It shows a monster, whose paws rest on human heads, eating a corpse. It seems to combine the Roman funerary theme of a lion (death) eating its prey (e.g. on the Corbridge lion, but common over much of the western Empire) with the Celtic fascination with corpses and severed heads seen at Entremont or Roquepertuse. The soldier from Vachères (see Alpes-de-Haute Provence) is here, as are some interesting Romano-Celtic gods and Imperial portrait busts. Perhaps the most memorable item though is the relief from a tomb at Cabrières-d'Aigues. A group of men haul the towropes of a riverboat carrying barrels of wine, whilst a steersman sits in the stern. Above are a row of amphorae, some of the distinctive Gallic type with footrings, others in wicker casings like a modern Chianti flask. The Calvet Museum (65, Rue Joseph Vernet) is housed in the Hôtel Villeneuve-Martignan of 1741-54. It contains the art collections of Esprit Calvet, Professor of Medicine, art collector, bibliophile and archaeologist, who left them to the city on his death in 1810. The painter Joseph Vernet, some of whose paintings are on display, was a maternal ancestor of the celebrated detective Sherlock Holmes.

Rivet 265-71.

## Carpentras

(Colonia Julia Meminorum;
Carpentorate) M81 12-13 IGN67 A1

The Memini were a branch of the Cavares, whose pre-Roman centre may have been at la Lègue outside

Carpentras. Later a Roman Colonia, by late Roman times the city was known by its present name. The Triumphal arch at the Palais de Justice, of the early first century AD, was moved here from elsewhere, like the tetrapylon at Cavaillon. It shows military trophies and chained captives representing conquered peoples. The weapons and costumes of those on the W face are particularly striking. One, possibly a Parthian, has a long cloak and a double axe; another is a German in a coarse shaggy knee-length garment with a curved falchion or short sword. The more worn E reliefs seem to be Greeks or Syrians. Inscriptions from the town include one erected by its Jewish community to Decimus Valerius Dionysus, who built an auditorium of some sort for them, and decorated it with murals. One thinks of the third-century synagogue paintings from Dura Europos on the Euphrates, now in Damascus museum.

## Cavaillon (Cabellio)
M81 12 IGN66 B2

Almost synonymous in France with melons, Cavaillon originated as a hillfort of the Cavares on the Colline-St-Jacques, overlooking the town, where pre-Roman remains have been found (A. Demoulin, *Gallia* 23 (1965), 1-86). Commanding an important crossing of the River Durance, it was a trading dependency of Marseilles. The only visible Roman monument is a four-arched tetrapylon, two of whose arches remain, of around AD 1-10. This now stands in the Place du Clos in the centre of town, but was moved there from the bishops palace in 1860. The acanthus frieze, with birds and butterflies, links it to the Maison Carrée at Nîmes. A worn early Christian inscription has been cut on one face. There is a display of material from the town in the Museum. Rivet, *Gallia Narbonensis* 262-71;

Bromwich 1993, 163-4.

## Orange (Arausio)
M80 20/93 19 IGN59 D10

Orange contains two outstanding Roman monuments — the celebrated Triumphal Arch with its rich sculpture, and the Theatre. Both only survive because they were incorporated in medieval fortifications by a thirteenth-century Prince of Orange, Raymond de Baux. The arch is dated to AD 26-7 by an inscription of Tiberius. There may have been an earlier arch on the site. The theatre is probably slightly earlier. The town walls, of which a few remnants still survive, were Augustan, though they were obscured by their inclusion first in the walls of Raymond de Baux and then in the fortifications erected by Maurice of Nassau in the 1620s. One circular gate tower survives beside the Rue St Clement on the SW.

Arausio originated as a hillfort of the Cavares, sited on the hill of St-Eutrope, in the S part of the present town. About 35 BC Octavian, the future Emperor Augustus, founded a military colony here for veterans of *Legio II Gallica*, the Second Gallic Legion. Its full title was *Colonia Julia Firma Secundanorum Arausio* ('The stalwart Julian colony of the Second (Legion) at Arausio'). Augustus renamed the legion *Legio II Augusta*, the Second Augustan Legion, after himself, and its capricorn badge appears on the shield of one of the Roman soldiers on the arch. *II Augusta* went on to become one of the three permanent British legions, with its base at Caerleon in south Wales.

The *Triumphal Arch* stands at the N end of the town. The road which ran under it led S to a T-junction at the town centre, next to the Theatre and another large building, probably a temple, at the foot of the hill of St Eutropius. The sculptures on the arch represent naval

43 Orange
(Vaucluse)
— Roman
theatre.
Copyright
Chris Dunn

and military battles in a style deriving ultimately from the school of Pergamum in Asia Minor. The triple arches are topped by a cornice and central pediment, with socket holes for a bronze lettered inscription on the architrave, interpreted from these as referring to Tiberius. There is a pedimented upper stage with a second cornice and, above that, an upper part which no doubt served to support the bronze statuary with which the arch was once crowned. Both faces are covered with sculpture showing military trophies above the arches; naval battles on the pediment and battle scenes at the top. One Roman soldier on the left of the N frieze has a shield with the Capricorn badge of *Legio II Augusta*. On the sides are bound barbarian prisoners and military trophies on T-shaped frames, like those at Carpentras. Above are Jupiter, and pairs of Tritons matching the land and naval battles on the main fronts. The theme is Roman victory by sea and land. Some of the shields of defeated enemies in the trophies on the S face bear personal names such as Mario, Avot and Sacrovir, showing that reference to real events was intended. Sacrovir was the leader of a revolt among the Aedui in AD 21.

In the town itself, the *Theatre*, built to hold 9,000 spectators, is one of the most spectacular sites of Roman Gaul. The cliff-like stage building (*frons scaenae*) survives intact, its huge scale dwarfing even the twice life-size statue of Augustus put there by M.J. Formigé during his restorations in the 1920s. Louis XIV described it as the finest wall in his kingdom. Its outside face, arcaded and of warm brown stone, towers over the adjacent square. Inside, its present austere bareness is in sharp contrast to its appearance in antiquity, when it would have been embellished with superimposed rows of marble columns (a few fragments have been re-erected), marble veneering and perhaps mosaic. The stage building itself represented, at ground level, a street scene with columns and three doors of houses (which survive) for exits and entries. The stage building of an Elizabethan theatre would have been very similar. Even the grooves and mast seatings for the stage curtains survive, though they are normally hidden by the modern staging.

Next to the theatre is the *Hemicycle complex*, with the rock face cut back in a semicircle and the remains of a small temple. Its purpose is uncertain. Opposite the museum, the narrow Rue

Pontillac is crossed by a high Roman wall, which has been traced as far as the Rue Victor Hugo. It was probably part of the forum N of the theatre. One vanished monument is the amphitheatre W of the town. In 1639 its walls were still 12ft high, and some remains were found in 1823, but nothing is now visible. It was probably Augustan in date (Grenier III, 646).

N of the central temple of the city stood the town's Public Record Office. In 1949, in digging a bank vault, fragments were found of three large marble cadastral plans showing the grid plans of three successive land allotments (centuriations) to veterans settled in the colony. Some elements of these have now been recovered by aerial photography. The earliest, Cadastre A, from the time of Vespasian, in AD 77, probably deals with land near Avignon. Cadastre B, probably of the time of Trajan, may relate to land N of Orange. Cadastre C is somewhat later. The three plans were the subject of a definitive analysis by André Piganiol. The fragments are now well displayed in the Municipal Museum (Place des Frères-Mounet — same ticket as theatre) along with sculptures from the theatre.

The medieval title of Prince of Orange was inherited by Maurice of Nassau and by the Dutch royal family. This French town has thus given its name to the Orange Free State in South Africa and to the Protestant Orange Order in Northern Ireland.

R. Amy et al 1962, *L' Arc d'Orange* (27th supplement to *Gallia*, 1962); S. Piganiol, *Les documents cadastraux de la Colonie Romaine d'Orange* (16th supplement to Gallia, 1962); Rivet, *Gallia Narbonensis* 272-6; M.-E. Bellet, *Orange Antique* (G.A.F.); J.C. Anderson, 'The date of the arch at Orange', *Bonner Jahrbücher* 187 (1987), 159-92; Bromwich 1993, 181-94.

## Pont Julien Roman bridge
M84 2 IGN67 C2

Three-arched bridge of massive masonry on the Roman road from north Italy into Gaul by the Mt Genèvre Pass. Off the N100 W of Apt.

## Voison-la-Romaine (Vasio)
M81 2-3 IGN60 B2

Canon Joseph Sautel spent nearly 50 years (1907-55) of his long life excavating Roman Voison. As is said on Sir Christopher Wren's tomb in St Paul's Cathedral, 'If you seek his monument, look around you'. In 1929 the town added 'La-Romaine' to its name in honour of the past that he had revealed. Inevitably at such a date, this was a one-dimensional picture of Vasio in its greatest flowering, and it has been left to later hands to reveal the story of its growth and decline. There may have been an oppidum of the Vocontii here, in the Haute Ville area to the S. By about 50 BC, a scatter of houses of Italian peristyle type, but built in poor quality local masonry, were beginning to appear. Better quality stonework and refinements such as baths show increasing Roman influence in the early decades AD and by Flavian times the developed Roman town had appeared.

There are two areas of excavated buildings. The Puymin area on the E contains the museum, the Theatre and a number of shops and houses. The *House of the Messii* is so named from honorific inscriptions found here to Lucius Messius, and a kinswoman Messia Alpina. Presumably it was their family home. It contains a porticoed garden with a pool, a series of reception rooms, one with a floor of red marble tiles, a possible cult room for the *lar* or guardian spirit of the house, and a set of lavatories. Next to it is *Pompey's Portico* (named from a misreading of an inscription to a lady named Pompeia), with re-erected columns around the central formal garden of another large house. To the E is a row of shops and a structure identified by Sautel as a Nymphaeum. Nearby a 2m high pottery store jar (dolium) has been re-erected on the site of its discovery. Beyond is the newly excavated *Thés Area*, with a row of shops, the corner of a temple precinct, and part of another large house, the *Peacock Villa*. Both the shops and the villa date from Flavian times, around AD 60-80. The 'Villa' has a series of mosaics. It takes its name from one with a series of birds — ducks, partridges, a peacock, and even parrots. Other mosaics show theatre masks, various other animals and birds and a cupid riding a dolphin. They are rather later than the house itself, probably second century. The shops probably included an oil-seller, a clothes shop and a butcher's.

The *Theatre*, excavated by Sautel in 1911-12, was heavily restored by Jean Formigé in 1932. The seating and rear gallery are almost entirely new. The tunnel behind the theatre is however Roman, with niches for oil lamps. On the other side of the museum is another large peristyle house, wrongly named the *Praetorium* (Governor's residence) by Sautel. Late first-century in date, with rooms including baths and a kitchen around a small courtyard, it was later extended with rooms looking out on to a porticoed garden court with an exedra and fountain. A latrine with a row of 4 seats is nearby.

The second excavated area is *La Villasse*, across Avenue Général de Gaulle. It contains several large and impressive houses, particularly the *House of the Dolphin* and the *House of the Silver Bust*. The former is a classic Pompeian style house, with atrium, peristyle, tablinium (reception room) and triclinium (dining room). It began in

Flavian times around a central court and was then expanded. The atrium has a small fountain and an ornamental stone table with lions. The adjacent row of 20 latrines was probably, from its size, a public lavatory rather than part of the fittings of the house. Nearby, a re-paved road runs uphill past a row of shops. In the *House of the Silver Bust* (named from one of the finds), the garden court with its pool has been re-planted with hedges, flowers and grass, whilst bulrushes mark the area of the pool. Public baths are known in the Avenue Coudray, but have not yet been fully explored, and the round arched bridge over the Ouvèze may also be Roman.

Though most of the visible remains belong to the early Roman Empire, a collection of Early Christian epitaphs in the cathedral cloister is a reminder that the town continued into later times. The Romanesque cathedral of Notre-Dame, of *c.*1150-60 contains much reused Roman stonework, and several of its walls, particularly at the E end, rest on a foundation of reused Roman column drums.

C. Goudineau, *Les fouilles de la Maison du Dauphin à Voison-la-Romaine* (Paris 1979); C. Goudineau and Y. Kisch, *Voison-la-Romaine* (G.A.F. Voison 1984).

# 12 Roussillon and the Narbonnaise
## (Narbonensis Prima)

## ARIÈGE

For archaeologists, the Ariège is most famous for the cave systems along the limestone belt on the northern flanks of the granites and schist of the Pyrénées. Many, like Niaux and the Mas d'Azil, have Palaeolithic deposits, cave paintings and engravings. Ruled by the Counts of Foix from the eleventh century, the Pays was attached to the French crown in 1607. In 1790 it was renamed after the river which forms its main axis. The Musée Départmental de l'Ariège is housed in part of the former castle of the counts at Foix.

### St Lizier
(Lugdunum Consorannorum)
M86 3 IGN71 A3

Lugdunum sits on top of a steep hill above the modern town, like the other two Lugdunums, St Bertrand de Comminges and Lyon. It changed its name after its sixth-century bishop, Glycerius, was canonised under the name of St Lizier. The late Roman walls enclose a pear-shaped area. Though they have been much altered by medieval rebuilding and refacing, a number of towers are visible.

A black marble, veined with white, is said to have been quarried here in Roman times. It may be the type referred to by some ancient writers as 'Marmor Celticum' — Celtic marble. Possible examples are known from Bordeaux and Voison-la-Romaine.
Johnson 1983 110-11; West 1935 137, 143.

## AUDE

*Carte Archéologique de la Gaule Romaine* XII (1959)

### Carcassonne
M83 11 IGN72 B1/64 D11

Famous for its Roman and medieval walls, restored by Viollet le Duc in the nineteenth century, Carcassonne began life in the sixth century BC as a hillfort of the Volcae Tectosages, and excavation has produced Etruscan, Phocean, Attic and Massiliot pottery. In the early Empire, it was a Colonia, by the fourth century a mere *castellum*, absorbed by its larger neighbour Narbonne. The only visible remains of the Roman town are its walls, and the mosaic floor and walls of a first-century house excavated within the Château Comtal and left on view.

The main double circuit of walls date from the time of St Louis (1226-70) and Philip III, le Hardi (1270-85). The Roman work followed the line of the inner circuit. In their final form, the medieval defences were a superb example of the concentric style of fortification which marked the high point of medieval military architecture in western Europe, and which can be seen for example in some of the North Welsh castles of Edward I. A higher inner line of defence was protected in front by a lower outer line, separated from it by a clear space. This space, known at Carcassone as the Lists, was flat, to allow rapid redeployment to any threatened sector. Where the defences were built on sloping ground, the space between the walls had either to be built

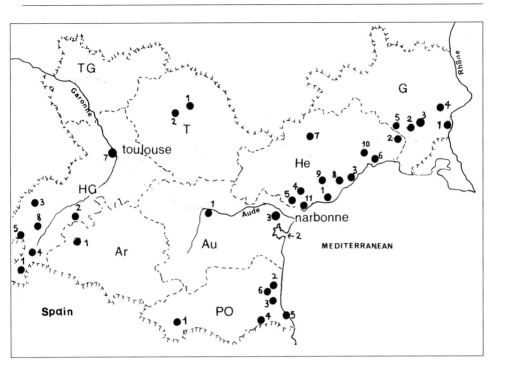

44 Roussillon and the Narbonnaise (Narbonensis Prima)

**Ar** Ariège *1 St Lizier*

**Au** Aude *1 Carcassone 2 Etange de Sigean 3 Narbonne*

**G** Gard *1 Beaucaire 2 Nages 3 Nîmes 4 Pont du Gard 5 Sommières*

**HG** Haute-Garonne *1 Bagnières- de Luchon 2 Matres Tolosane- Chiragan 3 Montmaurin*
*4 St Béat 5 St Bertrand de Comminges 6 St Michel du Touch 7 Toulouse 8 Valentine*

**He** Hérault *1 Agde 2 Ambrussum 3 Balaruc les Bains 4 Béziers 5 Enserune*
*6 Lattes and Maguelonne 7 Lodève 8 Loupian 9 St Thibéry 10 Substantion 11 Vendres*

**PO** Pyrénées-Orientales *1 Amélie les Bains 2 Château Roussillon 3 Elne 4 Perthus-L'Ecluse*
*5 Port Vendres 6 Théza*

**T** Tarn *1 Albi 2 Montans*

**TG** Tarn-et-Garonne

up, or the ground cut away, to form a level terrace. The relevance of this to understanding the Roman walls will be seen later.

Entry to Carcassone, whether for medieval carts or modern tourists, is by the Porte de Narbonne, a large gatehouse with distinctive beaked towers, built by Philip III. The red tile roofs of this and of the Tour de Trésau to the right are recent restorations. Viollet le Duc's original choice of conical slate roofs, as seen elsewhere on the circuit, was criticised as being out of keeping with local building traditions and geology, and more recent conservation work has replaced them with red tiles, as here, or, on some of the late Roman towers, low pitched roofs clad in Roman style roofing tiles.

In this sector, the Roman walls were removed by Philip III, but beyond the

Tour de Trésau, along the N sector of the walls, the Roman work can be distinguished by its regular courses of small squared masonry and red brick levelling courses. There has been much later patching and refacing. The levelling courses, which in late Roman walls of this kind are normally very regular, marking each 'lift' or stage in building the wall, are often far from regular, and in places, as on the Saint-Sernin tower S of the Narbonne Gate, areas of herringbone brickwork, set in alternate diagonal courses, have been introduced. Herringbone work is a medieval rather than Roman technique. This, and the irregular brick courses, have led to claims that parts of the walls are not Roman but Visigothic. Most of the irregularity is due to later refacing however, as is the herringbone work, but a full survey with drawn or photogrammetric elevations would be useful. One further complication is that in places the cutting away of the sloping ground surface to produce the level Lists made it necessary to underpin the Roman walls. As a result, they sit on top of what appears as first glance to be earlier masonry, but is in fact medieval underpinning.

Immediately beyond the *Tour de Trésau* an incurving stretch of the Inner curtain was straightened out by Philip III, and the earlier wall inside it, already remodelled by St Louis, demolished. This has now been re-excavated and left on display, with its two towers. A little further on is the *Tour du Vieulas*. Its exterior can be seen from the Listes (reached through the Porte du Rodez a little further on), and presents an extraordinary hotchpotch of masonry. The leaning late Roman tower, with its brick courses, can readily be distinguished. Below this the ground has been cut away by Philip III to form a flat terrace, and the larger medieval masonry underpinning it looks at first glance as if it belongs to an earlier wall and tower. The undercutting caused the Roman tower to tilt forward, though fortunately it did not collapse. At an earlier stage, both the adjacent curtain wall and part of the face of the tower had been refaced, the latter with some of the irregular brick courses sometimes said to indicate a Visigothic date. Here at least they are clearly the result of later rebuilding. Above this, the wall returns to the vertical, with a thirteenth-century curtain wall and tower, itself topped by the more regular stonework of Viollet le Duc.

Beyond is a well-preserved stretch of Roman curtain wall, with three towers, the *Tour de la Marquière*, the *Tour de Samson* and the *Tour du Moulin d'Avar*. The first of these has also been affected by the medieval underpinning, and leans to one side. The towers, which were normally placed every 20-30m, were solid to first-floor level. The three large windows at wall walk level, through which arrows or other missiles could be fired, are normal on late Roman towers of this kind, as can be seen for example at Le Mans, though here the upper parts have been much restored by Viollet le Duc. The near collapse of the Tour du Vieulas had evidently caused concern, for the underpinning of the Tour de Samson was strengthened with a rectangular block of masonry serving as a buttress. In the flank of the Tour du Moulin d'Avar is a Roman postern, the *Avar Postern*, with jambs and lintel of large sandstone blocks and a relieving arch above with alternate voussoirs of brick and stone. Again the best parallels are at Le Mans. From here, the Roman wall continues past the *Tour de la Charpentière* to the Castle of the Counts.

The castle probably dates from 1226-45. Its walls form a rectangle, with the W face against the Roman curtain wall. There is another Roman postern gate, now blocked, next to the Tour Pinte, and one Roman tower was used as the apse of the castle chapel, now the *Tour de la Chapelle* at the northern angle of the castle. Beyond the castle, the W town wall is largely rebuilt, though the *Tour Wisigothe* beyond the Tour de la Justice is of Roman type. However, it is smaller than the other Roman towers, and may be an addition. At the S angle of the walls, outside the Tour Mipadre, are the remains of a Roman tower which collapsed during the levelling work. This shows that Phillip III's curtain wall was here on a different alignment to the Roman work, allowing more space between the two curtains. The other main surviving stretch of Roman walling is on the E face, between the *Tour St Martin* and the *Tour Saint-Sernin*, though these have been much altered by later rebuilding.

After a siege in 1240, St Louis removed the inhabitants of Carcassonne to a new town or *bastide* across the Aude. The cité was now a fortress, not a town. It retained its role as a strongpoint on the Spanish-French border until the Treaty of the Pyrénées in 1659 finally settled its line and ceded Roussillon to France. Neglect followed, and by the 1830s it was a warren of ruined towers and poor cottages. There were proposals to demolish the whole complex and put the stone to more profitable use, but the efforts of the Inspector of Ancient Monuments Prosper Mérimée and others led to positive steps for its protection. In 1844, Viollet le Duc was put in charge of the restorations, which he continued until his death in 1879. Even that was not the end of the story however. In March 1944, the German area commander removed the inhabitants once more and until the liberation in August, Carcassonne was again a fortress.

J.-P. Panouillé 1992, *Carcassonne in the days of the siege* (Caisse Nationale des Monuments Historiques et des Sites, Paris).

# Etang de Sigean
M86 9-10 IGN72 C-G3
South of Narbonne, a series of coastal lagoons or Etangs lie behind the coast, almost to Perpignan. Separated from the sea only by a long narrow spit of alluvium, these were attractive to early settlement. Two *oppida* on hills fronting the lagoon have been excavated. The material from the Oppidum du Moulin at Peyriac-de-Mer is in a private museum there. Further S at Sigean is the Oppidum of Pech de Mau, with Hellenistic occupation.

# Narbonne
M83 14 IGN72 C4
Narbonne was the first Roman Colonia in Gaul, founded in 118 BC on the line of the early road linking Italy and Spain, the Via Domitia. Its probable predecessor, the hillfort of Montlaurès, capital of the Elisyces, occupied from the sixth century BC lies 4km NE of the city. Italian colonists were brought in, and traces of centuriation in the surrounding countryside, oriented on the early line of the Via Domitia, show how the land was divided among the new settlers. Later, Julius Caesar reinforced the settlers with veterans of his Tenth Legion.

The site of the Hadrianic or Antonine forum is known from excavation. Its site is marked in the Place Bistan by a display of architectural fragments, and a mural showing Roman builders at work. Adjacent was the Capitoleum, with temples to Jupiter, Juno and Minerva. This was the largest of the group of Augustan Greek-style neo-Attic temples, which includes the Maison Carrée at Nîmes, the Temple of Augustus and Livia at Vienne and that near the Arch of Orange. The Narbonne temple, of Carrara marble from Italy, and twice the size of the Maison Carrée, may have been left unfinished, and completed only in the time of Hadrian. Another temple to the Imperial cult, dedicated in AD 11, is known from an inscription (C.I.L. XII, 4331). A large amphitheatre was found in 1838, but the site is now built over, whilst another inscription (C.I.L. XII, 4342) records the rebuilding of the public baths by Antoninus Pius after a fire.

There is a collection of Roman inscriptions and sculptures in the Musée Lapidaire (former church of Notre Dame de Lamourgier, Place Lamourgier), many from the demolition of the late Roman city walls, whose polygonal shape overlay the much larger earlier street grid, as at Amiens or Bordeaux. The Museum of Archaeology, in the Hotel de Ville, the old archbishop's palace, contains an outstanding collection, including impressive Roman wall paintings from the Clos de la Lombarde site, sculptures and inscriptions, and an informative display of Roman pottery. There are also a number of good Roman mosaics in the Musée des Beaux Arts.

The main Roman building currently visible is the elaborate underground *horrea* or warehouse, of first-century date. This, (signposted, entrance at 14 Rue Rouget de Lisle) probably originally comprised four ranges of multiple underground chambers around a large central courtyard. Only the N and W galleries now remain. The modern entrance leads into the N gallery, with some 30 barrel-vaulted cells, whose entrances show no sign of having been

fitted with doors. The storerooms were still in use in medieval times, when each range was fitted with a goods hoist, and the partitions between cells in the W gallery removed. The underground walling may also have served as foundations for ranges of above ground buildings, perhaps a market.

Two early church sites are also visible. At Clos de la Lombarde (junction of Avenue de Lattre de Tassigny and Rue Chanzy on the city outskirts) a large peristyle house was occupied from about 40 BC to the late third century. It produced a collection of superb wall paintings, which it is hoped to exhibit on site. The house was then demolished and a Christian church built over it. This could be another example of a local magnate giving the site of a house to the Church, though equally the house may have been already demolished, and the site a vacant lot. The church, which may be as early as the fourth century, consists of an aisled nave, a long transept-like crossing (also seen in Lyon churches a little later) and an internal (not projecting) apse flanked by a pair of vestries (the *prothesis* and *diaconicon*). Below the altar is a crypt or *martyrium*.

The church of St Paul in the Place Dupleix also has an early crypt, and some early tombs are visible, including two amphora burials. There is a major collection of fifth-/sixth-century 'Aquitanian' or 'SW Gallic' sarcophagi and other late Roman types in the Musée Archéologique.

M. Gayraud, *Narbonne Antique des origines à la fin du IIIe Siècle* (1981); Y. Solier, *Narbonne: Monuments et Musées* (G.A.F.).

# GARD
## Beaucaire (Ugernum)
M83 10 IGN88 B8

The castle, La Redoute, stands on the site of an oppidum occupied since the

*45  Nages (Gard) — Round tower on walls of oppidum. Copyright Chris Dunn*

Bronze Age, with Greek finds from the seventh century BC onwards. On its S side is the podium or buttressed enclosure wall of a Roman temple.

The Roman road between Beaucaire and Nîmes, the Via Domitia, is followed for most of its length by the D999. However, the 11km stretch W of Beaucaire, marked on maps as the 'Chemin Romain', survives with a remarkable number of inscribed milestones still in situ. For detailed instructions see Bromwich 1993, 59-60, who recommends the IGN Blue map 2942 est. From the D38 a right-hand turn leads to the Marroniers cemetery, at the edge of which are two milestones of Claudius, marking 15 Roman miles to Nimes. Two (Roman) miles further on at the Clos de Melettes are the 'Colonnes de César', a group of four milestones.

## Nages Hillfort
M83 8 IGN66 B5

A complicated drystone fort surrounded by a massive outer wall 6m thick, with double or triple facing, enclosing a rectangular area 300m square (the S rampart has been destroyed). The defences are of several periods (hence their complexity), but grew from an initial inner enclosure, concentric to the main rampart, dating from 300 BC (Nages I). A demolished N rampart under the later enclosure must represent an initial extension of this. About 250 BC the site was destroyed, but was immediately rebuilt on a grander scale, with outer enclosures and bastions (Nages II). In its fully developed phase, Nages was concentric, with the original inner enclosure, and three outer compartments divided off by cross-walls. Entrance was from the NW, where three half-round towers project to the field, guarding narrow gateways each 1.4m wide. These give access to a small barbican-like ward forming the NW quadrant. The two other outer quadrants were entered at the junctions of their cross-walls with the inner enclosure, where in each case a large semicircular tower guards the entry at very close range indeed.

Inside were rows of parallel streets in long narrow insulae, associated with imported Italian Campanian ware and amphorae. The final phase (Nages III) dates from after the Roman conquest in 120 BC. A small square temple at the centre of the site was built about 70 BC and demolished about AD 10 when the site was abandoned.

Occupation then moved down to a settlement around a spring at the foot of the hill, known in the ninth century as the *Villa Anagia*. This has produced much Roman material, starting with Augustan Arretine and other pottery and continuing to the end of the Roman period. A mosaic and marble architectural fragments show the existence of substantial buildings, and a cremation cemetery with a series of inscribed tombstones is known. There is a museum of site finds in the Mairie.

M. Py 1978, *L'oppidum des Castels à Nages (Gard)* (Paris); A. Parodi et al 1987, 'La Vaunage du IIIe siècle au milieu du XIIe siècle, habitat et occupation des sols', *Archéologie du Midi Médiéval* V, 2-59 (p63).

# Nîmes (Nemausus)
M83 9 IGN66 B6

Nîmes developed from an Iron Age settlement on Mont Cavalier, trading with Marseilles from the fifth century BC. It became a Roman Colonia under Julius Caesar, with coins inscribed COL(onia) NEM(ausus). New veterans from the eastern legions arrived from Egypt under Augustus, and later coins show a crocodile and a palm tree. Nîmes became a distinguished city, possibly the birthplace of Trajan's wife Plotina, and the home of the family of Antoninus Pius.

The Augustan *City Walls*, of durable local limestone from newly opened quarries, were 6km in length, enclosing 220ha, and have recently been the subject of definitive recording and study. An inscription on the *Porte d'Auguste* recorded in bronze letters that Augustus built the gates and walls of the Colonia in 16 BC. Presumably this records their completion. The gate has twin main arches, with a smaller pedestrian arch each side, flanked by semicircular towers. The arches have both portcullis grooves and door sockets, and fragments on site suggest that there was a gallery above with a series of arches, like those on the gates of Autun. Some of the wall's 40+ external circular towers are still visible. A single arch gateway, the Porte de France, survives on the S.

Within the city, the Augustan temple known as the *Maison Carrée* marks the central area around the forum. A bronze letter inscription, of which the holes remain, dates it to AD 2-4 by its dedication to Gaius Caesar and Lucius Caesar, Augustus's two adopted sons. Lucius died of fever in Marseilles in AD 2, whilst consul designate, as on the inscription. Two years later Gaius also died. The temple belongs to a group of Greek style neo-Attic temples in a style favoured by Augustus and found both in Rome (Apollo in Circo, Mars Ultor in the Forum of Augustus) and in S Gaul (Narbonne, Vienne, Orange). The temple of Mars Ultor, dedicated in 2 BC, may even have served as the immediate model. In turn, the Maison Carrée is said to have been the model for Napoleon's church of the Madeleine in Paris. The six Corinthian columns on its portico are matched by similar engaged columns on its other sides. Above is an acanthus frieze. It may have been the work of local craftsmen under the supervision of an Italian architect, and close study of its carvings by Amy and Gros suggested three teams of craftsmen were involved. It is now a

*46  Nîmes (Gard) — 'Temple of Diana'. Copyright Chris Dunn*

museum of Roman antiquities, with mosaics, busts and statuary (the bronze head of Apollo is particularly fine), and inscriptions.

To the NW, just within the city walls, was a religious cult centre focused on *Mont Cavalier* and the sacred spring below it. The *Tour Magne* is a 33m high octagonal tower in a series of stages. Its core is a prehistoric conical tower of rubble walling (visible from the modern internal staircase), possibly a religious monument, later encased within the Roman tower. Below was a sacred complex dedicated to the water goddess Nemausus, still partially visible in an eighteenth-century guise, having been laid out as an ornamental water garden in 1740. The *Nymphaeum* was originally in the centre of a temenos or temple precinct, surrounded on three sides by porticoes. There was a monumental

gateway on the S and the pool of the Nemausus spring on the N, with a Romano-Celtic temple in front of the spring. A small theatre to one side is now hidden under the steps up to the Tour Magne. The Nymphaeum was a rectangular platform surrounded by an ornamental pool, with a central altar or statue base.

The so-called *Temple of Diana* projected out from the W portico. An elegant building of the late first century, with a series of internal pedimented niches, one suggestion is that it may have been a library, with the niches serving for the storage of scrolls, though the most recent view is that it was an Augusteum or Imperial shrine. Its roof, which partly survives, was a series of structurally separate arches, a technique also seen in the Pont du Gard and the Amphitheatre. It was used as a church from 991 until

*47  Nîmes (Gard) — Maison Carrée. Copyright Chris Dunn*

sacked by the Protestants in 1562 (F.O.R. VIII, 110-12; Grenier 1960, 502-6).

On the SW of the city were very different buildings, a 'leisure complex' of amphitheatre, public baths and circus, again just within the Augustan walls. The *Amphitheatre* is still used for bullfights and other events. It could have held 20,000 spectators and, unusually, two inscriptions in its underground chambers record the name of the architect, T. Crispius Reburrus. It probably dates from the time of Domitian or Nerva (AD 79-97), when the Roman Colosseum had made amphitheatres prestigious and fashionable. It is of two storeys, each of 60 arches, with an attic story above. The main entrance on the N, leading direct to the box for the president of the games, is emphasised by corbels with bull carvings and a pediment. Inside an elaborate complex of passages and staircases

ensured that the crowds found their seats quickly and safely. The arena was fitted with a cruciform cellar (no longer visible), reached by tunnels, from which animals and scenery could be raised to the arena by lifting gear. The various tiers of seating were divided according to rank and status, from the reserved seats for notables in the front stalls to the slaves and workmen in the gallery. On top of the walling, the socket holes for the *velarium* are visible This was a structure of masts and large sails, operated by sailors, which provided shade.

Much of the Circus was still visible in the seventeenth century. It has now vanished, though something of its outline is preserved in the lines of houses. The colossal marble head of a Julio-Claudian Emperor, now in the museum of the Maison Carrée may be from it. The Baths lie under the present Lycée Alphonse Daudet. FOR VIII, 94 *Gallia* 42 (1985) 396-8.

*48  Pont-du-Gard from the south-west. Copyright Chris Dunn*

One unusual monument is the *Castellum Divisiorum* — the circular water settlement and distribution tank at the end of the aqueduct whose most celebrated feature is the Pont du Gard. This, found in 1844, is in the Rue de la Lampèze, across the Boulevard Gambetta from the Maison Carrée and below the seventeenth-century fort. The water entered the originally roofed 1m deep tank from the end of the aqueduct channel, where there was a sluice gate to control the flow, and was distributed through a series of outlets originally fitted with lead pipes. The holes in the floor were for drainage for maintenance. The Musée Archéologique, due to move to a new site, has an outstanding collection of material from the city, and from Iron Age and Roman sites in the surrounding area.

Esperandieu, *L'Amphitheatre de Nîmes* (Paris 1933); R. Amy and P. Gros, *La Maison Carrée de Nîmes* (Paris 1979);

Varène, *L'enceinte gallo-romaine de Nîmes: les murs et les tours* (53rd supp. to *Gallia*, 1992).

## Pont-du-Gard Aqueduct
M80 19/83 9 IGN66 A7

The Pont du Gard, carrying the Nîmes aqueduct over the River Gard, is one of the best known monuments of Roman France, yet is only one element of a 50km aqueduct bringing water from the Fontaine d'Eure just east of Uzès to Nîmes. Wherever possible, the water channel was below ground in an arched stone tunnel, but where the fall of the ground or the crossing of a valley made it necessary, the channel was carried on a solid wall, or, as here, on an arched bridge. The date of the aqueduct, and of the Pont du Gard, is uncertain, suggested dates ranging from Augustus to Trajan, but the Flavian period in the late first century seems most likely.

A small water pumping station now marks the site of the Fontaine d'Eure,

*49  Pont du Gard — the water channel. Copyright Chris Dunn*

and the first visible part of the aqueduct is at Bornègre (IGN66 A7), just off the bend of the D3 bis to Argilliers, where it emerges from a tunnel to cross a stream by a bridge of three arches of dressed ashlar, with cutwaters upstream and downstream to resist the torrents resulting from heavy seasonal rains on the karst limestone terrain. Further remains are visible at Le Pont Rou, just E of the D227 at Vers, where it is cut by the D981 and the railway. There are good stretches both above and below these, with some of the arches filled in by later alterations. From here, it is only a short distance to the Pont du Gard itself.

Pont du Gard is one of the monuments where a consummate work of engineering and architecture is set against a natural background of great beauty, blending the work of nature and of man. Three superimposed rows of arches carry the waters of the aqueduct over the Gardon Valley at a height of nearly 50m. The lowest tier of broad arches is over 20m high, with massive rectangular piers founded on bedrock and solid cutwaters against winter floods. The river itself flows in a perhaps artificially deepened channel beneath one even wider arch. Above are a series of slightly smaller arches, whose span however corresponds with those below, included an extra wide one above the river arch. The water is carried in a concrete lined channel in an upper tier of much smaller arches. Unlike, say, a cathedral, much of the evidence of how the feat of building such a structure was achieved is left on view. Blocks of pale yellow limestone weighing up to 6 tonnes were quarried and taken to the masons yard for rough dressing. Many archstones had short coded inscriptions to identify where they should be placed, and some are still visible. Projecting

*50  Sommières (Gard) — Roman bridge. Copyright Chris Dunn*

blocks in the walling supported wooden scaffolding for construction or repairs, and similar projecting ledges were left for the timber centring of the arches, though there are also rows of putlog holes for scaffolding on the upper piers. The bridge is something of an object lesson in Roman engineering techniques. It is possible to walk across on the thoroughfare above the lower row of arches.

Below the Pont du Gard, the aqueduct follows the D981 S of the river towards Remoulins. There is a single arch bridge just off the road at La Sartanette and several stretches of aqueduct tunnel are visible near Sernhac. Thereafter, it followed broadly the line of the N86 and the motorway to Nîmes.

G.F. Hauck 1988, *The Aqueduct of Nemausus* (Jefferson, North Carolina); G. Fabre et al 1992, *The Pont du Gard: Water and the Roman Town* (Caisse Nationale des monuments historiques et des sites, Paris 1992 — in English or French); Bromwich 1993, 110-20.

**Sommières** Roman bridge
M83 8 IGN66 B4

A somewhat restored Roman bridge, originally of 17 arches, still carries the D40 road to Lodève.

## HAUTE-GARONNE

Around the headwaters of the Garonne in the central Pyrénées, the Haute-Garonne is notable both for the extensive remains of the Roman town of St Bertrand de Comminges and for a series of huge luxury villas like Chiragan, Montmaurin and Valentine.

**Bagnères-de-Luchon** (Ilixo)
M85 20 IGN70 D9

This spa town and winter sports resort had its Roman predecessor in the form of a luxurious suite of baths utilising the hot springs.

**Martres-Tolosane — Chiragan**
Villa M82 16 IGN71 A2

Chiragan, on the N bank of the Garonne,

excavated 1826-99, was the largest great prodigy villa of SW Gaul. Its earliest phase was a fairly small Augustan peristyle house, centre of an agricultural estate, with rows of dwellings for farm hands. It was much enlarged under Trajan, when a second courtyard was added, plus a colonnaded court running down to the Garonne on the S. At the end of this, overlooking the waters of the Garonne, was a six-sided gazebo or summer house. An entrance courtyard was added E of the main house, with a colonnade and cryptoporticus along the facing side.

Antonine and Severan extensions added new complexes of rooms, including a large bath suite, tripling the size of the villa, and an elaborate fountain was added in the entrance court. Occupation continued until the end of the fourth century, but may have ended in a fire. The parallel rows of 40 sheds, barns, farm buildings and labourer's cottages running out in regimented lines from the main buildings recall that this was not only a country house, but also the centre of a large working estate. Some were weaving sheds, as large numbers of loom weights testify, there was a large barn and granary, and space for 30 yoke of oxen. In all, the establishment covered an area of 16ha. The site was backfilled after excavation.

An early medieval church with E apse, surrounded by a cemetery of sarcophagi and earth graves, in use until the thirteenth century, overlay the villa. It included 25 fifth-/sixth-century sculptured 'Aquitanian' sarcophagi. Most accessible account — Grenier II (1934), 888-97; J. Boussard, 'Les sarcophages paléochrétiens de Matres Tolosane', *Cahiers Archéol* 9 (1948), 33-72.

## Montmaurin Villa
M82 15 IGN70 B11
Montmaurin is one of the great luxury villas of SW Gaul, purchased by the state and laid out for visitors after excavation. What is visible is the main part of a grand 'prodigy house' (to borrow a much later English term) of about 350, but there were earlier phases, starting in the time of Claudius or Nero. The first period 'Villa Rustica' consisted of an enclosure wall around an area on the N bank of the River Save. Inside were agricultural and residential buildings, the centre of a large rural estate. No main residential building was identified.

### The first villa
Not long after the mid-first century, Montmaurin was transformed into a villa of about 120 rooms, ranged round a courtyard, with private apartments around a lesser court to the rear. These correspond to the atrium and peristyle of contemporary town houses in Italy and parts of S. Gaul. Thus far, Montmaurin II recalls a very grand town house, but it was transformed by two pairs of ostentatious wings, only a single room deep, springing out from each side of the house. (Only the left-hand pair of wings have been excavated, and even these are no longer visible, but the other pair can be assumed for reasons of symmetry.) On the S., the entrance gateway led to a grand forecourt 160m wide, surrounded on three sides by the first pair of wings. On the analogy of later country houses, these probably held stables, carriage houses and the like. In the centre was the main house, and to its rear, a second 'mirror image' pair of wings, elaborated, like the other, with an arcaded front and projecting central pavilions.

### The fourth-century villa
The villa saw various alterations in the course of its life, and about 350 was remodelled in its present form. The visitor approached the house from the SW (one now enters obliquely from the side, and may need to reorient). Passing through a lodge, he entered a spacious

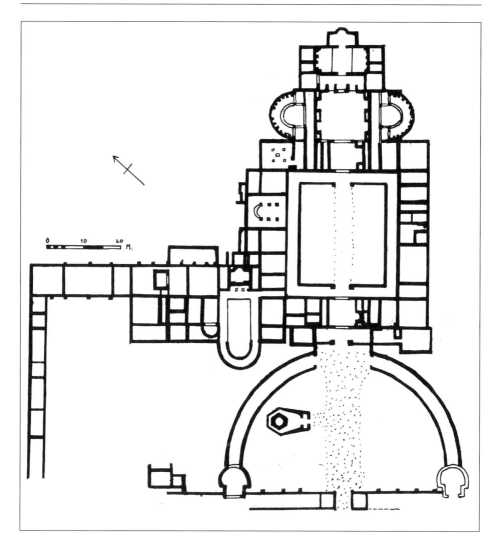

*51  Montmaurin (Haute Garonne) — plan of fourth-century villa. After Fouet*

*Cour d'Honneur*, with the facade of the main house in front, and two colonnades sweeping round to enclose a semicircular court, each ending in a little porticoed pavilion. On the left are the foundations of a domestic shrine, a circular *tholos* or perhaps an open-air altar, within a small kite-shaped enclosure. Two periods of enclosure foundations are visible.

The most striking features of the villa plan are its axial nature and symmetry, though the latter has been affected to some extent by changes made during the building's long life. In theory (allowing for open doors and eye levels) someone seated in the apse of the furthest room of the palaestra should have been able to see across the Palestra Court and the Garden Court beyond, to the main entrance, and the *Cour d'Honneur*. Nothing is now visible of the buildings around the *Estate Court* ('Cour de Communs') which held the usual agricultural buildings of a rural estate in the outer pair of wings. Some were heavily buttressed, suggesting granaries and barns. The visitor's eye will however be caught by the re-erected pillars of the *Nymphaeum*, an elaborate water feature between the main house and projecting wing. It was a rectangular open-air pool, paved with large slabs of marble, and surrounded by ranges of columns, and a covered walk, also paved in marble. The apse at the upper end may have held a statue. Venus bathing was a favourite and appropriate subject in such a position and a statue of Venus in a rare amber coloured calcite, fragments of which are now in the museum, may have been from here. The naked figure (or 'idol' as one early clerical excavator described it) had given offence at some date, and fragments of the smashed statue were found scattered over much of the villa. At the upper end of the nymphaeum, two intact pillars stand before the entrance to an apsidal room, with some of the moulded marble panelling of the door surround still in situ.

## The main house and Garden Court

The main house, grouped around the central court, derived its basic form from the first-century villa, though there had been alterations and elaboration in the course of time. On the SW was an entrance portico, and the apse of the nymphaeum and the S corner room of the main block projected at each end of the main facade. The main court was no doubt laid out as a Garden Court. Many of the surrounding rooms had hypocausts (mostly of the underfloor channel type rather than with brick *pilae*) and mosaics. Early records suggest that there may have been about a dozen mosaics, but only four survived.

## The Peristyle Court

The large square room (33) at the upper end of the court may have been a *triclinium*

or dining room. Beyond, the rooms around a second court or peristyle are more like a summer pleasance than a normal residential building. The peristyle, originally paved in marble, sloped gently downwards towards a central drain with a perforated drain cover which carried away rain water from the surrounding roofs. On its upper side, directly opposite the entry from Room 33, were two sets of steps up to a raised corridor or gallery leading to the other rooms. The draped Venus now in the museum may have stood on the little platform between the sets of steps. Each side of the peristyle three rectangular rainwater basins project into the court, and behind them are two apsidal porticoes, which would have opened on to a view of the central court through colonnades along their inner sides. From the raised corridor, other stairs led to flanking rooms paved in mosaic and to a smaller and more intimate version of the peristyle-portico theme. A central paved open-air space (17) is flanked by two niched rooms which may have corresponded to the porticoes flanking the central peristyle. Each would have provided space for dining or relaxation in the agreeable summer climate, either side of a central open-air space for games or entertainment.

The coin sequence ends under Gratian (367-83) and, unlike some of the other great Pyrenean villas, there is no subsequent Christian phase, though several post-Roman burials are recorded. Though it is rash to try to tie numismatic data for the end of villas to historical events, it may be permissible to recall that Magnus Maximus, the murderer of Gratian, had a bad reputation for confiscating the estates of rich supporters of the previous regime.
G. Fouet, *La Villa Gallo-Romaine de Montmaurin* (20th supp. to *Gallia* Paris 1969).

## St Béat Marble quarries
M85 20 IGN70 C11

St Béat marble first appears in St Bertrand in the peribolos of the temple *c*.100 and at the villa of Montmaurin at about same time. The white, grey, or veined grey-white marble was in much demand throughout Gaul. Examples have been recognised as far away as Poitiers, Nantes and Lillebonne. In the fifth and sixth centuries it was used for the sculptured 'Aquitanian' or 'South West Gallic' sarcophagi. The quarries continued in use in later centuries, the marble being used extensively in the gardens of Versailles, and they are still operational today. In 1946 a Roman cave sanctuary was discovered in a modern quarry, with heads and busts sculptured in the rock and many altars dedicated to a local god, Erriapus, one by the corporation of marble workers (*Marmo(rarii) Omnes*), or to Silvanus, the god of wild places.
*I.L.T.G.* 1-23.

## St Bertrand de Comminges
(Lugdunum Convenarum)
M85 20 IGN70 C10

According to St Jerome, writing in the fourth century, Lugdunum was founded in 72 BC by Caesar's rival Pompey the Great after his conquest of the Pyrénées. So far, no trace of this alleged colony has been found in excavation, and occupation seems to begin in Augustan times. The present name derives from the twelfth-century bishop Bertrand de l'Isle-Jourdain, who built the present cathedral and established a community of canons there. M.R. James's superb ghost story set in St Bertrand concerns one of those canons. 'Canon Alberic's Scrapbook' (*Ghost Stories of an Antiquary*) tells how a Cambridge don, visiting the cathedral in search of early manuscripts, is offered a scrapbook containing pages taken from many of the treasures of the former cathedral library. Needless to say, there is a catch — and a nasty one.

St Bertrand is an acropolis town. From a distance, the walled medieval town and cathedral, on their isolated hill of Jurassic limestone, stand out against the beginnings of the Pyrénées. Lugdunum lay on the flat plain to the N, but the assumption that it moved from the plain up to its present site in late Roman times, leaving the lower town deserted, is not wholly supported by new excavations. The 70ha Roman town is covered in fields and scattered houses, making large-scale excavation possible. Much was uncovered by Bertrand Sapène between 1920-70, with a number of major buildings being left on display. In 1985 new excavations and conservation work began, conducted by a large collaborative team of French and foreign scholars. This new work has made possible a reassessment of the chronology of individual buildings and the early development of the town under Augustus and his successors.

Any pre-existing oppidum or Pompeian colony must have lain on the hill, under the modern town, where excavation is difficult, though a little late Republican occupation is now known under the lower town. Augustan Lugdunum focused on a crossroads at its foot, where a road from Toulouse crossed one from Dax. The Toulouse road formed one of the main streets (*Cardo Maximus*) of the new town. To its W was a large temple, perhaps of the Imperial cult, in a rectangular enclosure, which may have been the E element of a tripartite forum-basilica complex, and a set of public baths, the 'Forum' or 'Temple'. Baths E of the road was a rectangular cobbled open space like a Greek *agora* or market square. Standing on its edge, opposite the baths, were two monuments — a small rectangular building and the square foundation of a pillar or column. The temple was built in the last two decades before Christ, and the first phase of the Temple Baths was also Augustan. Under Tiberius (AD 14-37), the baths were enlarged and a *macellum* or market hall built along the N side of the market square. Private houses of this period are also known, e.g. under the North Baths.

In the Flavian period, the town continued to develop. The Temple Baths were rebuilt in their present form, whilst S of the market square a large private house appeared, presumably the residence of a local magnate. The square was a busy spot, and the plinth of the monument was given a circular curb, perhaps to protect it from traffic. Sapène believed that the temple was renovated under Trajan, with the first use in the town of St Béat marble, and there are a number of dedications to Trajan and his wife Plotina from the Forum area (*I.L.T.G.* 70-4). The second century saw the building of the North Baths. There is a first-century theatre S of the city centre complex, and the possible site of an amphitheatre has been identified.

The site has so far produced little evidence of a 'third-century crisis' or of the shrinkage seen in other towns. Possibly early in the fourth century, the macellum was demolished and replaced by a rectangular enclosure with a rectangular piazza (Sapène's 'Pi-shaped portico') to the S, and a rectangular 'vestibule', perhaps a public or religious building, at its far end. Otherwise, the fourth century saw minor alterations to the Temple Baths and elsewhere, but little major change. The large private house S of the market square was rebuilt in luxurious style. This part of the town saw considerable activity in the fifth century. A polychrome mosaic was laid in one of the rooms of the private house,

whilst the market square has produced a marked concentration of fifth-/sixth-century grey stamp-decorated pottery (terre sigillée paléochrétienne). W of the house a small Christian church was built, impinging on its garden.

## Forum Baths

These were first built under Augustus, rebuilt and enlarged under Tiberius and again in the 70s. The main structure dates from this third phase. It consists of an elaborate colonnaded palaestra on the E, followed by the usual cold, tepid and hot rooms in a simple linear sequence. To their W is a *Macellum* or shopping precinct built around 30-50 AD. A rectangular complex measuring 62 x 27m, flanked on the S by a row of shops, its three entrances led to an open court with mosaic floor, flanked by rows of shops — 22 in all. The space within the court was divided up by two aedicules — monumental square-pillared structures — and further articulated by three broad shallow apses inside the entrances. The central space was ornamented with a square pool and a shrine.

## North Baths

These occupy an entire insula among housing 150m N of the main city-centre complex. Possibly Antonine, though the chronology of the complex is still being worked out, they were entered from the W through a roadside portico with pre-existing (Claudian) shops, leading to a courtyard (*Palaestra*) for exercise and games. The main block is of *opus mixtum*, with triple brick courses at regular intervals. On the S is a large natatio or swimming pool. The baths themselves follow the normal pattern of *Frigidarium* with cold bath, *Tepidarium*, a circular dry hot room (*Laconicum*) and an impressive *Caldarium*, with two hot baths in its E wall and a large apse at one end. The smaller apses in the side walls would have housed circular stone-raised basins

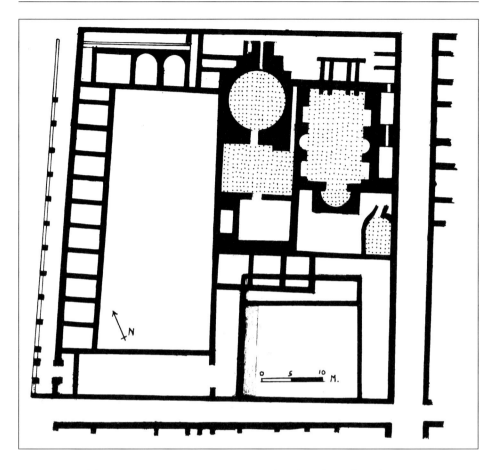

*52  St Bertrand de Comminges (Haute-Garonne) — North Baths. After Paillet and Guyon*

in which bathers could have washed themselves down. Later repairs and alterations suggest that the baths continued in use until late Roman times.

St Bertrand also has the remains, rare in France, of a Roman auxiliary fort of playing card shape. E of the Roman town, at a place called *Encraoustos* ('the enclosure') are the wall and earth bank of a fort of 2.85ha, thought to be Severan in date.

## The Christian church

This had a simple plan, with a rectangular nave and narrower square-ended chancel — one which was to remain standard for smaller churches

throughout the Middle Ages. There was probably a small narthex on the W. Later, the chancel was extended by a three-sided apse and rooms were added each side of the chancel. These were probably transeptal vestries.

Guyon et al, 'From Lugdunum to Convenae: recent work on Saint-Bertrand-de Comminges', *J.R.A.* 4, (1991), 89-122; S. Esmonde Cleary, M. Jones and J. Wood, 'The late Roman defences at Saint-Bertrand-de-Comminges: interim report', *J.R.A.* 11, (1998), 343-54; D. Schaad and G. Soukiassian, 'Encraoustos: un camp militaire Roman à Lugdunum — civitas

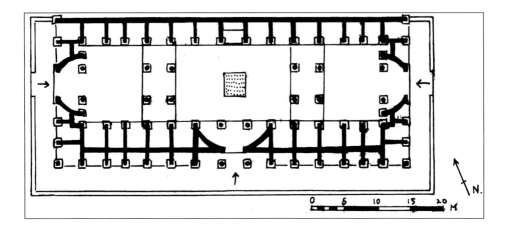

53 *St Bertrand de Comminges (Haute-Garonne) — Macellum (shopping precinct). The central water basin is stippled. After Paillet and Guyon*

Coinvenarum (Saint Bertrand de Comminges)', *Aquitania* 8 (1990).

## St Michel du Touch
Rural sanctuary M82 7 IGN64 B4

Four km from Toulouse, on the opposite bank of the Garonne, is a brick-built complex including an amphitheatre and a large bath suite of late first-/early second-century date with black and white mosaics.

*Gallia* 24 (1966), 425-7; 26 (1968), 534; 28 (1970), 410-13; 34 (1976), 477; Amphitheatre — *Gallia* 20 (1962), 571-2.

## Toulouse (Tolosa)
M82 8 IGN64 C3

The pre-Roman capital of the Volcae Tectosages was a large settlement along the banks of the Garonne. Somewhere within it was a sanctuary with a sacred pool from which the Roman general Q. Servlius Caepo removed a huge treasure in 106 BC, after suppressing a revolt by the Volcae. When the treasure vanished en route to Rome, Caepio was suspected of having a hand in its disappearance.

Roman Tolosa lies under the modern city. Its walls ran in a huge semicircle backing on to the Garonne, with almost 50 large circular towers, one of which is visible in the Place St-Jacques. They enclosed an area of some 90ha. The N gate was excavated in 1971 in the Place du Capitole (*Gallia* 30 (1972), 486-8). The site of the S Gate is known, and a triumphal arch was recorded in front of it in 1556. Until recently, the walls were thought to be second century in date, in part because of the use of brick, but recent excavation, and archaeomagnetic dating, suggests that they were under construction around AD 30. In the fourth century, as in London, the undefended river frontage was protected by a curtain wall, whose foundations contained reused sculptures and column fragments. A length of this wall, with a postern, is visible at the Institut Catholique.

Within the walls, there is little to see. The sites of the Theatre and Baths are known from excavation, but the great circular rotunda of la Daurade ('the Golden one'), which may have been a Roman temple reused as a Christian church, was demolished by the Benedictines in 1761, when they wanted a more modern and fashionable church.

La Daurade was an oval decagonal brick structure, with a cupola pierced by a central opening or oculus, like Hadrian's Pantheon in Rome. Its interior was decorated with three ranges of mosaics, comprising around 100 life-size figures, set in niches framed by marble columns decorated with spiral fluting or vine-scrolls. The upper range comprised nativity scenes, with Christ and St Mary flanked by Archangels and Prophets below, and Prophets and Old Testament figures in the bottom register. This sophisticated and ambitious brick structure was surely Gallo-Roman rather than Merovingian, and a Hadrianic or Antonine date is likely. The refurbishment of the interior with mosaics and marble columns must be later than the Council of Ephesus in 431, when the cult of the Virgin as Theotokos 'Mother of God' was first promulgated, and the columns (some of which survive) resemble those from villas such as Matres-Tolosane or Montmaurin, occupation of many of which is now thought to extend into the fifth century. Its purpose is unknown, though various suggestions have been made, including a baptistery or the Palatine chapel of the Gothic kings of Toulouse, perhaps part of the palace of Theoderic II (453-66) mentioned by Sidonius.

In the same period, Toulouse was one of the centres of production for the 'South West Gallic' or 'Aquitainian' sculptured sarcophagi, and an important collection of these can be seen in the Musée des Augustins (Rue d'Alsace-Lorraine). The main Gallo-Roman collections are in the Musée Saint-Reynaud (Place Saint-Sernin).

The patron saint of Toulouse was the martyr Saturninus, originally buried in a timber coffin within a small wooden oratory. Bishop Hilary built a brick vault over his remains about 402, but early in the sixth century Bishop Exsuperius translated them to a new basilica, now the medieval church of St Sernin, 300m to the N. An early apse was found under St Sernin in 1970.

Outside Toulouse was the amphitheatre of Purpan, built in AD 50-100, with an elaborate external elevation of alternate buttresses and rounded recesses. Largely brick-built (like much of Toulouse), it was enlarged in the mid-third century and occupied to the end of the fourth (*Gallia* 44 (1986), 320-1; *Gallia Informations* 1989, part 1 106-7). M. Labrousse, *Toulouse antique* (Paris 1968); E. James, *The Merovingian Archaeology of SW Gaul* 272-5; D. Cazes et al, 'La topographie urbain de Toulouse pendant l'Antiquité tardive et l'Haut moyen age' in P. Périn (ed), *Gallo-Romains, Wisigoths et Francs en Aquitaine, Septimanie et Toulouse* (Rouen 1991), 161-70; R. de Filippo 'Nouvelle definition de l'enceinte romaine de Toulouse', *Gallia* 50 (1993), 181-204.

## Valentine Villa
M85 20/86 1 IGN70 C10
The large luxury villa of Arneso in the Garonne valley W of St Gaudens was described by Eydoux as 'Un Versailles Pyrénéen'. Partly excavated in 1864 and again, by G. Fouet, in the 1950s. An early third-century villa was enlarged in the fourth. A late-Roman mausoleum in its SW corner was overlain by a possible Carolingian chapel and a medieval church, with an associated late Roman and early medieval cemetery. The site is on display.
*Gallia* 17 (1959), 430-3 (with plan); 19 (1961), 199.

## HÉRAULT
*Forma Urbis Romani* X (1946).
## Agde (Agatha)
M83 15 IGN65 B8
A Greek settlement near the mouth of

*54  Ambrussum (Hérault) — Roman bridge. Copyright Chris Dunn*

the Hérault, its ancient name was Agatha Tyche ('Good luck'). It lies under the modern town, and apart from the ramparts, of the fourth to second centuries BC, not a great deal survives. In Roman times, the port was a centre for export of basalt millstones. The excellent museum of underwater archaeology (Musée d'Archéologie Sous-marine, Mas de la Clape) has a model of a Roman merchant ship and a collection of material from local shipwrecks, including anchors, sounding leads, metal ingots, many stamped with the names of producers, locally produced millstones and an important collection of amphorae. The bronze figure of a youth may be a Hellenistic original.

## Ambrussum
Hillfort, Roman vicus and bridge
M83 8 IGN66 C4-5
A small town on the *Via Domitia*,

between Nîmes and Substantion, with remains of a Roman bridge, the Pont Ambroix. Ambrussum began as a hillfort, first occupied in Neolithic times, on a triangular plateau defended by a rampart with a series of rounded towers like those of Constantine and Nages. Excavation inside the hillfort has revealed solidly built cobbled roads and large Greek style houses. Settlement moved downhill when the road was built. Only one arch of the bridge survives, but it was equipped with cutwaters upstream and storm apertures to resist the force of the Vidourle.
Rivet 1988, pl 19; Hodge 205-8.

## Balaruc-les-Bains
M83 16 IGN66 D1
A Roman building found whilst building a new school near the town centre has been conserved and laid out on display. It may be a temple of Neptune.
Bromwich 1993, 82.

## Béziers (Baeterrae)
M83 15 IGN65 D6

Béziers, on its prominent hill, started life, like many cities of the region, as a hillfort. Etruscan and Greek pottery is known, with coins bearing the name of the city. It lay on the Roman trunk road from Italy to Spain, the Via Domitia, and in 36 or 35 BC became a colony for veterans of the Seventh Legion. Baeterrae lies under the modern city, and though the site of the Forum is known at its centre, and a theatre and amphitheatre to the south, nothing is visible, though ruins of the amphitheatre still existed in 1625. Fragments of an Augustan monumental arch are also known. The late Roman walls enclosed a polygonal area at the centre of the Roman city. Some traces can be seen in the W wall of the church of La Madeleine and there are two late Roman sarcophagi at the church of St Aphrodise. One has a hunting scene, with horsemen and lions; the other is a fifth-/sixth-century 'Aquitanian' sarcophagus of Pyrenean marble. A battered statue of an unknown Roman Emperor stands near the Hôtel de Ville.

Rivet 1988 149-59; M. Clavel, *Béziers et son Terretoire dans l'Antiquité* (1970).

## Ensérune Hillfort
M83 14 IGN65 D6

Iron Age hillfort along the crest of a long ridge, signposted from the D62 E. Occupied since the sixth century BC, its first phase had rectangular mud-brick houses, but from *c*.425 BC these were replaced by dry stone structures. Phase 3 (*c*.220 BC), following a destruction, saw a rebuilding of the rampart, the use of Roman building techniques such as tiled roofs and the occasional column, and the use of imported Greek and Italian pottery, Iberian and Greek inscriptions and Massiliot coins. A remarkable feature of the earlier periods is the use of large rock-cut silos.

Ensérune lay on the coastal route to Spain at the junction of a route leading to Atlantic Gaul. Catalan influence was strong. The lines of terraced houses have many Spanish parallels, and graffiti show that its people spoke Iberian. At its zenith, the population may have been 10,000. Occupation ended early in the first century AD. The site museum shows the pottery and finds from the site and its burials.

J. Jannoray, *Ensérune, contribution à l'étude des civilisations préromaines de la Gaule Méridionale* (1965). Subsequent work was the subject of interim reports in *Gallia* in alternate years.

## Lattes (Latara) and Maguelone
M83 7/17 IGN66 C3 and D2/3

Lattes, in the delta of the Lez S of Montpellier, boasts an archaeological centre and museum. It was receiving Greek imports from the sixth century BC onwards, and was walled from the beginning. The oval area within the walls contains crowded ranges of rectangular buildings and in Roman times had a temple of Mercury and was a centre for river traffic. It began to decline rapidly from about 200 AD, when changes in the coastline led to its replacement by Maguelone (Magalona) now at the tip of a long peninsula between the coastal lagoons and the sea, which already had a bishop in the fifth century. The display of Roman glass from the cemetery is outstanding.

Rivet 1988, 171; M. Py and D. Garcia, 'Bilan des recherches archéologiques sur la ville portuaire de Lattara (Lattes)', *Gallia* 50 (1993), 1-93.

## Lodève (Colonia Claudia Luteva or Forum Neronis)
M83 5 IGN65 B6

The Nero who gave his name to this

town was not the emperor, but Tiberius Claudius Nero, sent to Gaul by Augustus in 46 BC with the remit of founding Colonies. Little is known of its later history, and the only known Roman site is a mausoleum under the outlying church of St Martin de Combas (*Gallia* 22 (1964), 491-3).

Rivet 1988, 160-1.

## Loupian Les Près-Bas villa
M83 16 IGN65 D9

The elaborate villa, still under excavation, began in the early first century AD and reached its peak in the fourth, when at least a dozen rooms were equipped with lavish carpet-like spreads of mosaic and a large peristyle garden with central marble pool was added. The excavated parts are dominated by two large triclinia or dining rooms, the larger with triple apses for the diner's couches, summer and winter dining rooms perhaps. Occupation continued into the fifth century, when some of Sidonius's friends still had villas in this area. By now however, the mosaics were becoming worn, and some were covered with new floors of *opus signinum*.

H. Lavgne et al, 'La Villa gallo-romaine des Près-Bas à Loupian', *Gallia* 34 (1976), 215-35; Rivet 1988, 155-6 and fig. 16.

## St Thibéry Bridge
M83 15 IGN65 C7

The 'Roman' bridge over the river Hérault here, near the Roman settlement of *Cessero*, is probably medieval.

Rivet 1988 153-4 and plate 9.

## Substantion (Sexantio) Hillfort
M83 7 IGN66 C2

This hillfort, now in a suburb of Montpellier, stood where the Roman Via Domitia crossed the river Lez. Occupied from the seventh century BC onwards, excavation has produced

important prehistoric remains, but also evidence of Roman occupation.

## Vendres
M83 15 IGN65 D6

The remains of a Roman building on the coast south of Béziers are a supposed temple of Venus, as the place name indeed suggests (it was *de Veneris* in 1140), but it may be a villa.

*Forma Orbis Romanis* X, no 96; Rivet 1988 154-5.

# PYRENEES-ORIENTALES

In the SE tip of France, sandwiched between the Spanish border and the Mediterranean, Roussillon (Pyrénées-Orientales) is still strongly Catalan. It became part of France at the Treaty of the Pyrénées in 1659.

## Amélie-les-Bains
Thermal establishment
M86 18-19 IGN72 J2

Parts of the Roman bath complex are incorporated in the modern Thermes Romains. The modern changing rooms are in a Roman room with intact brick barrel vault and niched walls, which may have fulfilled the same purpose. The swimming pool next door also had a Roman predecessor.

## Château-Roussillon (Ruscino)
M86 20 IGN72 G3

Capital of the small tribe of the Sordones, the remains of Ruscino belong wholly to the Julio-Claudian period, and its later history is obscure. The most important are those of the Forum, an exceptionally early example, of 25-20 BC. It has a rectangular basilica, entered by an open portico and steps on its long E side. Rows of rectangular piers support the roof and a rectangular chamber at the N end was the Curia or council chamber. To the E was the forum, a porticoed courtyard dominated by a series of statue bases, with a row of shops at the E end replacing the temple precinct normal later. Dedications to the Imperial family and to local officials and dignitaries, whose statues no doubt once stood on the bases, were found. Below the forum is the main sewer of the town. Nearby, a group of Julio-Claudian houses have been excavated, producing a rich collection of painted wall plaster.

G. Barroul, *Ruscino: Château-Roussillon* (*Rev. Archéol de Narbonnaise* supplement 7, 1980); R. Marichal, 'Ruscino, capitale du Roussillon antique', *Archéologia* 183 (1983), 34-41.

## Elne (Illiberis, Vicus Helenae)
M86 19-20 IGN72 I I1-2

Named after Helena, mother of Constantine the Great, it was the scene in 350 of the murder of her grandson Constans, in flight from the usurper Magnentius. Material from excavations in the town is in the archaeological museum (Chapel of St Lawrence) in the cathedral cloisters.

## Le Perthus — L'Ecluse
Late Roman fort and customs post
M86 19 IGN72 J3

The pass of Le Perthus, the Roman Summum Pyrenaeum, crosses from France into Spain. The modern N9 road follows this route along the stream valley of the Rom. Just beyond the hamlet of Les Cluses, a ruin, the Castell dels Moros ('castle of the Moors') can be seen on a height to the right of the road. This was a late Roman frontier post, with a stone curtain wall and series of square towers enclosing a roughly rectangular area. Access involves crossing the stream, and a scramble up a steep scarp, but there are views from a lay-by on the N9 and from the Romanesque chapel of L'Ecluse Haute on the D71b about 1km from Les Cluses.

The Roman road ran immediately below the scarp, across the Rom from the N9, where a rock cutting and the remains of what may have been the Roman customs post are visible. The three towers on the E face of the fort are well preserved, with stairs to the rampart walk, and a gateway. There is a postern in the W wall. In 409, Constans, son of the usurper Constantine III, replaced the soldiers guarding the Pyrenean passes with barbarian troops, who allowed their fellow barbarians, who had been ravaging Gaul since 407, to pass into Spain. For one of the customs officers collecting the import duty on goods entering Gaul on this road see Théza below.

R. Grau 1978, 'Un fort romain à sauver: le Castell dels Moros de l'Ecluse', *Archéologia* 124, 64-70; Bromwich 1993, 76-8.

## Port Vendres (Portus Veneris)
M86 20 IGN72 I4

A series of shipwrecks found here give a remarkable picture of coastal trade in Roman times between Spain and southern France. The ships are numbered (A-E) not chronologically, but in the order in which they were found. They carried amphorae, the contents of which are known from elsewhere, so it is possible to identify parts at least of the cargo. In two cases, quantities of fish bones inside the amphorae confirmed the identification as fish sauce. The two earliest (*Port Vendres D and E*) date from around the time of Augustus or Tiberius, and carried amphorae of Spanish wine and fish sauce (Dressel 2-4 and Pascual 1). *Port Vendres B* sank between AD 42-8 in the reign of Claudius, laden with a mixed cargo of Spanish olive oil (Dressel 20 and 28 and Haltern 70) and mackerel sauce (Beltran 2A), south Spanish pottery, glass bowls, and ingots of tin, copper and lead. Some of the lead ingots were stamped with the name of a slave of the Empress Messalina, wife of

Claudius, a reminder of how much Roman trade was in official or aristocratic hands, with slaves occupying the roles of modern businessmen or entrepreneurs. A fourth wreck (*Port Vendres C*) sank in the mid-second century with a cargo of Gaulish amphorae and iron bars. One surprising find was a bronze statuette of an African black rhinoceros. The fifth wreck, *Port Vendres A*, was the first and the last — the first found and last in date. A 'good luck' coin in the mast step shows that it was built after 313-17, and other coins showed that it sank about 383-392 — a working life of about 75 years. Its main cargo (it could carry around 70-5 tons) was amphorae of Spanish fish sauce (Almagro 50 and 51C). Many contained sardine bones.

Parker (1992), 874-8.

**Théza** Inscription
M86 19 IGN72 H1

The S wall of the church of Théza, just off the N114 between Elne and Perpignan, contains an unusual record of a Roman customs officer. He was stationed on the road from Spain via the Col de Perthus, collecting the *quadragesima Galliarum*, the 2.5% import duty on goods entering Gaul. Found at St Julien, 5km to the W in the fifteenth century, it is a dedication to Mercury, the god of trade, by Evhangelus 'slave of the society of the tax of the one fortieth' — Soc(io) XXXX Ser(vus).

C.I.L. XII 5362.

## TARN

The present département of Tarn was not particularly important in Roman times. There was some industry in the Tarn valley itself, with a centre for the production of samian ware at Montans, and mines of argentiferous lead around Ambialet further east.

*Guide Répetoire* 17 (1968).

**Albi** (Albiga) M82 10/83 1 IGN64 A9
The capital of the Ruteni became the *Civitas Albigensium* under the late Empire, giving its name to the medieval religious dissidents the Albigensians. It occupied the triangular tip of a high promontory between the Tarn and a tributary. First-century occupation and pottery kilns are known, and the will of a seventh-century bishop suggests that it once had walls. There are Roman finds in the Musée Henri de Toulouse Lautrec.

F. Prevot, T.C.C.G. VI (Aquitania Prima), 51-6.

**Montans** Samian ware kilns M82 9 IGN64 A7
Montans, on the Tarn west of Albi, was a pioneer centre in the production of south Gaulish *terra sigillata* (samian ware). Production began in the period AD 1-20 with wares closely imitating Italian models, and continued to the early second century.

## TARN-ET-GARONNE

There are no major Roman sites in the département. A number of small earthworks are known, indicating a scattered rural population, but their date is usually unclear. The Musée Ingres at Montauban contains Roman material from local sites.

*Guide Répetoire* 26 (1971).

# 13 Alps, Savoie and the Côte d'Azur
## (Narbonensis Secunda and Alpes-Maritimae)

The diminutive province of Alpes-Maritimae originated after Augustus's conquest of the Ligurians and other Alpine tribes on the borders of Italy and Gaul. It became a procuratorial province, governed by an *eques* (a Roman knight) rather than by a senator, under Claudius or Nero. Its original capital was at Cimiez (Alpes-Maritimes) on the outskirts of Nice, where there are impressive remains, but its interior was mountainous country, notorious for its bandits. By the late Empire, its capital had shifted to Embrun, and though it could by now boast eight civitates, according to the *Notitia Galliarum*, most of these could have been no more than mountain villages.

In modern terms, Savoy and the southern Alps form the SE corner of France, between the Mediterranean beaches of the Côte d'Azur and the mountains of the Swiss and Italian borders.

## PROVINCE OF ALPES-MARITIMAE
## ALPES-DE-HAUTE-PROVENCE (BASSES-ALPES)

Apart from Riez and Digne, the département contains several Roman small towns, including Barcelonnette (Rigomagus) and Castellane (Salinae), the name of the latter recalling salt mining in the Alps. Castellane had its own magistrates, and for a while in the fifth century a bishop, but was probably little more than a village.

*Carte Archéologique de la Gaule Romaine* 6 (1937); Rivet (1988), 342-3.

**Digne** (Dinia)
M81 17 IGN60 C10
A Roman small town of 5ha, Digne appears in the *Notitia Galliarum* as the *Civitas Diniensium*, but when it acquired this dignity is unknown. The town museum has Roman material from the site.
Rivet (1988), 247-50; Inscriptions — *I.L.N.* III, ed. A. Chastagnol 1992.

**Riez** (Colonia Julia Augusta Apollonis Reiorum, Civitas Regensium)
M84 5 IGN60 D9
The oppidum of the small tribe of the Reii may have lain on Mont St Maxime, NE of the Roman town, which was on the flat ground below, at the junction of two streams. Nearby are four first-century Corinthian columns of grey granite, with their entablature intact — a typical Mediterranean classical ruin, standing in an empty landscape. They formed part of the temple of Apollo implied in the place name. Granite is not local, and the columns may be from the quarries of Pennafort near Callas (Var), 117km away.

To the E are an excavated fifth-century cathedral, and a still standing baptistery of the same date. The cathedral was built over the demolished public baths at the centre of the town, as at Cimiez, and cathedral and baptistery use grey granite columns recycled from the Temple of Apollo. The baptistery is a simple cube-like building, octagonal inside, with angle niches and a ring of eight columns around the central baptismal pool. It is now a museum. The

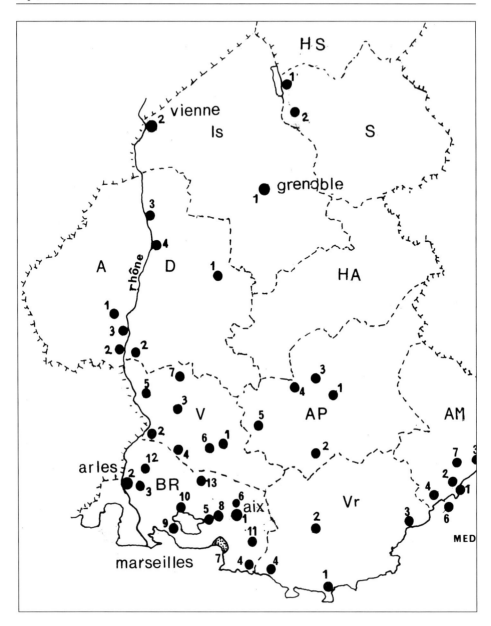

55  Alps, Savoie and the Côte d'Azur

    **AP** Alpes-de-Haute-Provence *1 Digne 2 Riez 3 St Geniez-Pierre Ecrit 4 Sisteron 5 Vachères*

    **AM** Alpes-Maritimae *1 Antibes 2 Biot 3 Cimiez 4 La Napoule 5 La Turbie 6 Lerins 7 Vence*

    **HA** Haute-Alpes

    **HS** Haute Savoie

    **S** Savoie *1 Aix-les-Bains 2 Chambéry*

    **VR** Var *1 Hyères-Olbia 2 Bagnoles-La Gayole 3 Fréjus 4 St Cyr sur Mer* present roof is modern. Before restoration in 1818 there was a central lantern like cupola, resting on the octagon of columns. The only evidence for late Roman defences is a reference to 'walls and gates' in the life of bishop St Maximus (434-60), written about 580-90 (*Patrologia Latina* 80, cols 31-40). No trace has been found, but they were probably on Mont St Maxime, where Maximus built a church. His successor, the British-born Faustus of Riez, says that he also built a second church, of St Peter and St Paul, within the old town. This was probably the excavated cathedral. Both bishops were ex-monks of Lerins and Faustus, a theologian of repute. One of Sidonius's letters records him sending a complementary copy of one of his works (perhaps that on Grace) back home to 'his Britons'.

Baptistery — G. Bailhache, *Congrès Archéol de France* 95 (1933 Aix and Nice) 75-8; Bishops — Griffé II, 1966, 260-4; G. Barroul, 'Un centre administratif et religieux des Alpes du Sud: Riez', *Archéologia* 21 (1968), 20-7; Inscriptions — *I.L.N.* III ed. A. Chastagnol 1992.

## St Geniez — 'Pierre Ecrit'
M81 6 IGN60 B9

Claudius Postumus Dardanus was a far from popular man among his fellow Gallic aristocrats. The praetorian prefect and former provincial governor of Viennensis, and his brother Claudius Lepidus, ex-governor of Germania Prima, had been among the few of their number to remain loyal to the Emperor Honorius when Constantine III revolted against him in 407. After Constantine's defeat in 411, Dardanus carried out a bloody purge among his supporters in Gaul, probably including the grandfather of Sidonius Apollinaris.

A devout Christian, and correspondent of St Augustine and St Jerome, Dardanus, his wife Nevia Galla,

and his brother later retired to live in religious seclusion at a place called *Theopolis* ('City of God') in a narrow valley, the Riou de Jabron, E of Sisteron. Sidonius records other Christian aristocrats who retired to their estates to live in semi-monastic retirement in this way. Theopolis may have been a villa, fortified with walls and a gate. Dardanus cut a road E from Sisteron through the valley, and commemorated this with an inscription (C.I.L. XII, 1524) which can be seen by the side of the road on the cut back rock face at the Défilé de Pierre Ecrit. The site of Theopolis is not known, but it may have lain near St Geniez, further along the road. A farm called Théous 4km NE of the village could preserve the name, but nothing is known there. A chapel 2km SE of St Geniez has a crypt with early columns, and could mark the mausoleum of Dardanus and his wife, but so far Theopolis remains to be found.

Benoit, 'La crypte en triconique de Theopolis', *Rivista di Archéologia Cristiana* 27 (1951), 69-89; F.O.R. VI, no 70; Rivet (1988), 254.

## Sisteron (Segustero)
M81 5-6 IGN60 B8
See chapter 11.

## Vachères
M81 15 IGN67 C3

The fine sculpture of a Gallic warrior from this remote upland valley between Apt and Sisteron is now in the Musée Calvet at Avignon, but is recorded here in its proper context. Depicted in the round in classical style, but with the tension of native sculpture, he stands holding a long oval shield with a round boss set with large circular rivets, exactly like some of the shields from Alesia. He wears a torque around his neck and has a knee-length coat of mail with elaborate mail shoulder straps. His military cloak and belt, the latter with a dagger suspended from it, suggest service in the Roman army. Of Augustan date, he is probably from a mausoleum like several others known in this area. Since he is missing from the knees down, the original site may one day be identified. Roman structures and inscriptions are recorded around a chapel at Conseillère here, and this could be the original context.

Reddé 1996, 152.

# ALPES-MARITIMES

The present département lay partly in Narbonensis II (Antibes), partly in Alpes Maritimae (Cimiez, Glandeve, Senez, Vence). Both parts are included here.

*Carte Archéologique de la Gaule Romaine* 1 (1931); *Guide Répetoire* 21 (1969); F.C.E. Octobron, *Castellaras et camps: enceintes celto-ligures du Département des Alpes-Maritimes* (1962).

## Antibes (Antipolis)
M84 9 IGN68 B10

Antibes, like Marseilles, was a colony of the Greek city of Phocea in Asia Minor. 'Antipolis' means 'the city opposite', though it is not clear opposite what. In 154 BC Antibes appealed to the Romans for help against Ligurian attacks. In Roman times it was famous as a tunny fishing port, and writers like Martial and Pliny refer to the tuna of Antipolis, the *garum* or fish sauce made from it, and the salt used in its manufacture, which was a delicacy in its own right. A series of rock-cut circular and rectangular basins near the old port may be *vivaria* for keeping fish alive until they were required. The Greek or Roman theatre, now under the bus station, and the sites of an amphitheatre and public baths are known. The museum (Bastion St Andrée) has material from local shipwrecks.

Hodge 1998, 182-6; Inscriptions — *I.L.N.* III ed. A. Chastagnol 1992.

## Biot Roman mausoleum
M84 9 IGN68 B10

At Biot, N of Antibes, is a first-century Roman tower-tomb known as 'la Chèvre d'Or' ('the Golden Goat'), of a type familiar along the Mediterranean coastlands from Spain to Syria. It contains a funerary chamber for cremation urns and has niches outside for statues.

Clébert (1970), 96-7.

## Cimiez (Cemenelum)
M84 10 IGN61 D9

The original capital of Alpes Maritimae outside Nice has been the site of important excavations, and remains of houses, three sets of baths and an amphitheatre are visible. There is also an attractive site museum. The amphitheatre, in its first-century form, may have been military, for its seating capacity, 500, would have accommodated the First Cohort of Ligurians, *Cohors I Ligurum*, stationed here until the Civil War after the death of Nero. The biggest surprise of the excavations however was the prosperity of the town in the third century, when the western Empire was, it is often assumed, in terminal crisis. The amphitheatre was extended, the Northern Baths built early in the century, and the Western Baths in the late third. The latter was converted into a small cathedral in the fifth century and a baptistery inserted into one of its rooms.

The amphitheatre is of two distinct phases. In its earlier form, two simple retaining walls held back an earth fill, with an overall width of 5m, around an oval arena. There were two opposed main entrances, two lateral openings, one of which supported the box for the president of the games, and pairs of walls in the thickness of the bank, probably to support stairs. Overall, it is a smaller version of legionary amphitheatres like those at Caerleon or Chester, save that it was for a unit of 500 men, not 5,000. In the secondary phase, the amphitheatre was enlarged by a series of radial walls added outside the earlier structure, in the manner of later urban amphitheatres. The new work is in *opus mixtum* — stone with bands of brick — and the similarity of the work to that of the nearby baths suggests a date in the early third century.

Duval, *Gallia* 4 (1946), 77-136; F. Benoit, *Fouilles de Cemenelum 1: Cimiez, la ville antique*, 1977; G. Laguerre 'L'occupation militaire de Cemenelum (Cimiez-Nice)', *R.A.N.* 2, 1969, 165-84.

## La Napoule (Neapolis, Ad Horrea)
M84 8 IGN68 B7

Now a fashionable seaside resort outside Cannes, Neapolis ('the New City') was a Greek foundation. In Roman times it became an important staging post on the coast road, midway between Antibes and Fréjus. The Roman name ('at the Granaries') suggests that grain was shipped out from the port here, perhaps for Rome.

## La Turbie Monument of the Alps
M84 10 IGN61 D9

The trophy (*tropaea*) of the Alps was erected by Augustus to mark the boundary between Italy and Gaul and his conquest of the Alpine tribes. It stands in the hills W of Monaco, close to the A8 motorway. The inscription listing the 45 peoples subdued by Augustus in geographical order was copied by Pliny, and has been restored from the many fragments found during conservation.

The *tropaea,* clad in white Carrara marble, stood 50m high, with staircases leading from its square base to the upper storeys. The tall rectangular podium carries on its W face the restored inscription, flanked by trophies of arms. Above a series of offsets is a circular

colonnade of 24 columns, between which were statues of the Imperial family (a head of Drusus has been found). The tall entablature above originally supported a stepped base and a bronze statue of Augustus with two captives, taken by one monastic writer for an idol and the demons Beelzebuth and Matafellon.

J. Formigé, *La Trophée des Alpes (La Turbie)* 1949 (2nd supplement to *Gallia*).

## Lerins Monastery
M84 9 IGN68 B9

Between 400 and 410, Honoratus, a well-travelled Gallo-Roman of senatorial family from the Trier region, established a monastery on this small coastal island of 105ha. Its Roman occupation had left a useful legacy of building stone. There was a church, novice house, baptistery, refectory and a number of outlying chapels, each probably serving a group of monks living in cells. The establishment of Lerins coincided with the disintegration of the western Roman Empire. It attracted many able men, who might earlier have gone into the service of the Emperor. Lerins became a 'nursery of bishops', and its monks occupied many of the sees of southern Gaul. Their influence reached as far as Britain. Abbot Faustus, later bishop of Riez, was British (or Breton) born and Lupus of Troyes accompanied Germanus of Auxerre to Britain. In the seventh century, Benedict Biscop, later the founder of Monkwearmouth and Jarrow in Northumbria, was a monk here for two years, at about the time Lerins became a more conventional Benedictine monastery.

Lerins shared the decline of southern Gaul in the seventh century. Repeated Arab raids followed. By the time the present Cistercians arrived in 1869, most of the buildings had been long in ruins.

There are seven scattered chapels on the island, but access is restricted due to the modern monastery.

A.C. Cooper-Marsdin, *The History of the Islands of Lérins* (Cambridge 1913); Lord Fletcher, 'The monastery at Lerins', *J. Brit Archaeol Assoc.* 133 (1980), 17-29.

**Vence** (Vintium) M84 9 IGN68 A8

The medieval walls may follow the line of a Roman predecessor. Among the many inscriptions, one records the building of an aqueduct for the town by a local magnate, M. Claudius Faventinus (C.I.L. XII, 6). There were other small Roman towns at *Senez* (Sanitium), *Thorame* (Eturamina), *Briançonnet* (Brigomagus) and *Glandève* (Glanate), but there are no visible remains, though some have produced collections of inscriptions.

Rivet 1988 335-49.

## HAUTES-ALPES

Only the E part of the département lay in Alpes-Maritimae, the W part being in Narbonensis II. Neither Gap (in Narbonensis) nor Embrun (in Alpes-Maritimae) have left any visible remains.

## HAUTE-SAVOIE

The County of Savoie, now the départements of Haute-Savoie and Savoie, was Italian until 1860, when it became part of France in return for Napoleon III's military help in expelling the Austrians from Italy. In Haute-Savoie there are archaeological collections in the museums at Annecy and Thonon-les-Bains, including prehistoric material from wetland sites ('lake dwellings'). The museums are housed in the respective castles.

## SAVOIE

The area contains several early Roman sites, sometimes with N Italian links, as at Aix. The shrine of the native god

Limetus at Châteauneuf was taken over early in the first century AD by Mercury and his consort Maia, only to be demolished in Flavian times (Mermet *Gallia* 50 (1993), 95-138). The double temple recalls that of the same couple at Berthouville (Eure). A bathhouse, theatre and houses are also known there.

## Aix-les-Bains

(Vicus Aquensis, Aquae Gratinae) M89 15 IGN51 B11

The modern spa town on the Lac du Bourget had an impressive Roman predecessor, renamed in late Roman times after the Emperor Gratian like nearby Grenoble. Parts of the Roman baths survive under the Thermes Nationaux of 1864, including a brick calderium or hot room, and a circular swimming bath (conducted tours). Between the baths and the Hôtel de Ville is an inscribed arch set up by Lucius Pompeius Campanus. The Hôtel de Ville, once part of the château of the Marquess of Aix, but now a museum, includes a much-altered Roman building known as 'Temple of Diana'. Excavations in the car park to its east have revealed a temenos wall separating it from the large open space between it and the Baths. This contained the Arch of Campanus, and the general arrangement in Roman times may not have been far removed from that today.

The arch of Campanus dates from around 25 BC. A single arch, it was erected by Campanus during his lifetime in memory of his parents. The best parallels are in north Italy, as Prieur points out. The rectangular piers carry an arch with the forepart (*protome*) of a bull on the keystone. Above is the badly worn inscription (C.I.L. XII, 2473) and on the W face rectangular recesses perhaps meant to hold funerary inscriptions.

Wuilleumier, *La Passée d'Aix-les-Bains*

(Lyon 1950); Prieur 1982, 460-75; Rivet 1988, 323.

## Chambéry Museum
M89 16 IGN51 B11

The *Musée Savoisien d'histoire et d'archéologie* (1, Boulevard de Théatre) contains material from prehistoric wetland sites in the Lac de Bourget and local Gallo-Roman sites.

# VAR
*Carte Archéologique de la Gaule Romaine* II (1932).

## Hyères Almanarre — Olbia
M84 16 IGN68 D2

The Greek and Roman town of Olbia was first identified in 1909, when a dedication to its *Genius* or Guiding Spirit was found. Founded about 350 BC, it was planned with military precision, perhaps as a counter to the Ligurian oppidum of Costebelle, 2km N. Within a square of walls, each side 160m long, with rectangular towers, was a street grid of 40 long rectangular insulae, with two main streets intersecting at the centre. Its Greek character is shown by its shrines to Artemis, Aphrodite, and Arasteus, son of Apollo and to the nymph Cyrene. Destroyed about the time of the Roman siege of Marseilles in 49 BC, Roman occupation was slight, though it included a large baths and continued until the sixth century (there is a church on the site). Much of the site has been laid out on display beside the RN559 coast road.

J. Coupy, 'Fouilles à Olbia', *Gallia* 12, 1954, 3-33 and 'Les fouilles d'Olbia', *C.R.A.I.* 1964, 313-21.

## Brignoles — La Gayole
Early Christian sarcophagus and crypt
M84 15 IGN67 J3

The farm of La Gayole was once a Grange of the Abbey of St Victor at Marseilles. A chapel on the farm contained a sculpted Roman sarcophagus often claimed as one of the earliest Christian memorials in Gaul. Now in Brignoles, it has Christian scenes (a seated teacher, orante, Good Shepherd, St Peter fishing). Dates as early as the end of the second century have been claimed, and the crypt identified as the funerary chapel of an aristocratic family, but it is probably much later, and could have been brought to the chapel from somewhere else in the vicinity. The sarcophagus probably belongs to the late Roman Marseilles school, most of whose products were destroyed at the Revolution, making it difficult to put surviving examples into context.

D.A.C.L. VI, 668-95; *Gallia* 20 (1962), 702-3.

## Fréjus (Forum Julii)
M84 8 IGN68 B7

Julius Caesar used Fréjus as a port at the time of his siege of Marseilles in 49 BC. His successor, Octavian, the future Augustus, established a naval base here, with barracks for naval troops which have been found recently S of the city. Its full title was *Forum Julii Octavanorum Colonia Pacensis Classica* — 'the Julian Forum of Augustus, the Colony of Peace and of the Fleet'. After the battle of Actium, around 30 BC, the city became a Roman colony for veterans of the 8th Legion. The Augustan city walls enclose an irregular area, with circular towers along at least part, at an average of about 50m. The ruinous remains of two gates survive, the Porte de Rome on the E and the Porte des Gaules on the W. Both were a distinctive Augustan type, with two circular towers flanking a broad semicircular recess, with the actual gate — a central arch flanked by two lesser arches for pedestrians — at its centre. The Porte de Rome is approached by an aqueduct, of which piers and an intact arch remain.

The theatre is within the Augustan walls, near the Porte de Rome, and is probably contemporary with them. The Amphitheatre on the other hand is just outside the walls on the NW, and probably a later addition to the amenities of the city in the late first century, when many urban amphitheatres were built in Gaul. It consists of a series of radiating vaulted passages around the arena, supporting tiers of seats, intersected by circular galleries around the circumference for the circulation of the crowds. Above this was a broad gallery, with columns towards the arena, which provided a walkway or portico. There may have been further tiers of wooden seating above this, supported by the columns.

The aqueduct begins at the Source du Neissoun near Beauregard, N of Fayence, where the water was impounded. After 3km it flows through a lengthy 3m high rock-cut channel known as the Roche Taillée before following a sinuous course, 40km overall, to Fréjus. Its final 10km, in the hilly country NE of Fréjus, is marked by a series of eight short aqueduct-bridges carrying the channel over streams and valleys, before it enters Fréjus by the Porte du Rome.

Grenier III 606-12 (amphitheatre), 734-41 (theatre); Inscriptions — *I.L.N.* 1 ed. J. Gascou and M. Janon 1985.

## St-Cyr-sur-Mer Villa

M8414 IGN67 J3

Large villa E of La Ciotat near Les Lecques. Locally identified as the Greek site of Tauroentum (which was probably at Le Brusc) and so signposted. Displayed for visitors, with site museum.

# Appendix: A brief gazetteer of pottery types

Since much of recent advances in our knowledge of Roman Gaul depends upon pottery from excavations, non-specialists may find a brief explanation of some of the pottery types involved useful. The bulk of pottery in all periods comprised locally produced coarse wares in reduced (grey or black) or oxidised (orange) fabrics, depending on the amount of oxygen present in the kiln. Imported fine wares and amphorae are however more closely dateable and give invaluable data on the chronology and external contacts of particular sites. The best concise introduction to these is J.W. Hayes's *Handbook of Mediterranean Roman Pottery* (British Museum 1997). For reasons of space, I have not attempted a bibliography, save for works particularly relevant to Gaul.

## African Red Slip Wares
From the late first century AD new and simplified forms of red-gloss pottery based on *terra sigillata* began to be produced in the Carthage area, and later in other parts of Tunisia and eastern Algeria. This was exported in huge quantities, and in late Roman times was the standard fineware over the whole Mediterranean basin. Various types are known (African red slip A, C and D), but generically it can readily be distinguished from *terra sigillata* by its coarser fabric, more matte glaze and distinctive stamped or moulded decoration.
J.W. Haynes, *Late Roman Pottery* (1972) and *Supplement* (1980).

## Argonne Ware
Lavoye (Meuse) on the edge of the Argonne forest had been producing samian ware since the time of Hadrian. When this ended in the third century, various workshops in the Argonne continued to produce a range of samian forms in red-slipped ware, sometimes with complex rouletted patterns, including Christian symbols. These were made until about AD 530, and detailed studies of the individual roulette-wheels used have made it possible to divide the industry into a series of datable phases.
G. Chenet and G. Gaudron, *La céramique sigillée d'Argonne des IIe. et IIIe. siècles* (6th supp. to *Gallia* 1955); G. Chenet, *La céramique Gallo-Romain d'Argonne du IVe. siècle et la terre sigillée décorée à la molette* (Mâcon 1941); E. Hübener, 'Eine studie zur spätromische Radchensigillata (Argonnesigillata)', *Bonner Jahrbucher* 168 (1968), 240-98; D. Bayard, 'L'ensemble du Grand Amphithéâtre de Metz et la sigillée d'Argonne au Ve. Siècle', *Gallia* 47 (1990), 271-319.

## Arretine Ware
From around 40 BC, red-gloss pottery of high quality was made at Arretium (Arezzo) in northern Tuscany. Between about 25 BC and AD 25, pottery from Arezzo and Pisa was exported to Gaul, where it is something of an archaeological type-fossil for the period of Augustus and Tiberius. For a while, it was also produced in a branch factory at Lyon. A variety of plates and dishes were made, together with vessels with moulded relief decoration, in a glossy sealing-wax red ware which formed the basis for the later Gaulish 'terra sigillata' or 'samian' wares.

## Campanian Ware
A black-gloss pottery produced mainly in the Naples region of southern Italy in 200-50 BC, and a common find in shipwrecks of the period, often associated with Italian Dressel 1 amphorae. A

slightly later version (Campanian B) from Etruria may have played a role in the transition to red gloss *terra sigillata*.

J.P. Morel, 'Le céramique campanienne en Gaule interne' in *Les âges du Fer dans la vallée de la Saône* ed L. Bonnamour et al, *Rev. Archéol Est* supplement 6 (Paris 1985), 181-7.

## Dressel 1 Amphorae

In 1899, the German scholar Heinrich Dressel produced a pioneer typology of Roman amphorae, mainly as the basis for publishing the various stamps and inscriptions found on different types. Though most of this has now been superseded, the term Dressel 1 is still used for the tall cylindrical amphorae in reddish fabric in which prodigious quantities of Caecuban and Falernian wine (on whose merits see Pliny *Natural History* XIV, 8) were exported to Gaul and even to southern England. This came from the estates of Republican senators in south-central Italy. One modern estimate is that between 50,000 and 100,000 hectolitres of wine were imported annually into Gaul in the first century BC.

Two main broadly successive types are known, Dressel 1A (*c.*150-50 BC), and 1B (*c.*70-10 BC), making a useful chronological marker on late Iron Age and early Roman sites. Type A was reaching Carthage by 146 BC and Gaul before the destruction of Entremont in 122 BC, and is often seen as characteristic of the La Tène III/D period from *c.*125-100 BC onwards to the time of Caesar. Since Type B begins about 70 BC, it is largely post-Caesar, though reliable dating depends on a large enough site assemblage, with enough of the amphorae preserved to identify the type. By about 10 BC on the Augustan fort sites in Germany and elsewhere, Dressel 1 amphorae were facing competition from Spanish sources, and were in any case being phased out by the equally distinctive Dressel 2-4 amphorae.

On amphorae generally see D.P.S. Peacock and D.F. Williams, *Amphorae and the Roman Economy: An Introductory Guide* (London 1986); A.P. Fitzpatrick, 'The distribution of Dressel 1 amphorae in NW Europe', *Oxford Journal of Archaeology* 4 (1985), 343-50.

## Samian Ware

The wholly illogical English name for this red-gloss pottery, familiar to anyone who has ever visited a museum with Roman collections, derives from an eighteenth-century confusion with pottery produced on the Greek island of Samos, as described by classical authors. In France, it is *terre sigillée*. It was produced in great quantities in centres in southern, central and eastern Gaul (e.g. La Graufesenque, Lezoux, Lavoye. ). Some 50 centres of production are known, large and small. For these see:

C. Bémont and J.-P. Jacob (eds), *La terre sigillée gallo-romaine. Lieux de production du Haut-Empire: imlantations, produits, relations* (Documents d'Archéologie Française 6, Paris 1986).

## Terra Sigillata

Meaning literally 'stamped pottery', *terra sigillata* is a generic term for the red gloss wares, often with moulded decoration, produced in Italy and Gaul in the earlier Roman period. It covers both Arretine and Samian wares, as well as some more localised types produced in Spain and the east.

## Terre Sigillée paléochrétienne grise et orangée

This somewhat unwieldy title ('early Christian grey and orange stamped wares'), current in several variants, covers a range of orange or grey slipped wares, with distinctive stamped decoration, made in S and central Gaul in the late fourth to sixth centuries AD. Three main variants are known, associated with the cities of Marseilles, Narbonne and Bordeaux, and there are other smaller production sites inland. A little of the 'Atlantic type' from Bordeaux was exported to western Britain (Insular D ware).

# Sources and bibliography

## SOURCES

### Maps

The *Tabula Imperii Romani* ('Map of the Roman Empire') provides a series of maps to a uniform scale of 1:1,000,000 with a gazetteer and bibliography. Sheets include L31 (Lugdunum); M30-1 (Condate, Glevum, Londinium, Lutetia); M31 (Lutetia, Atuatuca, Ulpia Noviomagus); M32 (Mogontiacum); and L32 (Mediolanum). These however show the ancient topography and landscape, and are not intended for use in the field, or for finding one's way. For maps for use in the field see Introduction.

### Guides

For general guidebooks, the Michelin *Guides de Tourisme* (the 'Green Mich' as opposed to the 'Red Mich', giving hotels and garages), available either in French or English, cover France in 22 pocket-sized volumes. Concise introductions cover all aspects of the region, from geology to the types of Breton fishing boat. Among British guidebooks, the dependable *Blue Guide* gives unrivalled detail. My well-worn 1958 edition covered northern France in one volume, but more recent editions cover various regions, as do the very readable Companion Guides.

Among site guides, the official series *Guides Archéologiques de la France* are excellent, concisely written by the leading authority on a site (often the excavator) and well illustrated. I have noted them (abbreviated G.A.F.) in the site bibliographies. Like the English Heritage/Cadw/Historic Scotland equivalents they can usually be bought on site.

### Source books

Bibliographies are given for all sites dealt with here, but for full catalogues of Roman sites and finds for a particular département, the series *Carte Archéologique de la Gaule* is indispensable. The series now covers most French départements.

## Abbreviations

A.N.R.W.    *Aufsteig und Niedergang der Römischen Welt* (Berlin)
Arch. Med.  *Archéologie Médiévale*
B.A.R.      *British Archaeological Reports* (Oxford)
B.M.        *Bulletin Monumental*
C.A.F.      *Congrès Archéologique de la France*
C.B.A.      Council for British Archaeology
C.I.L.      *Corpus Inscriptionum Latinarum* Vols XII, Gallia Narbonensis (Berlin 1888) and XIII (Berlin 1899-1916), Three Gauls and Germany
C.R.A.I.    *Comtes rendus de l'Académie des inscriptions et belles lettres*
D.A.C.L.    *Dictionnaire d'Archéologie Chrétienne et du Liturgie* ed. F Cabrol and H. Leclerq (Paris 1913-53, 15 vols)
F.O.R.      *Forma orbis Romani* (= *Carte archéologique de la Gaule Romaine*)
G.A.F.      *Guides Archéologiques de la France*
G.R.        *Guide-Répetoire d'Archéologie Antique* (Touring Club de France)
I.L.N.      *Inscriptions Latines de Narbonnaise* (44th supplement to Gallia, 4 vols 1985-97)
I.L.S.      *Inscriptiones Latinae Selectae* ed. H. Dessau
I.L.T.G.    *Inscriptions Latines des Trois Gaules* ed. W. Wuilleumier (Paris, 17th supplement to *Gallia*

1963)
J.R.A.    *Journal of Roman Archaeology*
J.R.S.    *Journal of Roman Studies*
M.S.A.P.  *Mémoires de la Société des Antiquaries de Picardie*
R.A.     *Revue Archéologique*
R.A.E.   *Revue Archéologique de l'Est* (before 1993 *'et du Centre Est'*)
R.A.N.   *Revue Archéologique de Narbonnaise*
R.A.O.   *Revue Archéologique de l'Ouest*
R.A.P.   *Revue Archéologique de Picardie*
R.E.A.   *Revue des Études Anciennes*
R.G.M.G. *Recueil Général des Mosaiques de la Gaule*
T.C.C.G. *Topographie Chrétienne des Cites de la Gaule*

## Books and Articles

Agache, R. 1970, *Détection aérienne de vestiges protohistoriques gallo-romains et médiévaux dans le bassin de la Somme et ses abords* (*Bull. Soc de Préhistoire du Nord* 7)

Agache, R. 1975, 'La campagne à l'époque romaine dans les grandes plaines du Nord de la France', A.N.R.W. II, 4, 658-713.

Agache, R. 1978, *La Somme Pré-Romaine et Romaine* (M.S.A.P. 24 Amiens)

Amy, R. et al 1962, *L'Arc d'Orange* (27th supplement to *Gallia*)

Amy, R et al. 1979, *La Maison Carrée de Nîmes*

Balmelle, C. 1980, *R.G.M.G. IV Aquitaine 1*

Balmelle, C. 1987 do. *Aquitaine 2*

Bedon, R. 1984 *Les carrières et les Carriers de la Gaule Romaine* (Paris)

Bedon, R. 1997 (ed), *Les Aqueducs de la Gaule Romaine et des régions voisines* (*Caesarodunum* 31, Limoges 1997)

Bedon, R., Chevallier, R. and Pinon, P. 1988, *Architecture et Urbanisme en Gaule Romaine* (Paris, 2 vols)

Bémont, C. and Jacob, J.P. 1986 (ed), *Terre-sigillée Gallo-Romain. Lieux de production du haut-empire: Implantation, produits, relations* (Documents d'archéologie française 6, Paris)

Bender, B. 1986, *The Archaeology of Britanny, Normandy and the Channel Islands*

Benoit, F. 1954, *Sarcophages paléochrétiens d'Arles et de Marseilles* (5th supplement to *Gallia*)

Bessac, J.-C. 1988, 'Influences de la conquête romaine sur le travail de la pierre en Gaule Méditerranéenne', *J.R.A.* 1, 57-72

Blanchard-Lemée, M. et al 1991, *R.G.M.G II Province de Lyonnaise part 4 (west)*

Blanchet, A. 1907, *Les enceintes romaines de la Gaule*

Blanchet, A. 1907a, 'Recherches sur les aqueducs romaines en Gaule', *C.A.F* Avallon

Blanchet, A. 1907, 354-457.

Bouley, E. 1983, 'Les théâtres cultuels de Belgique et des Germanies: Reflections sur les ensembles architectonique théâtres-temples', *Latomus* 42, 546-71

Brogan, O. 1953, *Roman Gaul*

Bromwich, J. 1993, *The Roman Remains of southern France: A Guidebook*

Brulay, R. 1991, 'Le Litus Saxonicum continental' in V. Maxfield and M.J. Dobson (eds) *Roman Frontier Studies 1989* (Exeter), 155-69.

Butler, R.M. 1959, 'Late Roman town walls in Gaul' *Archaeol. J.* 116, 25-50.

de Caumont, A. 1870, *Abécédaire ou rudiments d'archéologie, époque gallo-romaine*

Chevallier, R. 1957, 'Gallia Lugdunensis, Bilan des 25 ans de recherches historiques et archéologiques', *A.N.R.W.* 2:3 (1957), 860-1060.

de Caumont, A. (ed) 1976, *Le Vicus Gallo-Romain: Actes du Colloque* (= *Caesarodunum* 11)

Clébert, J.-P. 1970, *Provence Antique: 2, l'époque gallo-romaine*

Cliquet, D. et al (eds) 1993, *Les Celtes en Normandie: Les rites funéraires en Gaule* (*R. A. O.* supplement no 6)

Cochet, Abbé 1866, *La Seine-Inférieure historique et archéologique* (2nd ed, Paris)

Collis, J. 1975, *Defended sites of the later La Tène in central and western Europe* (B.A.R. Supp. Series 2)

Cotton, M. 1957, 'Muri Gallici' in Wheeler and Richardson 159-216

Cotton, M.A. and Frere, S. 1961, 'Enceintes de l'âge du Fer au pays des Lémovices', *Gallia* 19

(1961), 31-54

Cunliffe, B. 1988, *Greeks, Romans and Barbarians: Spheres of Interaction*

Cunliffe, B. and Rowley, T. (eds) 1976, *Oppida: The beginnings of Urbanisation in Barbarian Europe* (B.A.R Supp. ser 2 Oxford)

Darmon, J.P. and Lavagne, H. 1977, *R.G.M.G. II Province de Lyonnaise Part 3 (central)*

Davies, W. et al 2000, *The Inscriptions of Early Medieval Brittany/Les inscriptions de la Bretagne du Haut Moyen Âge* (Oakville, Connecticut and Aberystwyth)

Déchelette, J. 1927-31, *Manuel d'archéologie préhistorique, celtique et gallo-romaine* vols 4 and 5

Desbordes, J.-M. 1975, 'La Picardie antique', *Archéologia* 80, 44-60

Desbordes, J.-M. 1985, 'Les fortifications du second Âge du Fer en Limousin: caractères et fonctions', *Gallia* 43 (1985), 25-47

Drinkwater, J.F. 1978, 'The rise and fall of the Gallic Julii', *Latomus* 37, 4, 817-50

Drinkwater, J.F. 1983, *Roman Gaul: The Three Provinces 58 BC-AD 260*

Drinkwater, J.F. 1987, *The Gallic Empire: Separatism and Continuity in the North-Western Provinces of the Roman Empire AD 260-274* (Stuttgart)

Dubois, J. 1965, 'La carte des diocèses de France avant la Revolution', *Annales* 20, 680-91

Duby, G. 1980, *Histoire de la France Urbaine* 1 (Paris)

Duchesne L.M. 1900, *Fastes Episcopaux de l'ancienne Gaule*

Dumasy, F. 1975, 'Les édifices théâtraux de type gallo-romain. Essai de definition', *Latomus* 34, 4, 1010-19

Duval, N. 1993, 'Le context archéologique: les villas du Sud-Ouest' *Antiquité Tardive 1: les sarcophages d'Aquitaine*, 29-36

Espérandieu, E. et al 1907-1981, *Recueil Général des bas-reliefs, statues et bustes de la Gaule romaine* Vols 1-16

Février, P.-A. 1973, 'The origin and growth of the cities of southern Gaul to the third century AD', *J.R.S* 63, 1-28

Fichtl 1994, *Les Gaulois du Nord de la Gaule*

Galliou, P. 1983, *L'Armorique Romaine* (Braspars)

Garmy, P. and Maurin, L. 1996 (ed) *Enceintes Romaines d'Aquitaine: Bordeaux, Dax Périgueux, Bazas* (Documents d'Archéologie Française 53)

Gayraud, M. 1981, *Narbonne antique, des origines à la fin du IIIe siècle* (7th supplement to *R.A.N.*)

Giot, P.R., Briard, J. and Pape L. 1995, *Protohistoire de la Bretagne* (Rennes)

Golvin, J.C. 1988, *L'amphithéâtre romain* (Paris, 2 vols) 226-36

Goudineau, C. 1979, *Les fouilles de la Maison du Dauphin à Voison-la-Romaine* (37th supplement to *Gallia*)

Golvin, J.C. 1984, *Voison-la-Romaine*

Grenier, A. 1931, *Manuel d' archéologie gallo-romaine I* (travaux militaires)

Grenier, A. 1934, do. II. (routes, navigation, occupation du sol)

Grenier, A. 1958, do III. (Capitole, forum, temple, basilique, théâtres, amphithéâtres, cirques)

Grenier, A. 1960, do. IV (Aqueducs, thermes, villes d'eau, sanctuaries d'eau)

Grenier, A. 1937, 'La Gaule Romaine' in *An Economic Survey of Ancient Rome* Vol 3, ed. Tenney Frank (New Jersey)

Griffe, E. 1964-6, *La Gaule Chrétienne à l'époque romaine* (Paris, 3 volumes)

Gros, P. 1979, 'Pour une chronologie des Arcs de Triomph de Gaule Narbonnaise', *Gallia* 37, 55-83

Haselgrove, C. 1990, 'The Romanization of Belgic Gaul: some archaeological perspectives' in *The Early Roman Empire in the West* ed. T. Blagg and M. Millett (Oxford), 45-71

Hatt, J.J. 1986, *La Tombe Gallo-Romaine* (2nd ed.)

Hodge, A.T. 1998, *Ancient Greek France*

Horne, P.D. and King H.C. 1980, 'Romano-Celtic temples in continental Europe: a gazetteer of those with known plans' in W. Rodwell (ed) *Temples churches and religion: recent research in Roman Britain* (Oxford)

Humphrey, J.H. 1986, *Roman Circuses: arenas for chariot racing* (London) 388-431

James, E. 1977, *The Merovingian Archaeology of SW Gaul*, B.A.R. Supp. Series 25 (2 vols)

Johnson, J.S. 1973, 'A group of late Roman city walls in Gallia Belgica' *Britannia* 4, 210-13

Johnson, J.S. 1976, *The Roman Forts of the Saxon Shore*

Johnson, J.S. 1983, *Late Roman Fortifications*

Jones, A.H.M. 1954, 'The date and value of the Verona list', *J.R.S.* 44, 21-9

Jullian, C. 1906-26, *Histoire de la Gaule* (8 vols)

Kenyon, K.M. 1934, 'The Roman theatre at Verulamium, St Albans', *Archaeologia* 84, 213-61

King, A. 1990, *Roman France and Germany*

Knight, J.K. 1999, *The End of Antiquity: Archaeology, Society and Religion in Early Medieval Western Europe, AD 235-700*

Koethe, H. 1933, 'Die keltische Rund und Vieleck tempel der Kaiserzeit', *Bericht der Römisch-Germanischen Kommission* 23, 10-108

Krencker, D. and Krüger, E. 1929, *Die Trierer Kaiserthermen* (Augsberg)

Labrousse, M. 1968, *Toulouse antique des origines à l' établissement des Wisigoths*

Lancha, J. 1981, *R.G.M.G. III Narbonnaise part 2 (Vienne)*

Lavagne, H. 1979, *R.G.M.G. III Narbonnaise part 1 (central)*

Loriot, X. and Nony, D. 1997, *La crise de l'Empire Romain 235-85* (Paris)

Mertens, J. 1980, 'Recherches récentes sur le limes en Gaule Belgique' in W. Hanson and L. Keppie (eds), *Roman Frontier Studies 1979* (B.A.R. Int. Ser. 71)

Mertens, J. 1983, 'Urban wall circuits in Gallia Belgica in the Roman period' in J. Maloney and B. Hobley (eds), *Roman urban defences in the west* (London) 40-57

Middleton, P.S. 1979, 'Army supply in Roman Gaul' in *Invasion and Response: The case of Roman Britain* ed. B. Burnham and H. Johnson (B.A.R. Brit ser. 73), 81-97

Nash, D. 1978, *Settlement and coinage in Central Gaul c.200-50 BC* (Oxford)

Olivier, A. and Rogers, G. (1978), 'Le monument romain de Vaugrenier', *R.A.N.* 11, 143-94

Parker, A.J. 1992, *Ancient Shipwrecks of the Mediterranean and the Roman Provinces* (B.A.R. Int. ser. 580)

Percival, J. 1976, *The Roman Villa: An Historical Introduction*

Picard, G.C. 1969, 'Les théâtres ruraux sacrés en Gaule', *Archéologia* 28, 68-77

Picard, G.C. 1970, 'Les conciliabula en Gaule', *Bull. Nat. Soc Antiq. Francais* 66ff

Piggott, S., Daniel, G. and McBurney, C. (eds) 1974, *France Before the Romans*

Prieur, J. 1982, 'Les arcs monumentaux dans les Alpes occidentales: Aoste, Suse, Aix-les-Bains', *A.N.R.W.* 12, 1, 443-75

Provost, M. 1993, *Le Val de Loire dans l'Antiquité* (52nd supplement to *Gallia*)

Raepsaet-Charlier, M.-Th. and G. 1975, 'Gallia Belgica et Germania Inferior. Vingt-cinq années des recherches historiques et archéologiques', *A.N.R.W.* 2, 4, 3-299

Ralston, I. 1981, 'The use of timber in hillfort defences in France' in *Hillfort Studies: Essays for A.H.A. Hogg* ed. G. Guilbert (Leicester) 78-103

Ralston, I. 1988, 'Central Gaul and the Roman Conquest: conceptions and misconceptions', *Antiquity* 62 (1988), 786-94

Ralston, I. and Büchsenschütz, O. 1975, 'Late pre-Roman Iron Age forts in Berry', *Antiquity* 44 (1975), 8-18

Reddé, M. (ed) 1996, *L'Armée Romaine en Gaule* (Paris)

Rivet, A.L.F. 1988, *Gallia Narbonensis: Southern France in Roman Times*

Rolland, H. 1946, *Fouilles de Glanum* (1st supplement to *Gallia)*

Rolland, H. 1958, *Fouilles de Glanum 1947-57* (11th supplement to *Gallia*)

Rolland, H. 1969, *La Mausolée de Glanum* (21st supplement to *Gallia*)

Rolland, H. 1977, *L'Arc de Glanum* (31st supplement to *Gallia*)

Roymans, R. 1990, *Tribal Societies in Northern Gaul: an anthropological perspective* (Amsterdam)

Stern, H. 1957-63, *R.G.M.G. I: Province de Belgique, parts 1-3* (10th supplement to *Gallia*)

Stern, H. 1967-75, *R.G.M.G. II: Province de Lyonnaise, parts 1 (Lyon) and 2 (SE)* (see also Darmon and Lavagne 1977 and Blanchard-Lemée 1991)

Symonds, R.P. 1992, *Rhenish Wares: Fine Dark Coloured pottery from Gaul and Germany* (Oxford)

Turcan, R. 1972, *Les religions de l'Asie dans la Vallée du Rhône* (Brill)

Vallat, F. and Kazanski, M. (ed) 1993, *L'Armée Romaine et les Barbares du IIIe. au VIIe. Siècle* (Mem. Assoc Français d'Archéol Merov. 5)

Viellard-Troiekouroff, M. de 1976, *Les monuments religieux de la Gaule d'après les oeuvres de Grégoire de Tours*

Von Petrikovits 1971, 'Fortifications in the north-western Roman Empire from the third to the fifth centuries AD', *J. Roman Studs* 61, 171-218

Walters, V. 1974, *The cult of Mithras in the Roman Provinces of Gaul* (Leiden)

Ward Perkins, J.B. 1938, 'The sculpture of Visigothic France', *Archaeologia* 87, 79-128

Ward Perkins, J.B. 1970, 'From Republic to Empire: some reflections on the early provincial architecture of the Roman west' *J.R.S.* 60, 1-19 (= 1994, 53-74)

Ward Perkins, J.B. 1981, *Roman Imperial architecture*

Ward Perkins, J.B. 1994, *Studies in Roman and early Christian architecture*

Watson, A. 1999, *Aurelian and the Third Century*

West, L.C. 1935, *Roman Gaul: The Objects of Trade* (Oxford)

Wheeler, R.E.M. and Richardson, K. 1957, *The Hillforts of Northern France*

Wightman, E.M. 1970, *Roman Trier and the Treveri*

Wightman, E.M. 1977, 'Soldier and civilian in early Roman Gaul', *Limes: Akten des XI Internationalen Limeskongressus* (Budapest), 75-86

Wightman, E.M. 1985, *Gallia Belgica* (London)

Woolf, G. 1998, *Becoming Roman: The Origins of Provincial Civilization in Gaul* (Cambridge)

Yegül, F. 1992, *Baths and Bathing in Classical Antiquity*

(The very substantial British journal *Archaeologia*, published by the Society of Antiquaries of London should not be confused with the French *Archéologia*, whose nearest British equivalent is *Current Archaeology*)

# Index